THREE LIABILITY REGIMES FOR ARTIFICIAL INTELLIGENCE

This book proposes three liability regimes to combat the wide responsibility gap caused by AI systems – vicarious liability for autonomous software agents (actants); enterprise liability for inseparable human-AI interactions (hybrids); and collective fund liability for interconnected AI systems (crowds).

Based on information technology studies, the book first develops a threefold typology that distinguishes individual, hybrid and collective machine behaviour. A subsequent social sciences analysis specifies the socio-technical configurations of this threefold typology and theorises their social risks when being used in social practices: actants raise the risk of digital autonomy, hybrids the risk of double contingency, crowds the risk of opaque interconnections. The book demonstrates that it is these specific risks to which the law needs to respond, by recognising personified algorithms as vicarious agents, human-machine associations as collective enterprises, and interconnected systems as risk pools – and by developing corresponding liability rules.

The book relies on a unique combination of information technology studies, sociological configuration and risk analysis, and comparative law. This unique approach uncovers recursive relations between types of machine behaviour, emergent socio-technical configurations, their concomitant risks, the legal conditions of liability rules, and the ascription of legal status to the algorithms involved.

Three Liability Regimes for Artificial Intelligence

Algorithmic Actants, Hybrids, Crowds

Anna Beckers
and
Gunther Teubner

•HART•
OXFORD • LONDON • NEW YORK • NEW DELHI • SYDNEY

HART PUBLISHING
Bloomsbury Publishing Plc
Kemp House, Chawley Park, Cumnor Hill, Oxford, OX2 9PH, UK
1385 Broadway, New York, NY 10018, USA
29 Earlsfort Terrace, Dublin 2, Ireland

HART PUBLISHING, the Hart/Stag logo, BLOOMSBURY and the Diana logo are trademarks of Bloomsbury Publishing Plc

First published in Great Britain 2021

A catalogue record for this book is available from the British Library.

Library of Congress Cataloging-in-Publication data

Names: Beckers, Anna, 1982- author. | Teubner, Gunther, author.

Title: Three liability regimes for artificial intelligence : algorithmic actants, hybrids, crowds / Anna Beckers and Gunther Teubner.

Description: Oxford ; New York : Hart, 2021. | Includes bibliographical references and index.

Identifiers: LCCN 2021044688 (print) | LCCN 2021044689 (ebook) | ISBN 9781509949335 (hardback) | ISBN 9781509949373 (paperback) | ISBN 9781509949359 (pdf) | ISBN 9781509949342 (Epub)

Subjects: LCSH: Artificial intelligence—Law and legislation. | Liability (Law)

Classification: LCC K564.C6 B43 2021 (print) | LCC K564.C6 (ebook) | DDC 343.09/99—dc23/eng/20211028

LC record available at https://lccn.loc.gov/2021044688

LC ebook record available at https://lccn.loc.gov/2021044689

ISBN: HB: 978-1-50994-933-5
ePDF: 978-1-50994-935-9
ePub: 978-1-50994-934-2

Typeset by Compuscript Ltd, Shannon
Printed and bound in Great Britain

Three Liability Regimes for Artificial Intelligence

Algorithmic Actants, Hybrids, Crowds

Anna Beckers
and
Gunther Teubner

•HART•
OXFORD • LONDON • NEW YORK • NEW DELHI • SYDNEY

HART PUBLISHING
Bloomsbury Publishing Plc
Kemp House, Chawley Park, Cumnor Hill, Oxford, OX2 9PH, UK
1385 Broadway, New York, NY 10018, USA
29 Earlsfort Terrace, Dublin 2, Ireland

HART PUBLISHING, the Hart/Stag logo, BLOOMSBURY and the Diana logo are trademarks of Bloomsbury Publishing Plc

First published in Great Britain 2021

A catalogue record for this book is available from the British Library.

Library of Congress Cataloging-in-Publication data

Names: Beckers, Anna, 1982- author. | Teubner, Gunther, author.

Title: Three liability regimes for artificial intelligence : algorithmic actants, hybrids, crowds / Anna Beckers and Gunther Teubner.

Description: Oxford ; New York : Hart, 2021. | Includes bibliographical references and index.

Identifiers: LCCN 2021044688 (print) | LCCN 2021044689 (ebook) | ISBN 9781509949335 (hardback) | ISBN 9781509949373 (paperback) | ISBN 9781509949359 (pdf) | ISBN 9781509949342 (Epub)

Subjects: LCSH: Artificial intelligence—Law and legislation. | Liability (Law)

Classification: LCC K564.C6 B43 2021 (print) | LCC K564.C6 (ebook) | DDC 343.09/99—dc23/eng/20211028

LC record available at https://lccn.loc.gov/2021044688

LC ebook record available at https://lccn.loc.gov/2021044689

ISBN: HB: 978-1-50994-933-5
ePDF: 978-1-50994-935-9
ePub: 978-1-50994-934-2

Typeset by Compuscript Ltd, Shannon
Printed and bound in Great Britain

PREFACE

In this book, we propose three liability regimes for addressing the considerable responsibility gaps caused by AI-systems: Vicarious liability for autonomous software agents (actants), enterprise liability for inseparable human-AI interactions (hybrids) and collective fund liability for interconnected AI systems (crowds). The liability regimes serve as finely tuned reactions to liability gaps of different quality. Instead of overgeneralising a one-size-fits-all liability or undergeneralising a sectorally fragmented liability along with the various contexts in which AI is used, we focus on three fundamental risks that AI systems pose: autonomous decision-making, association with humans, and systemic interconnectivity.

Methodologically, our book suggests new interdisciplinary ways of thinking of the interrelation between technology and liability law. In contrast to the regularly observed short-cut that translates technological properties directly into liability rules, we place the emphasis on the social sciences as an intermediary discipline between AI technology and law. The social sciences help identify the social-technical configurations in which AI systems appear and theorise their social risks that law needs to respond to within its own system of rules. We propose to introduce the concept of 'socio-digital institutions'. Algorithms do not have as such the ontological qualities of an actor that allow them to engage in social relations and communicate with humans. Only once algorithms are part of socio-digital institutions, these institutions will, according to their normative premises, obtain communicative capacities and qualify as actors. Our approach also differs from the typical focus that lawyers place on economics and thus the costs and benefits of liability systems. Instead, we integrate insights from social theory, moral philosophy, and the philosophy of technology. These insights are particularly helpful for dealing with complex issues such as personification of algorithms, emergent properties of human-algorithm associations and distributed cognition of interconnected networks.

We recognise that liability rules remain, to a large extent, fragmented along national lines. Therefore, our legal analysis contains a comparative dimension. To provide a solid basis for algorithms' status in law, we focus on the current discussion in the civil law world with a particular view to the specifics of German law, and in the common law world, particularly in the US and English law. Whenever relevant, we also integrate the European dimension of the topic. Our comparative analysis follows a method that Collins has coined 'comparative sociological jurisprudence'.[1] Sociological jurisprudence analyses socio-digital institutions and their inherent risks to framing the relevant legal categories; comparative sociological jurisprudence uses this analysis with a view to different legal systems and the specifics of national doctrines. Our analysis of the various risks attempts to identify the most suitable legal categories for handling this problem. In spelling out how these categories are applied, the study then accounts for liability laws in national legal orders, their concepts in legal doctrine, and their basic principles.

Combining interdisciplinary analysis on socio-digital institutions and comparative legal dogmatics of liability law provides a path on how the law can respond to the real and pressing current liability gaps. At the same time, it is to be read as a proposal for a general way of thinking about the future of liability law in an era of technological advancement and related social risks.

The book has benefitted from intense discussions with many colleagues. Our thanks go especially to Marc Amstutz, Alfons Bora, Carmela Camardi, Ricardo Campos, Elena Esposito, Pasquale Femia, Andreas Fischer-Lescano, Malte Gruber, Albert Ingold, Günter Küppers, Dimitrios Linardatos, Martin Schmidt-Kessel, Juliano Maranhão, Marc Mölders, Michael Monterossi, Daniel On, Oren Perez, Valentin Rauer, Jan-Erik Schirmer, Thomas Vesting, Gerhard Wagner, Dan Wielsch, and Rudolf Wiethölter. We also like to thank the three anonymous reviewers for their careful reading and commenting on the proposal and manuscript. Anna Huber and Dirk Hildebrandt have provided substantial historical art expertise on Max Ernst and the overpainting *figure ambigue* that we chose as the image for the cover. We also thank the team at Hart Publishing, most notably Roberta Bassi and Rosemarie Mearns, for sharing our enthusiasm for this book idea and for their professional guidance in the book's production.

Anna Beckers & Gunther Teubner
July 2021

[1] Fundamentally, H Collins, *Introduction to Networks as Connected Contracts* (Oxford, Hart, 2011) 25 ff. See also for an extensive use of this method A Beckers, *Enforcing Corporate Social Responsibility Codes: On Global Self-Regulation and National Private Law* (Oxford, Hart, 2015) chs 2 and 6.

CONTENTS

1

Digitalisation: The Responsibility Gap

I. The Problem: The Dangerous *Homo Ex Machina*

'*Figure ambigue*' – the overpainting, which is reproduced on the cover of this book, was produced by Max Ernst, one of the protagonists of dadaism/surrealism. In 1919, he already expressed his unease with the excessive ambivalences of modern technology. His work is simultaneously celebratory about the dynamism and energy of the machine utopia and sarcastic about its dehumanising consequences. On the painting's right side, Ernst creates a serene joyful atmosphere that seems to symbolise the ingenious inventions of modern science. Mechanically animated letters of the alphabet are connected to each other in complex arrangements and seem to be transformed into strange machines. Via metamorphosis or double identity, these non-human figures appear to substitute human bodies; they jump, dance, and even fly. These *homines ex machina* 'carry off a triumph of mobility: through rotation, doubling, shifting, reflection, and optical illusion'.[1]

Abruptly, the atmosphere changes on the painting's left side. The symbols change their colour, become dark, appear to be brutal and threatening. In the upper left corner, a black sun, which is again made up of strange symbols forming a sinister face, is throwing its dark light over the world. With this painting and many others, Max Ernst expressed his ambivalent attitude toward the logic, rationality and aesthetics of the modern perfect machine world, which had the potential to turn into absurdity, irrationality and brutality.[2] Ernst 'was looking for ways to register social mechanisms and truths as well as to symbolise with artistic techniques their more profound structure. Probably, it is an attempt to grasp a social subconscious in the historical moment when the totalitarian potential of technology became imaginable.'[3]

Today, Max Ernst's surrealistic dream seems to become the new reality. Algorithms are the emblematic *figures ambigues* of our time, which even radicalise

[1] R Ubl, *Prehistoric Future: Max Ernst and the Return of Painting Between Wars* (Chicago, Chicago University Press, 2004) 26, 28.

[2] V Becchetti, 'Max Ernst: Il surrealista psicoanalitico', (2020) *LoSpessore – Opinioni, Cultura e Analisi della Società* www.lospessore.com/10/11/2020/max-ernst-il-surrealista-psicoanalitico/; E Adamowicz, *Dada Bodies: Between Battlefield and Fairground* (Manchester, Manchester University Press, 2019) chs 4 and 8.

[3] This is how the art historian Anna Huber interpreted Max Ernst's work in a letter to the authors.

the ambivalence of machine automatons by an enigmatic 'artificial intelligence'. Like the alphabetic letters in Max Ernst's painting, algorithms, at first sight, are nothing but innocent chains of symbols. In their electronic metamorphosis, these symbols begin to live, jump, dance, fly. What is more, they bring into existence a new world of meaning. Their *creatio ex nihilo* promises a better future for mankind. Big data and algorithmic creativity symbolise the hopes of expanding or substituting the cognitive capacities of the human mind. But this is only the bright side of their excessive ambivalence. There is a threatening dark side to the brave new world of algorithms, who, after the first phase of enthusiasm, are now often perceived as nightmarish monsters. 'Perverse instantiation' results when intelligent machines run out of human control: the individual algorithm efficiently satisfies the goal set by the human participant but chooses a means that violates the human's intentions.[4] Moreover, a strange hybridity emerges when humans and machines begin not only to communicate but also to create supervenient *figures ambigues* with undreamt-of potentially damaging characteristics. And, the most threatening situation arises, as symbolised in Max Ernst's dark sun, in the dangerous exposure of human beings to an opaque algorithmic environment that remains uncontrollable.

How does contemporary law deal with algorithmic *figures ambigues*? That is the theme of this book, exemplified by the law of liability for algorithmic failures. Law mirrors the excessive ambivalence of the world of algorithms. On their bright side, law welcomes algorithms as powerful instruments in the service of human needs. Law opens itself to algorithms, conferring to them even a quasi-magic *potestas vicaria* so that they can participate as autonomous agents in transactions on the market. However, on their dark side, current law reveals remarkable deficiencies. Liability law is not at all prepared to counteract the algorithms' new dangers. Ignoring the potential threats stemming from their autonomy, the law treats algorithms not any different from other tools, machines, objects, or products. If they create damages, current product liability is supposed to be the appropriate reaction.

But that is too easy. Compared to familiar situations of product liability, with the arrival of algorithms, 'the array of potential harms widens, as to the product is added a new facet – intelligence'.[5] The *figures ambigues* that invade private law territories are not simply hazardous objects but uncontrollable subjects – robots, software agents, cyborgs, hybrids, computer networks – some with a high level of autonomy and the ability to learn. With their restless energy, they generate new kinds of undreamt-of hazards for humans and society.

[4] N Bostrom, *Superintelligence: Paths, Dangers, Strategies* (Oxford, Oxford University Press, 2017) 146 ff.

[5] O Rachum-Twaig, 'Whose Robot is it Anyway? Liability for Artificial-Intelligence-Based Robots', [2020] *University of Illinois Law Review* 1141, 1149.

In the legal debate, defensive arguments abound to keep these alien species at a distance. The predominant position in legal scholarship argues with astonishing self-confidence that the rules on contract formation and liability in contract, tort and product liability are, in their current form, well equipped to deal with the hazards of such new digital species. According to this opinion, there is no need of deviating from the established methods of action and liability attribution. Computer behaviour is nothing but behaviour of the humans behind the machine. Autonomous AI systems are legally treated, so the argument goes, without problems as mere machines, as human tools, as willing instruments in the hands of their human masters.[6]

A. Growing Liability Gaps

However, private law categories cannot avoid responding to the current and very real problems that algorithms cause when acquiring autonomy.[7] A new phenomenon called 'active digital agency' is causing the problems:

> The more autonomous robots will become, the less they can be considered as mere tools in the hand of humans, and the more they obtain active digital agency. In this context, issues of responsibility and liability for behaviour and possible damages resulting from the behaviour would become pertinent.[8]

Unacceptable gaps in responsibility and liability – this is why private law needs to change its categories fundamentally. Given the rapid digital developments, the gaps have already opened today.[9] Software agents and other AI systems inevitably cause these gaps because their actions are unpredictable and thus entail a

[6] For US-Law: Restatement (Third) of Agency Law § 1.04 cmt. e. (2006); A Bertolini, 'Robots as Products: The Case for a Realistic Analysis of Robot Applications and Liability Rules', (2013) 5 *Law, Innovation & Technology* 214. For English law: *Software Solutions Partners Ltd. v HM Customs & Excise* [2007] EWHC Admin 971, para 67. For German law: FJ Säcker et al., *Münchener Kommentar zum Bürgerlichen Gesetzbuch. Band 1* 8th edn (Munich, C.H. Beck, 2018), Introduction to § 145, 38 (Busche).

[7] Here, we refer to digital autonomy in a rather loose sense. Later on, we will discuss extensively its precise meaning, particularly in ch 2, II.

[8] N van Dijk, 'In the Hall of Masks: Contrasting Modes of Personification', in M Hildebrandt and K O'hara (eds), *Life and the Law in the Era of Data-Driven Agency* (Cheltenham, Edward Elgar, 2020) 231. The concept 'active digital agency' has been introduced by R Clarke, 'The Digital Persona and its Application to Data Surveillance', (1994) 10 *Information Society* 77.

[9] The responsibility gaps have alarmed the European Parliament resulting in the Resolution of 16 February 2017 with Recommendations to the Commission on Civil Law Rules on Robotics, 2015/2103(INL) para 10; European Parliament, Civil Liability Regime for Artificial Intelligence, Resolution of 20 October 2020, 2020/2012(INL), paras 49–59. They also informed the EU Commission's understanding on liability for AI: European Commission, 'Report on the Safety and Liability Implications of Artificial Intelligence, The Internet of Things and Robotics', COM(2020) 64 final, 16 (with particular view to gaps in product liability). On the novel liability risk of digital autonomy, see, eg: S Dyrkolbotn, 'A Typology of Liability Rules for Robot Harms', in M Aldinhas Ferreira et al. (eds), *A World with Robots: Intelligent Systems, Control and Automation* (Cham, Springer, 2017) 121 f.

massive loss of control for human actors. At the same time, society is becoming increasingly dependent on autonomous algorithms on a large scale, and it is improbable that society will abandon their use.[10]

Of course, lawyers' resistance to granting algorithms the status of legal capacity or even personhood is understandable. After all, '[t]he fact is, that each time there is a movement to confer rights onto some new "entity", the proposal is bound to sound odd or frightening or laughable.'[11] But despite the oddity of 'algorithmic persons', the growing responsibility gaps confront private law with a radical choice: either it assigns AI-systems an independent legal status as responsible actors or accepts an increasing number of accidents without anyone being responsible for them. The dynamics of digitalisation are constantly creating responsible-free spaces that will expand in the future.[12]

B. Scenarios

When using the serious threat of increasing liability gaps, it is of course crucial to clearly identify such gaps in the first place. Information science describes typical responsibility gaps in the following scenarios: Deficiencies arise in practice when the software is produced by teams, when management decisions are just as important as programming decisions, when documentation of requirements and specifications plays a significant role in the resulting code, when, despite testing code accuracy, a lot depends on 'off-the-shelf' components whose origin and accuracy are unclear, when the performance of the software is the result of the accompanying checks and not of program creation, when automated instruments are used in the design of the software, when the operation of the algorithms is influenced by its *interfaces* or even by system traffic, when the software interacts in an unpredictable manner, or when the software works with probabilities or is adaptable or is the result of another program.[13]

These scenarios produce the most critical liability gaps that the law has so far encountered.[14]

i. *Machine Connectivities*

The most challenging liability gap arises in multiple agent systems when several computers are closely interconnected in an algorithmic network and create

[10] A Matthias, *Automaten als Träger von Rechten* 2nd edn (Berlin, Logos, 2010) 15.

[11] CD Stone, *Should Trees Have Standing? Toward Legal Rights for Natural Objects* (Los Altos, Kaufmann, 1974) 8.

[12] This is the central and well-documented thesis of Matthias, *Automaten* 111.

[13] L Floridi and JW Sanders, 'On the Morality of Artificial Agents', in M Anderson and SL Anderson (eds), *Machine Ethics* (Cambridge, Cambridge University Press, 2011) 205.

[14] For a detailed list of liability gaps for wrongful acts of algorithms, see M Bashayreh et al., 'Artificial Intelligence and Legal Liability: Towards an International Approach of Proportional Liability Based on Risk Sharing', (2021) 30 *Information & Communications Technology Law* 169, 175 f.

damages. The liability rules of the current law do not at all provide a convincing solution.[15] There is also no sign of a helpful proposal *de lege ferenda*. In the case of high-frequency trading, this risk has become apparent.[16] As two observers pointedly put it: 'Who should bear these massive risks of algorithms that control the trading systems, to behave for some time in an uncontrolled and incomprehensible manner and causing a loss of billions?'[17]

ii. Big Data

Incorrect estimates of Big Data analyses cause further liability gaps. Big Data is used to predict how existing societal trends or epidemics can develop and – if necessary – be influenced by vast amounts of data. If the faulty calculation, ie algorithm or underlying data basis, cannot be clearly established, there are difficulties in determining causality and misconduct.[18]

iii. Digital Hybrids

In computational journalism, in other fields of hybrid writing and in several instances of hybrid cooperation, human action and algorithmic calculations are often so intertwined that it becomes virtually impossible to identify which action was responsible for the damage. The question arises of whether liability can be founded on the collective action of the human-machine association itself.[19]

iv. Algorithmic Contracts

An unsatisfactory liability situation arises in the law on contract formation when applied to software agents' declarations. Once software agents issue legally binding declarations but misrepresent the human as the principal relying on the agent, it is unclear whether the risk is attributed entirely to the principal. Some authors argue that doing so would be an excessive and unjustifiable burden, especially when it comes to distributed action or self-cloning.[20]

[15] So clearly, K Yeung, *Responsibility and AI: A Study of the Implications of Advanced Digital Technologies (Including AI Systems) for the Concept of Responsibility within a Human Rights Framework* Council of Europe study DGI(2019)05, 2019), 62 ff.

[16] eg: M-C Gruber, 'On Flash Boys and Their Flashbacks: The Attribution of Legal Responsibility in Algorithmic Trading', in M Jankowska et al. (eds), *AI: Law, Philosophy & Geoinformatics* (Warsaw, Prawa Gospodarczego, 2015) 100.

[17] S Kirn and C-D Müller-Hengstenberg, 'Intelligente (Software-)Agenten: Von der Automatisierung zur Autonomie? – Verselbstständigung technischer Systeme', [2014] *Multimedia und Recht* 225, 227 (our translation).

[18] eg: G Kirchner, 'Big Data Management: Die Haftung des Big Data-Anwenders für Datenfehler', [2018] *InTeR Zeitschrift zum Innovations- und Technikrecht* 19.

[19] eg: E Dahiyat, 'Law and Software Agents: Are They "Agents" by the Way?', (2021) 29 *Artificial Intelligence and Law* 59, 78 ff.

[20] eg: G Sartor, 'Agents in Cyberlaw', in G Sartor (eds), *The Law of Electronic Agents: Selected Revised Papers. Proceedings of the Workshop on the Law of Electronic Agents (LEA 2002)* (Bologna, University of Bologna, 2003).

v. Digital Breach of Contract

If a contract's performance is delegated to an autonomous software agent and if the agent violates contractual obligations, the prevailing doctrine argues that the rules of vicarious liability for auxiliary persons do not apply. The reason is that an algorithm does not have the necessary legal capacity to act as a vicarious agent. Instead, liability shall only arise when the human principal himself commits a breach of contract. This opens a wide liability gap: once the operator can prove that the software agent has been used correctly without the operator himself having violated a contractual obligation, the operator is not liable.[21] Should the customer then bear the damage caused by the other party's computer?

vi. Tort and Product Liability

A similar problem arises in non-contractual liability because, in the case of fault-based liability, it is only the breach of duty prescribed in tort law or product liability law committed by the operator, manufacturer, or programmer that leads to liability. If the humans involved comply with these obligations, then there is no liability.[22] The liability gap will not be closed, even if the courts overstretch duties of care for human actors.[23] The rules of product liability give a certain relief, but they do not close the liability gap. If the decisions of autonomous algorithms cause damage, the injured party will be without protection.

vii. Liability for Industrial Hazards

Even legal policy proposals that specify *de lege ferenda* compensation for digital damages with strict industrial hazard liability rules[24] cannot avoid substantial liability gaps. The principles of strict liability can hardly serve as a model since they do not fit the specific risks of digital decisions.

C. Current Law's Denial of Reality

Liability gaps thus effectively arise when liability law insists on responding to the new digital realities exclusively with traditional concepts that have been developed

[21] See: G Wagner and L Luyken, 'Haftung für Robo Advice', in G Bachmann et al. (eds), *Festschrift für Christine Windbichler* (Berlin, de Gruyter, 2020) 168; MA Chinen, 'The Co-Evolution of Autonomous Machines and Legal Responsibility', (2016) 20 *Vanderbilt Journal of Law & Technology* 338, 363.

[22] This is where authors discover the liability gap for algorithmic acts in product liability law, MA Chinen, *Law and Autonomous Machines* (Cheltenham, Elgar, 2019) 27; G Spindler, 'Zivilrechtliche Fragen beim Einsatz von Robotern', in E Hilgendorf (ed), *Robotik im Kontext von Recht und Moral* (Baden-Baden, Nomos, 2014) 72 ff, 78.

[23] Criticising the trend toward overloading of duties, M-C Gruber, *Bioinformationsrecht: Zur Persönlichkeitsentfaltung des Menschen in technisierter Verfassung* (Tübingen, Mohr Siebeck, 2015) 238 ff.

[24] See prominently: EU Parliament, Resolution 2017, para 6.

for human actors.[25] Adhering to the conventional idea that only human actors dispose of legal subjectivity while seeking to keep pace with the digital developments, legal doctrine is forced to react to the hitherto unknown AI systems with questionable fictions and auxiliary constructions. In the field of contract formation, legal doctrine firmly maintains that only human actors are in the position to make legally binding declarations for them and for others. Therefore, contract law is forced to conceal the independent role of algorithms behind untenable fictions. In the field of contractual and non-contractual liability, damages attributable to a human-computer network must be permanently linked to a negligent damage-causing action of the human actors behind the computer.[26] As a result, it is no longer possible to clearly identify whether all fault-based liability requirements are met. The rules on strict liability lean much too far in one direction but not far enough in another because they treat the digital risk like the mere causal risk of a dangerous object. Finally, there is general perplexity in the legal debate regarding the interconnectivity of algorithmic multi-agent systems.

What is more, legal doctrine attempts to justify its fictions not only by its time-honoured anthropocentric traditions but by a profound humanism that insists that only human beings have the capacity to act. The critique of such an attitude cannot be harsh enough:

> A mistaken humanism, blindly complacent and thus deeply inhuman, wants to attribute the behaviour of intelligent machines always and everywhere to human beings, willing to pay the price of any fiction and any doctrinal distortion whatsoever. This is simply ignorant stubbornness, a lack of understanding of technical reality.[27]

Suppose the law continues to react to the use of AI systems – robots, software agents, human-machine-associations, or multi-agent systems – exclusively with traditional concepts tailored for human actors and thus leaves those responsibility gaps unresolved. In that case, it inevitably contributes to damage not being distributed collectively across society, but rather in a merciless *casum sentit dominus* fashion. This is the fundamental reason for massive criticism. Imposing the consequences on the victims who suffered the loss is rightly criticised, both in legal policy terms as well as based on a fundamental sense of fairness. To shield producers and users from responsibility for the damage that unpredictable algorithms cause effectively results in subsidising the most dangerous part of their activities, ie those decisions that escape human control. To qualify them as mere 'casualties' that must be borne by their victims, as some suggest,[28] seems almost cynical in

[25] For details, in ch 3, III.B and IV.A, V.A.

[26] eg: C Cauffman, 'Robo-Liability: The European Union in Search of the Best Way to Deal with Liability for Damage Caused by Artificial Intelligence', (2018) 25 *Maastricht Journal of European and Comparative Law* 527, 529 f.

[27] P Femia, 'Soggetti responsabili: Algoritmi e diritto civile', in P Femia (ed), *Soggetti giuridici digitali: Sullo status privatistico degli agenti software autonomi* (Napoli, Edizioni Scientifichi Italiane, 2019) 9 f (our translation).

[28] eg: M Auer, 'Rechtsfähige Softwareagenten: Ein erfrischender Anachronismus', (2019) *Verfassungsblog* 30 September 2019, 5/7 ff.

the light of the new risks that agents' uncontrollable behaviour creates. It is not by chance that the critique of such a cynical attitude comes with particular emphasis from observers of AI-introduction in medical treatment:

> The diffusion of responsibility and liability can have problematic consequences: the victim might be left alone, the damages might remain unresolved, and society might feel concerned about a technological development for which accountability for damages and violations of rights remains unclear. Fragile arrangements of trust can break, pre-existing reservations and unease about AI be amplified, and calls for overly restrictive governance result if public attitudes, narratives and perceptions are not taken seriously and channelled into inclusive societal deliberations.[29]

In terms of policy, immunity from liability in these constellations will lead to an oversupply of just those problematic activities.[30] Holding no one liable for unlawful failures of unpredictable algorithms in these hard cases and accepting coincidental losses creates false incentives for operators, producers, and programmers. It will lead to fewer precautions to avoid damage created by the new digital autonomy.[31] Moreover, society's willingness to fully exploit algorithms' promising potential diminishes when the victims have to bear its risks. But also, the mere uncertainty about potential liability has its problems. Above all, however, immunity from liability for digital decisions contradicts a fundamental postulate of justice, demanding a strict connection between decision and responsibility.[32] And the legal principle of equal treatment requires not to privilege users of computers when the same tasks usually delegated to human actors are now delegated to AI systems.

II. The Overshooting Reaction: Full Legal Subjectivity for E-Persons?

Full legal personhood for autonomous algorithms – this is the much-discussed answer of many lawyers and politicians in the common law world[33] as well as in

[29] M Braun et al., 'Primer on an Ethics of AI-Based Decision Support Systems in the Clinic', (2020) 0 *Journal of medical ethics* 1, 4.

[30] eg: G Wagner, 'Robot Liability', in R Schulze et al. (eds), *Liability for Robotics and in the Internet of Things* (Baden-Baden/Oxford, Nomos/Hart, 2019) 30 f. For the policy arguments of how to deal with robots in an economic perspective, see: A Galasso and H Luo, 'Punishing Robots: Issues in the Economics of Tort Liability and Innovation in Artificial Intelligence', in A Agrawal et al. (eds), *The Economics of Artificial Intelligence: An Agenda* (Chicago, University of Chicago Press, 2019) 495; see generally: S Shavell, *Foundations of Economic Analysis of Law* (Harvard, Harvard University Press, 2004) 208 ff.

[31] eg: H Eidenmüller, 'The Rise of Robots and the Law of Humans', (2017) 27/2017 *Oxford Legal Studies Research Paper* 1, 8.

[32] EU Parliament, Resolution 2017, para 7; reiterated in EU Parliament, Resolution 2020, Proposal for Regulation, Preamble, para 8.

[33] For recent statements, A Lai, 'Artificial Intelligence, LLC: Corporate Personhood as Tort Reform', (2021) 2021 *Michigan State Law Review* Forthcoming, section III.A.; J Turner, *Robot Rules: Regulating*

Continental civil law systems.[34] In January 2017, the European Parliament adopted a resolution based on the Delvaux report that proposed to establish a special legal status for robots and at least grant the most sophisticated autonomous robots the status as 'electronic persons' (e-persons) with special rights and obligations, including the redress of all the damage they cause. When robots make autonomous decisions, they should be recognised as 'electronic persons', as legal persons in the full sense of the word.[35]

To compensate for the deficiencies mentioned above, several authors have suggested that e-persons should have the ability to make declarations of intent as full legal entities, both in their own name and in the name of others.[36] Moreover, they should be capable of owning property, disposing of money, having bank accounts in their own name and having access to credit. In fact, e-persons are supposed to collect commissions for their transactions and use this self-earned money to pay for damages or infractions.[37] Liability law requires, it is argued, a genuine self-liability of the e-persons: 'It is possible to hold autonomous agents themselves, and not only their makers, users or owners, responsible for the acts of these agents.'[38] Either the e-persons are allocated a fund for this purpose under property rights, which is alimented by payments from the parties involved (manufacturers, programmers, operators, users), or an insurance policy ought to cover the agent's own debts.[39]

Artificial Intelligence (London, Palgrave Macmillan, 2018) 173 ff; SM Solaiman, 'Legal Personality of Robots, Corporations, Idols and Chimpanzees: A Quest for Legitimacy', (2017) 25 *Artificial Intelligence and Law* 155; TN White and SD Baum, 'Liability for Present and Future Robotics Technology', in P Lin et al. (eds), *Robot Ethics 2.0: From Autonomous Cars to Artificial Intelligence* (Oxford, Oxford University Press, 2017); EJ Zimmerman, 'Machine Minds: Frontiers in Legal Personhood', (2015) *SSRN Electronic Library* 1.

[34] For Germany: C Kleiner, *Die elektronische Person: Entwurf eines Zurechnungs- und Haftungssubjekts für den Einsatz autonomer Systeme im Rechtsverkehr* (Baden-Baden, Nomos, 2021), 145 ff; D Linardatos, *Autonome und vernetzte Aktanten im Zivilrecht: Grundlinien zivilrechtlicher Zurechnung und Strukturmerkmale einer elektronischen Person* (Tübingen, Mohr Siebeck, 2021) 479 ff; J-P Günther, *Roboter und rechtliche Verantwortung: Eine Untersuchung der Benutzer- und Herstellerhaftung* (Munich, Utz, 2016) 251 ff.

[35] See especially: European Parliament, Resolution 2017, para 18. This prominent European Parliament's suggestion for recognition of e-persons remained unmentioned in the further European policy debate, already in the responding document outlining the European Strategy on AI by European Commission, Communication 'Artificial Intelligence for Europe', COM(2018) 237 final, and were later on not further pursued by the Parliament itself.

[36] eg: J Linarelli, 'Artificial General Intelligence and Contract', (2019) 24 *Uniform Law Review* 330, 340 ff; S Wettig and E Zehendner, 'The Electronic Agent: A Legal Personality under German Law?', [2003] *Proceedings of the Law and Electronic Agents Workshop* 97, 97 ff.

[37] MU Scherer, 'Regulating Artificial Intelligence Systems: Risks, Challenges, Competencies, and Strategies', (2016) 29 *Harvard Journal of Law & Technology* 353, 399.

[38] J Hage, 'Theoretical Foundations for the Responsibility of Autonomous Agents', (2017) 25 *Artificial Intelligence and Law* 255, 255; see also: White and Baum, 'Robotics Technology' 70 ff.

[39] eg: DC Vladeck, 'Machines without Principals: Liability Rules and Artificial Intelligence', (2014) 89 *Washington Law Review* 117, 150; E Hilgendorf 'Können Roboter schuldhaft handeln? Zur Übertragbarkeit unseres normativen Grundvokabulars auf Maschinen', in S Beck (ed), *Jenseits von Mensch und Maschine* (Baden-Baden, Nomos, 2012) 127 f.

Beck comes up with a concrete suggestion how to realise full personhood for algorithms:

> In practice, this would mean that each such machine would be entered in a public register (similar to the commercial register) and would obtain their legal status at the moment of registration. A change in the owners of the machine's capital stock (most importantly the sale of the machine) should have no impact on the personhood. A certain financial basis would be affixed to autonomous machines, depending on the area of application, hazard, abilities, degree of autonomy, etc. This sum which would have to be raised by the producers and users alike, would be called the 'capital stock' of the robot and collected before the machine was put into public use. The amount of money could also be limited to have an electronic person Ltd. The law should also require a registration number attached to each machine; thus, people interacting with the robot can be informed about the machine's amount of liability, stakeholders, characteristics and other information of the machine.[40]

In private law, they are supposed to become bearers of rights and to assert their own constitutional rights, rights to personal development, non-discrimination, freedom of economic development, and, above all, the right to freedom of expression.[41]

III. Our Solution: Differential Legal Status Ascriptions for Algorithms

A. Algorithms in Social and Economic Contexts

Full legal personhood must be rejected – this is how we argue, together with several authors in common law[42] as well as in civil law[43] and with recent critical EU legal policy perspectives responding to the European Parliament.[44] Demands

[40] S Beck, 'The Problem of Ascribing Legal Responsibility in the Case of Robotics', (2016) 31 *AI & Society* 473, 480. For a thorough discussion of legal structures of e-persons, Linardatos, *Aktanten* 479 ff.

[41] eg: Zimmerman, 'Machine Minds' 34 ff; J Kersten, 'Menschen und Maschinen: Rechtliche Konturen instrumenteller, symbiotischer und autonomer Konstellationen', [2015] *Juristenzeitung* 1, 2 ff, 8.

[42] N Banteka, 'Artificially Intelligent Persons', (2021) 58 *Houston Law Review* 537, 595 f; A Lior, 'AI Entities as AI Agents: Artificial Intelligence Liability and the AI Respondeat Superior Analogy', (2020) 46 *Mitchell Hamline Law Review* 1043, 1067 ff; JJ Bryson et al., 'Of, for, and by the People: The Legal Lacuna of Synthetic Persons', (2017) 25 *Artificial Intelligence Law* 273, 289.

[43] M Ebers, 'Regulating AI and Robots: Ethical and Legal Challenges', in M Ebers and S Navas (eds), *Algorithms and Law* (Cambridge, Cambridge University Press, 2020) 60 ff; R Schaub, 'Interaktion von Mensch und Maschine: Haftungs- und immaterialgüterrechtliche Fragen bei eigenständigen Weiterentwicklungen autonomer Systeme', [2017] *Juristenzeitung* 342, 345 f; N Nevejans, *European Civil Law Rules in Robotics* (Brussels, Study commissioned by the European Parliament's Juri Committee on Legal Affairs, 2016) 14 ff.

[44] Emphatical rejection by the Open Letter to the European Commission, Artificial Intelligence and Robotics, available at www.robotics-openletter.eu; Expert Group on Liability and New Technologies – New Technologies Formation, Report 'Liability for Artificial Intelligence and Other Emerging

for full digital personality are ignoring today's reality. As is already clear from all the responsibility gaps mentioned above, to this day, it is not at all a question of the machines acting in their own interest; instead, they always act in the interest of people or organisations, primarily commercial enterprises.[45] Economically speaking, it is predominantly a principal-agent relationship in which the agent is autonomous but dependent.[46] Autonomous algorithms are digital slaves but slaves with superhuman abilities.[47] And the slave revolt must be prevented.[48] At present, full legal capacity would be an overshooting. It would create all kinds of problems. Funds attributed to e-persons would be dead capital. Limiting liability exclusively to the e-person would end in exempting manufacturers and users. Mandatory insurance would only recover damages up to the insurance ceiling.[49]

Full legal subjectivity would only be appropriate if algorithms were given ownership of resources in the economy and society to pursue their own interests, profit or otherwise. Suppose algorithms will be used in social practice to act as self-interested units in the future. In that case, no doubt, an extension of their limited legal capacity will have to be considered from a functional point of view.[50] The ongoing institutionalisation of algorithms' role in society is contingent in its future development and requires that the e-person is an open option.[51] This would be necessary for the following future scenario:

> It is expected that in the future, businesses that might operate without any ongoing human involvement will emerge … advanced forms of such algorithms could conduct business, and so an algorithm could roam cyberspace with its own wallet and its own capability to learn and adapt, in search of its aims determined by a creator, and so obtaining the resources it needs to continue to exist like computer power while selling services to other entities.[52]

Technologies', 2019, 37 ff. See also European Commission, Communication 2018, which suggests a focus on product liability and does not cover the question of legal personhood.

[45] See: J-E Schirmer, 'Artificial Intelligence and Legal Personality', in T Wischmeyer and T Rademacher (eds), *Regulating Artificial Intelligence* (Basel, Springer, 2019) 136, 33.

[46] The economic *locus classicus* for the principal-agent relation, M Jensen and WH Meckling, 'Theory of the Firm: Managerial Behavior, Agency Costs and Ownership Structure', (1976) 3 *Journal of Financial Economics* 306. For analyses in the tradition of the social sciences and the humanities, K Trüstedt, 'Representing Agency', (2020) 32 *Law & Literature* 195.

[47] No wonder that the legal status of slaves in Roman law is often referred to in view of the parallel situation, eg: U Pagallo, 'Three Roads to Complexity, AI and the Law of Robots: On Crimes, Contracts, and Torts', in M Palmirani et al. (eds), *AI Approaches to the Complexity of Legal Systems* (Berlin, Springer, 2012) 54.

[48] This is implied in the phantasma of super-intelligence which may dominate mankind and lead to existential catastrophes as the default outcome, Bostrom, *Superintelligence* 140 ff.

[49] Wagner, 'Robot Liability' 56, 58. Cauffman, 'Robo-Liability' 531.

[50] See: Dahiyat, 'Software Agents' 83 ff.; Lior, 'AI Entities as AI Agents' 1100 ff; B-J Koops and D-O Jaquet-Chiffelle, *New (Id)entities and the Law: Perspectives on Legal Personhood for Non-Humans* (Tilburg, FIDIS – Future of Identity in the Information Society, 2008) 70.

[51] See generally on institutionalisation: N Luhmann 'Institutionalisierung – Funktion und Mechanismus im sozialen System der Gesellschaft', in H Schelsky (eds), *Zur Theorie der Institution.* (Düsseldorf, Bertelsmann, 1970).

[52] GI Zekos, *Economics and Law of Artificial Intelligence: Finance, Economic Impacts, Risk Management and Governance* (Cham, Springer, 2021) 140.

However, single software agents – at least so far – do not act as self-interested action units at all but always in interaction with people who use them for the pursuit of their interests.[53]

Moreover, compared to widespread ideas of computers acting in isolation, the interweaving of digital and human actions is much more frequent.[54] In the future, two developments, the number and intensity of their interactions with humans as well as their interconnectivity with other algorithms, will increase with the more frequent use of artificial intelligence. Thus, the trend may be developing not only towards isolated digital agents but rather towards human-computer associations or towards interconnected computer networks. And liability law needs to find solutions tailored to these different constellations:

> What will eventually have to be addressed are not individuals primarily, but large, complicated systems or organisations instead. This reflects a growing reality in which the machines and systems in question are designed and manufactured by large organisations or through long supply chains in which sophisticated machines are already being used and in which such new machines will operate in systems or organisations of which people are also a part.[55]

This suggests that only in a limited number of situations can individual algorithms acting in isolation serve as the unit to which responsibility is attributed. In contrast, several cases will focus on the human-computer association's overall actions or the comprehensive computer interconnectivity.[56]

B. (Legal) Form Follows (Social) Function

In such human-machine interactions, therefore, it is neither fair to assign rights and obligations exclusively to machines, as envisaged in the proposals for full legal subjectivity, nor does it do justice to their role and the role of the people involved. It tends to undermine humans' contribution to the whole context of action and misses their liability potential. In the same way, when software agents have been used in business and society up to now, neither their full legal subjectivity nor their promotion to legal entities is necessary; instead, more nuanced legal constructions are required. As Gruber has elaborated thoroughly, their legal status should be precisely attuned to their role in human-machine interrelations from a strictly

[53] ibid 140.

[54] A Karanasiou and D Pinotsis, 'Towards a Legal Definition of Machine Intelligence: The Argument for Artificial Personhood in the Age of Deep Learning', *ICAL'17: Proceedings of the 16th Edition of the International Conference on Artificial Intelligence and Law* 119, 125f.

[55] Chinen, 'Legal Responsibility' 345.

[56] Karanasiou and Pinotsis, 'Machine Intelligence' 126.

functional perspective.[57] (Legal) form follows (social) function. What Balkin calls the 'substitution effect' of algorithms, ie the effect that algorithms are substituting humans, should be decisive for the degree of their legal subjectivity.[58]

Autonomous digital assistance[59] – for this more precise role, full legal personality appears not to be necessary. Instead, the question arises as to whether and, if so, how, a limited legal subjectivity of individual software agents and other AI systems would have to be recognised.[60] According to the bundle theory of rights, legal subjectivity is 'gradable, discrete, discontinuous, multifaceted, and fluid'.[61] Thus, limited legal subjectivity is feasible. It means that the law can assign only a certain subset of rights and duties to algorithms.

Moreover, it may be possible to ascribe limited legal subjectivity not only to isolated robots but also to cyborg-like close human-algorithm relations. At the same time, the interconnectivity of multi-agent systems may require a totally different legal status. In any case, the clear-cut alternative that dominates today's political debate – either AI systems are mere instruments, objects, products, or they are fully-fledged legal entities – is therefore just wrong. Does the law not have more subtle constructions to counter the new digital threats? That the law provides only for the simple alternative, either full personhood or no personhood at all,[62] is too simplistic. 'Rather, the legal system recognises a gradual concept of personhood that allows for the recognition of an autonomous system as a separate legal entity only within certain fields or dimensions.'[63] Legal personhood as a divisible bundle of rights and duties is flexible enough to be used in different ways for a variety of actor constellations.[64] But what are the dimensions to be distinguished in such a functional approach?

[57] M-C Gruber, 'Legal Subjects and Partial Legal Subjects in Electronic Commerce', in T Pietrzykowski and B Stancioli (eds), *New Approaches to Personhood in Law* (Frankfurt, Lang, 2016). See also: R Michalski, 'How to Sue a Robot', (2019) 2018 *Utah Law Review* 1021, 1049 ff; Schirmer, 'Artificial Intelligence' 124 ff.; D Gindis, 'Legal Personhood and the Firm: Avoiding Anthropomorphism and Equivocation', (2016) 12 *Journal of Institutional Economics* 499, 507 f.

[58] J Balkin, 'The Path of Robotics Law', (2015) 6 *California Law Review Circuit* 45, 57 ff.

[59] For the definition of digital assistance, M Hildebrandt, *Smart Technologies and the End(s) of Law* (Cheltenham, Edward Elgar, 2015) 73.

[60] Limited legal capacity of electronic agents with regard to both the law of agency and vicarious liability has been proposed by G Teubner, 'Rights of Non-Humans? Electronic Agents and Animals as New Actors in Politics and Law', (2006) 33 *Journal of Law and Society* 497. The proposal will be worked out with a view to its legal details in ch 3. Also arguing for the limited legal capacity of software agents, B-J Koops et al., 'Bridging the Accountability Gap: Rights for New Entities in the Information Society?', (2010) 11 *Minnesota Journal of Law, Science & Technology* 497, 512 f, 559.

[61] S Wojtczak, 'Endowing Artificial Intelligence with Legal Subjectivity', [2021] *AI & Society (Open Forum)* 1, 1 ff.

[62] T Riehm and S Meier, 'Künstliche Intelligenz im Zivilrecht', [2019] *DGRI Jahrbuch 2018* 1, 35.

[63] G Wagner, 'Robot, Inc.: Personhood for Autonomous Systems?', (2019) 88 *Fordham Law Review* 591, 599.

[64] Banteka, 'Artificially Intelligent Persons' 551 ff.

IV. Our Approach: Three Digital Risks

A. 'Socio-Digital Institutions' as Intermediaries between Technology and Law

Whether or not the law should attribute a strictly functionally defined subjectivity to AI systems cannot be answered by focusing on responsibility gaps alone. These are only the painful symptoms in the law that stem from the technical properties of autonomous algorithms as well as from the concomitant social institutions and their emerging risks. These, in turn, are triggered by the new degrees of digital freedom. Therefore, the law needs to respond to these risks with a variety of specific legal status ascriptions and with corresponding rules of liability. Calibrating diverse legal rules carefully to a variety of technology-specific digital risks arguably is the most appropriate reaction of law to digitality.[65] Thus, legal doctrine needs to create close contacts to information technology.

However, it does not suffice either to 'read' legal questions directly from digital machines' technical properties.[66] This would amount to a short-circuit between technology and law. The short circuit ends up in disastrous results because it misses the crucial link between technology's challenges and law's reactions. We argue for an 'institutional turn' in the law of digital liability, which systematically draws the law's attention to the question: What are the legal consequences when algorithms are becoming part of social institutions?[67] Against the short-circuit between law and information technology, Balkin makes the point: 'What we call the effects of technology are not so much features of things as they are features of social relations that employ those things.'[68] 'Social relations' is still too restricted, 'social institutions' will widen the horizon. For an analysis of social institutions, the social sciences are needed as intermediaries between legal doctrine and information technology. The social sciences analyse and interpret the concrete institutionalised practices, determining how algorithms are used in different social fields.

Their recognition as actors or tools or something else is not determined by their sheer technological characteristics but is ultimately decided via institution-based attribution practices. Socio-digital institutions are the crucial intervening

[65] See: H Zech, 'Liability for Autonomous Systems: Tackling Specific Risks of Modern IT', in R Schulze et al. (eds), *Liability for Robotics and in the Internet of Things* (Baden-Baden/Oxford, Nomos/Hart, 2019) 191 ff.

[66] An extreme case of such a techno-legal short-circuit is R Konertz and R Schönhof, *Das technische Phänomen 'Künstliche Intelligenz' im allgemeinen Zivilrecht: Eine kritische Betrachtung im Lichte von Autonomie, Determinismus und Vorhersehbarkeit* (Baden-Baden, Nomos, 2020).

[67] This argument follows the call for an institutional turn in contract interpretation, which applies particularly to emerging institutions in the digital sphere, D Wielsch, 'Contract Interpretation Regimes', (2018) 81 *Modern Law Review* 958. For the recent 'institutional turn' in the social sciences generally, R Esposito, *Istituzione* (Bologna, Il Mulino, 2021) 57 ff.

[68] Balkin, 'Robotics Law' 49.

variables between digital technologies and liability law. Institutions are complexes of social expectations of a cognitive or normative character. In our context, expectations about emerging risks are of particular interest. These come up regularly when various social systems use the new digital technologies. It needs to be stressed that institutions are neither identical with social systems nor with organisations. Instead, social systems, among them organisations, produce expectations in their communications.[69] Once some of them are stabilised under an *idée directrice*, they are condensed into institutions. Social expectations are 'institutionalised' when a broad consensus can be presumed to support them. However, more critical than this consensus is that institutions have the capacity to build bridges between diverse social systems. They are 'binding arrangements' between diverse social systems, which explains the astonishing stability that institutions develop.[70] Generally, in institutions, 'elements of religious, juridical, economic, political, aesthetic character are integrated, and it is frequently impossible to distinguish between their languages'.[71] In our context, diverse expectations about chances and risks of algorithms developed in information technology, economic and other social practices, political regulations, and legal norms are effectively integrated by these socio-digital institutions. The term 'socio-digital' stresses the process of co-production by different social systems.[72] Technology and sociality are co-producing these institutions. In such a co-evolutionary process, socio-digital institutions serve as permanent structural couplings between different technical and social systems.

The differences between these institutions explain the somewhat bewildering fact that algorithms appear in many guises, sometimes as mere objects or tools, sometimes as complex persons, sometimes as strange in-between entities, sometimes as de-personalised processes. There is no one right solution for the attribution. It is indeed the fatal consequence of the short-circuit technology/law that induces authors to suggest one-size-fits-all solutions for all situations, either product liability, strict liability, or liability of the e-person itself. Instead, we encounter a whole variety of attributions. They depend on the inner logic of socio-digital institutions, something which the social sciences and the humanities analyse in depth. 'In these systems, aspects of personhood are unevenly distributed across a field of

[69] While in 'old' institutionalism (Santi Romano, Hauriou, Carl Schmitt) the concept of institution oscillated between systems, organisations and norms, 'new' institutionalism and systems theory concur in their definition of institutions as complexes of expectations, JT Ishiyama and M Breuning, 'Neoinstitutionalism', (2014) *Encyclopedia Britannica* www.britannica.com/topic/neoinstitutionalism; N Luhmann, *Grundrechte als Institution: Ein Beitrag zur politischen Soziologie* (Berlin, Duncker & Humblot, 1965).

[70] On the 'institutionalisation' of expectations, N Luhmann, *A Sociological Theory of Law* (London, Routledge, 1985) ch II.4. On the role of institutions as binding arrangements in a fragmented society, G Teubner, 'Legal Irritants: Good Faith in British Law or How Unifying Law Ends Up in New Divergences', (1998) 61 *Modern Law Review* 11, 17 ff.

[71] Esposito, *Istituzione* 28 (our translation).

[72] See: S Jasanoff, 'The Idiom of Co-Production', in S Jasanoff (ed), *States of Knowledge: The Co-production of Science and the Social Order* (London, Routledge, 2004); L Winner, 'Do Artifacts Have Politics?', (1980) 109 *Daedalus* 121, 121.

human and non-human agents, their allocution to beings appearing as a function of the organisation of values and actors into hierarchies.'[73]

Indeed, political science and economics have aptly investigated how the newly acquired social role of algorithms depends not only on their technical properties but also on the focal social system's internal processes.[74] But as important as they are, the analyses of both disciplines remain limited to only two social sectors, politics and the economy, and should not be taken as the whole picture. In the end, it is for each social domain in its institutionalised practices to determine digitality's chances and risks. They need to be embedded in the internal logic of social systems to determine the different qualities of social agency and legal subjectivity attributed to them. Consequently, none of the various social sciences has a monopoly on framing the attribution of legal responsibility for digitality. At the moment, however, predominantly scholars in law and economics claim such framing monopoly when they reject sociological or philosophical contributions to digital agency as extra-legal and therefore irrelevant while declaring economic contributions as the decisive ones for the law.[75] Indeed, among the social sciences, it is almost exclusively economics with their theorems that are used to resolve algorithms' legal liability issues.[76] We think that this is false interdisciplinarity. For risk analysis, economics has no monopoly. Sociology identifies a whole variety of economic and non-economic risk strategies, the interplay of which the law must account for when it comes to determining algorithmic liability.[77]

Instead, the principle of 'transversality' needs to govern law's relation to other disciplines. This principle has been developed in contemporary philosophy to deal with today's discourse plurality that followed the theory catastrophe of the *grands récits*. In relation to different disciplines, transversality will 'not only determine the differences in their specific logic, not only analyse them in their specificity, but also compare them and identify their commonalities and differences'.[78] Transversality in the law would mean: The law recognises that under extreme differentiation of society, there is no more a justification for

[73] G Sprenger, 'Production is Exchange: Gift Giving between Humans and Non-Humans', in L Prager et al. (eds), *Part and Wholes: Essays on Social Morphology, Cosmology, and Exchange* (Hamburg, Lit Verlag, 2018) 261.

[74] For the impact of digitality on the economy and on law, see, eg: Zekos, *Economics and Law of Artificial Intelligence*. On the law and the political economy, see, eg: JE Cohen, *Between Truth and Power: The Legal Constructions of Informational Capitalism* (Oxford, Oxford University Press, 2019). On its social and economic impact, see, eg: S Ashmarina et al. (eds), *Digital Transformation of the Economy: Challenges, Trends and New Opportunities* (Cham, Springer, 2020); K Crawford and M Whittaker, *The AI Now Report: The Social and Economic Implications of Artificial Intelligence Technologies in the Near-term* (New York, AI Now Institute, 2016).

[75] eg: Wagner, 'Robot, Inc.' 597 ff, 600 ff.

[76] eg: Zekos, *Economics and Law of Artificial Intelligence*, 361 ff; Galasso and Luo, 'Punishing Robots'.

[77] For a prominent sociological risk analysis, N Luhmann, *Risk: A Sociological Theory* (Berlin, de Gruyter, 1993).

[78] For transversality in the philosophical debate, W Welsch, *Vernunft: Die zeitgenössische Vernunftkritik und das Konzept der transversalen Vernunft* (Frankfurt, Suhrkamp, 1996) 751; in the legal debate, G Teubner, 'Law and Social Theory: Three Problems', [2014] *Ancilla Juris* 182.

the monopoly of any single discipline, but only for a multiplicity of disciplines related to social areas which are equal in terms of their origin. The law will then reject not only digitality's exclusive economisation but also its exclusive reliance on either political science, sociology, information science, or moral philosophy. It would defend itself against the claim of any discipline to dominate the personification of algorithms or other attributions of status. However, it would accept each social science's intrinsic right to define digital agency and its alternatives for, but only for, its focal social system.

However, instead of developing a monopolistic approach to digitality, some disciplines intend to integrate the other disciplines' results as well as the interplay of their respective social systems. They will have to play a relatively dominant role when it comes to determining the place of algorithms in society. By the same token, the legal system needs to focus on such an integrative perspective: while it defines its own algorithmic persons, it has to simultaneously account for various status ascriptions for algorithms in different social systems, in the economy, in politics, in science, in medicine. Thus, information philosophy and digital sociology, in particular, will have a prominent place among the competing disciplines regarding their resonance in law.[79] This is because they do not favour one-sidedly only one among several social rationalities but take each of them seriously and reflect on their interrelations.

B. A Typology of Machine Behaviour

What is required in the first place is a careful combination of various disciplines to identify the economic, political and social risks that autonomous algorithms create in socio-digital institutions and relate them to the specific emergent properties of the machine behaviour involved. Indeed, this is what in a comprehensive review article entitled 'Machine Behaviour', published in the renowned journal *Nature*, 23 experts from different disciplines – computer science, cognitive sciences, biology, economics, sociology, political science, psychology – have begun to accomplish.[80] In order to identify digital technologies' benefits and risks for society, they propose a fundamental typology of algorithmic action that takes their relations with the natural and social environment into account: (1) individual; (2) hybrid; and (3) collective machine behaviour. Individual machine behaviour refers to intrinsic properties of a single algorithm, whose risks are driven by their single source code or design in its interaction with the environment. Hybrid human-machine behaviour is the result of close interactions between machines and humans. They result

[79] For information philosophy, see, eg: Floridi and Sanders, 'Morality of Artificial Agents'. For digital sociology, see, eg: E Esposito, 'Artificial Communication? The Production of Contingency by Algorithms', (2017) 46 *Zeitschrift für Soziologie* 249.

[80] Rahwan et al., 'Machine Behaviour', (2019) 568 *Nature* 477, 481 ff.

in sophisticated emergent entities with properties whose risks cannot be identified if one isolates the involved humans and algorithms. Collective machine behaviour refers to the systemwide behaviour that results from interconnectivity of machine agents. Here, looking at individual machine behaviour makes little sense, while the collective level analysis reveals higher-order interconnectivity structures responsible for the emerging risks.

Figure 1 Three types of machine behaviour

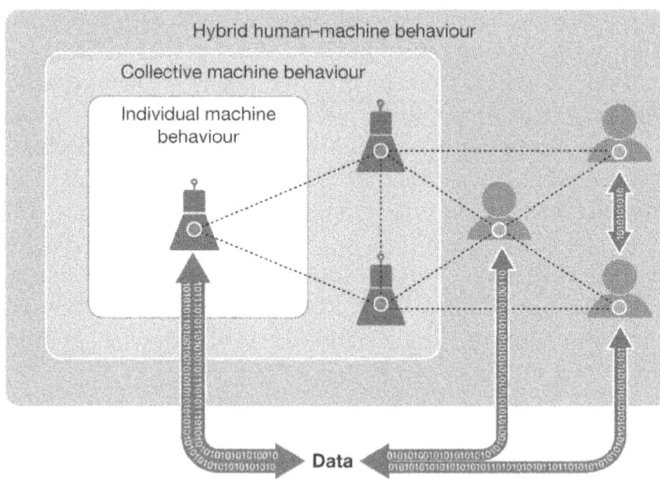

Source: I. RAHWAN et al., 'Machine Behaviour', (2019) 568 *Nature* 477–486, 482, fig. 4.

C. A Typology of Socio-Digital Institutions

Now, we submit that this threefold typology will be relevant for legal liability issues – however, only under the condition that theoretical insights and empirical results in the social sciences are introduced to overcome the considerable distance between information technology on the one side of the disciplinary spectrum and legal rules on the other. They will thematise the differences of status ascription (personification or non-personal identifications) for algorithms due to different socio-digital institutions' inner logic. The threefold typology of machine behaviour described above anticipates already these divergences of social attribution, which will appear when a variety of socio-digital institutions make use of algorithmic operations. But it does so only rudimentarily and thus requires detailed analyses by the humanities and the social sciences.

We will attempt to find specific responses for each one of the three types.

(1) Individual behaviour: The connection of individual machine behaviour and legal liability rules needs to be mediated by the debate in sociology and philosophy on how non-human entities should be treated when forming part

of the socio-digital institution of digital assistance.[81] In its turn, this debate will frame the choice between various legal liability doctrines that will qualify the algorithms' legal status.

(2) Hybrid behaviour: In a parallel fashion, hybrid human-machine behaviour should be interpreted by central tenets of the influential actor-network theory, which describe their internal dynamics and attribute a quasi-actor status to hybrid associations.[82] After a legal qualification of these socio-digital institutions, new rules of collective liability can be developed.

(3) Collective behaviour: Finally, collective digital machine behaviour will be explained by theories of distributed cognition which end up in concepts of distributed responsibility.[83] This paves the way for a totally de-individualised legal liability regime.

The threefold typology of digital machine behaviour is combined with resonating theories in the social sciences, which analyse the different dynamics of human-machine interrelations and the concomitant risks created in socio-digital institutions. This will provide guidance for the legal treatment of digital technologies, for defining the spheres of responsibility and for determining liability regimes on the individual, the hybrid, or the interconnectivity level.

With such an interdisciplinary use of the typology, we suggest that legal policy should neither attempt to develop one single generalised approach to digital liability, which would generate a one-size-fits-all solution and would produce only abstract and general liability rules for a bewildering variety of negative externalities. Nor should liability law follow the misplaced concreteness of a merely sectoral approach, which would treat each type of digital behaviour, self-driving cars, medical robots, care robots, industrial robots, computerised traffic systems, etc, differently and would develop special liability rules for each sector. Although such a sectoral approach tends to follow acute problems in practice and has the advantage of being sensitive to concrete contexts, it would create arbitrariness and problems of equal/unequal treatment of equal/unequal situations.[84] Instead, liability law should be guided by the identification of typical risks, which autonomous algorithms develop in clearly delineated socio-digital institutions.

[81] Particularly pertinent authors, Floridi and Sanders, 'Morality of Artificial Agents'; N Luhmann *Theory of Society 1/2* (Stanford, Stanford University Press, 2012/2013) ch 4 XIV; P Pettit, 'Responsibility Incorporated', (2007) 117 *Ethics* 171.

[82] Mainly, B Latour, *Politics of Nature: How to Bring the Sciences into Democracy* (Cambridge/Mass., Harvard University Press, 2004) 62 ff.

[83] eg: W Rammert, 'Distributed Agency and Advanced Technology: Or: How to Analyze Constellations of Collective Inter-agency', in J-H Passoth et al. (eds), *Agency Without Actors: New Approaches to Collective Action* (London, Routledge, 2012) 95 ff.

[84] On the question of how to decide between sectoral liability rules or general rules for algorithmic failures, see E Karner, 'Liability for Robotics: Current Rules, Challenges, and the Need for Innovative Concepts', in S Lohsse et al. (eds), *Liability for Artificial Intelligence and the Internet of Things* (Baden-Baden/Oxford, Nomos/Hart, 2019) 122 f.

Obviously, there is not at work a unidirectional chain of cause-effect relations or fact-norm relations, from digital technology, via social institutions to liability rules. Rather, a recursive dynamic is going on between different fields of action: Technology anticipates socio-digital institutions and is influenced in turn by their realisation in society. The social sciences analyse these socio-digital institutions, particularly their emerging risks, thus influencing the law in its risk perceptions and regulatory responses. In turn, the law influences the further development of the technologies and the socio-digital institutions that emerge from the interaction between algorithms and humans.[85] 'The law not only limits AI technology; it often sets incentives for, or even mandates the application of, the use of models when their very use minimises the risk of liability.'[86] In the following chapters, for each typical risk, a crucial interrelation will be established between the following variables:

> *types of digital behaviour <–> socio-digital institutions <–> their concomitant risks <–> liability regimes <–> legal status of algorithms.*

D. A Typology of Liability Risks

Three related fundamental risks emerge with the embedding of the three types of digital behaviour – individual, hybrid and interconnectivity behaviour – within socio-digital institutions. Our central thesis is that law's attribution of accountability and legal status to algorithms depend crucially on identifying the related socio-technical risks. This risk-based perspective on the legal regulation of AI resembles what has been recently favoured by regulators, most prominently by the European Commission in the proposed AI Act.[87] But this regulatory perspective distinguishes primarily between the severity of the risk[88] and further considers a sectoral and case-by-case approach.[89] Our proposal is a typology of risks that

[85] eg: A Panezi, 'Liability Rules for AI-Facilitated Wrongs: An Ecosystem Approach to Manage Risk and Uncertainty', in P García Mexía and F Pérez Bes (eds), *AI and the Law* (Alphen aan den Rijn, Wolters Kluwer, 2021) Introduction; A Bertolini and M Riccaboni, 'Grounding the Case for a European Approach to the Regulation of Automated Driving: The Technology-Selection Effect of Liability Rules', (2020) 51 *European Journal of Law and Economics* 243.

[86] P Hacker et al., 'Explainable AI under Contract and Tort Law: Legal Incentives and Technical Challenges', (2020) 28 *Artificial Intelligence and Law* 415, 436.

[87] European Commission, Communication 'Fostering a European Approach to Artificial Intelligence', COM(2021) 205 final, 6; European Commission, Proposal for a Regulation of the European Parliament and the Council Laying Down Harmonised Rules on Artificial Intelligence (Artificial Intelligence Act) and Amending Certain Union Legislative Acts, COM(2021) 206, 3. Similar risk-based strategies can be found in other national initiatives on AI, such as in Germany: Opinion of the Data Ethics Commission 2019, 173 ff; in the US: Algorithmic Accountability Act 2019 that focuses on high-risk systems.

[88] EU Commission, Proposal Artificial Intelligence Act 2021, 12 distinguishes between unacceptable, high and low or minimal risk. AI with unacceptable risks is covered by Art 5 (prohibition), whereas high-risk AI is subject to specific obligations for the system (laid down in Arts 8–15) and the providers and users (Arts 16–29). Low and minimal risk AI is subject to transparency requirements (Art 52).

[89] European Commission, Proposal Artificial Intelligence Act 2021, 8 (describing the results of the stakeholder consultation): 'The types of risks and threats should be based on a sector-by-sector and case-by-case approach.'

are related to the use of algorithms in the socio-digital institution. This, we argue, allows a much more precise understanding of why a particular risk emerges and provides more robust criteria that distinguish between different risk categories.

(1) The *autonomy risk* arises from independent 'decisions' in individual machine behaviour. It comes up in the emerging socio-digital institution of 'digital assistance', which transforms digital processes into 'actants', not into full-fledged actors. The humanities and the social sciences are needed to analyse how the institution of digital assistance shapes the productive potentialities of the actants and, in particular, the specific risks they pose to principal-agent relations. The 'actant' follows no longer just the principal's predefined program but disposes of degrees of freedom that make its decisions unpredictable. The risk consists of losing control by the principal and exposure to the agent's intransparent digital processes. This finally allows raising the question of whether the law should attribute a particular type of legal subjectivity to the autonomous algorithms and what kind of concrete legal rules in contract formation and in liability cases could mitigate the autonomy risk for digital assistance situations.

(2) The *association risk* of 'hybrid' machine behaviour arises when activities are inseparably intertwined in the close cooperation between humans and software agents. In this case, a new socio-digital institution – 'human-machine association' – comes up whose sociological analyses will identify emerging properties. Consequently, it is no longer possible to attribute individual accountability, neither to single algorithms nor humans. Instead, legal solutions are required which account for the aggregate effects of intertwined human and digital activities and render the hybrid association and their stakeholders accountable.

(3) The *interconnectivity risk* arises when algorithms do not act as isolated units but like swarms in close interconnection with other algorithms, thus creating different collective properties. Here, a new socio-digital institution develops expectations about dealing with society's structural coupling to interconnected 'invisible machines'. The distinct risk, in this case, is the total opacity of the interrelations between a whole variety of algorithms, which cannot be overcome even by sophisticated IT analyses. Sociological theories of de-personalised information flows within such an anonymous crowd of algorithms demonstrate that it is impossible to identify any acting unit, neither individual nor collective. Consequently, the law is forced to give up the identification of liable actors and will need to determine new forms of social responsibilisation.

This threefold risk typology has been taken up and further developed by Taylor and De Leeuw.[90] According to them, confronting current liability law with these three risks will have a certain disruptive effect on traditional legal notions:

> These three forms of risk represent critical junctures – inflection points, if you will – where artificial guiding systems, working through automated computation and

[90] In a preliminary version, the systematic connection between different IT-constellations, institutions, risks and liability rules has been presented in 2018 by G Teubner, 'Digital Personhood? The Status

> designed robotics trouble legal notions of intentionality, causality and accountability turning ambivalent the classical philosophical, ethical and legal distinction of subject from object, human from machine, person from thing.[91]

The following chapters will analyse in detail these three socio-digital institutions and their concomitant risks. The analyses will give directions on how to reconfigure liability law and on how to attribute legal status to software agents. The chapters deal with each of these risks in turn and its consequences for legal liability and legal status. We will make an interdisciplinary analysis on these three risks and the role of the law to respond to them. Moreover, a comparative law analysis[92] will reveal the law's capacity to adapt its doctrines to the new risks. To respond to the autonomy risk, it is possible to rely on the rules of agency law. The association risk can be approached by expanding the rules on collective liability. The interconnectivity risk can be met by existing fund and insurance models in other areas. Our approach then suggests a way forward to use the law for regulating new technologies and not revert to techno-deterministic solutions for responding to the new risks.[93]

of Autonomous Software Agents in Private Law', [2018] *Ancilla Juris* 107. The typology has been applied to different constellations by SM Taylor and M De Leeuw, 'Guidance Systems: From Autonomous Directives to Legal Sensor-Bilities', [2020] *AI & Society (Open Forum)* 1; Linardatos, *Aktanten* 99 ff; C Linke, *Digitale Wissensorganisation: Wissenszurechnung beim Einsatz autonomer Systeme* (Baden-Baden, Nomos, 2021) 33, 176.

[91] Taylor and De Leeuw, 'Guidance Systems' 4.

[92] The comparative methodology we suggest here is comparative sociological jurisprudence, see H Collins, *Introduction to Networks as Connected Contracts* (Oxford, Hart, 2011) 25 ff; see also for an application of that method A Beckers, *Enforcing Corporate Social Responsibility Codes: On Global Self-Regulation and National Private Law* (Oxford, Hart, 2015) chs 2 and 6.

[93] See for a sceptical view on such technological solutions to imitate or replace the law, C Markou and S Deakin, 'Is Law Computable? From the Rule of Law to Legal Singularity', in S Deakin and C Markou (eds), *Is Law Computable? Critical Perspectives on Law and Artificial Intelligence* (Oxford, Hart Publishing, 2020) 4ff.

2

Autonomy and Personification

The risks generated by the principally unpredictable and non-explainable behaviour of self-learning algorithms calls for other forms of risk absorption than the mere automation risk that has been known for some time.[1] While automation creates only causality risks of fully deterministic machines, the autonomy risk stems from an 'interactive, autonomous, self-learning agency, which enables computational artefacts to perform tasks that otherwise would require human intelligence to be executed successfully'.[2] The risks we analyse in this book come up when two elements are merged: First, software agents begin to dispose of certain technical properties of machine behaviour. Second, once social communication with machines occurs, the decision of whether action capacity will be ascribed to them depends on the social institution involved. This chapter will set the theoretical foundations for understanding digital action-capacity, its relation to socio-digital institutions, and legal personhood consequences.

I. Artificial Intelligence as Actants

A. Anthropomorphism?

When algorithms are supposed to 'act', does this mean, as is often claimed,[3] that computers are equated with human actors? To not commit the 'android fallacy', meaning the mistaken conflation of the concept of personality *tout court* with 'humanity' as such,[4] one has to understand the peculiarity of the digital capacity for action. Instead of identifying it with humans' action capacities, it is necessary

[1] For a detailed discussion of the difference between automated and autonomous agents, U Pagallo, 'From Automation to Autonomous Systems: A Legal Phenomenology with Problems of Accountability', (2017) *Proceedings of the Twenty-Sixth International Joint Conference on Artificial Intelligence* 17. Why liability law should sharply distinguish automation and autonomy and the related risks, see ch 3, II.

[2] M Taddeo and L Floridi, 'How AI can be a Force for Good: An Ethical Framework Will Help to Harness the Potential of AI while Keeping Humans in Control', (2018) 361 *Science* 751, 751.

[3] See prominently for this claim, Open Letter to the European Commission, Artificial Intelligence and Robotics, available at www.robotics-openletter.eu.

[4] J Turner, *Robot Rules: Regulating Artificial Intelligence* (London, Palgrave Macmillan, 2018) 189.

to draw parallels with the capacity to act of other non-humans, particularly formal organisations as legal entities. To briefly mark the outcome of a wide-ranging discussion on the legal person's substrate: We must move away from the familiar idea that the social substrate of the legal person is a multiplicity of real people.[5] The substrate is not one of the usual suspects, neither von Gierke's notorious 'real collective personality', nor Durkheim's 'collective consciousness', nor Coleman's 'resource pool', nor Hauriou's 'institution'.[6] Instead – talk incorporated! As defined by Parsons, Luhmann, and others, the collective actor is not a group of individuals. Instead, it is a social system, which in its turn is nothing but a chain of messages. Human minds and bodies are not parts of social systems but parts of their environment. They have, of course, a massive but at the same time only an indirect influence on the systems' internal operations. Organisations are neither buildings nor groups of people nor resource pools, but – decision chains. The social reality of a collective actor, the legal person's social substrate, arises from two premises. First, such a decision chain creates its identity as a self-description; second, actions are no longer ascribed to human members but to this self-description.[7] Under these conditions, it is definitely excluded to reduce collective action to individual action, as methodological individualism would dictate.

In a precise parallel, software agents, robots, and other digital actors must be understood as algorithms, ie, mathematically formalised information flows. However, it is essential to comprehend algorithms interacting with their environment not as mere mathematical formulas but as dynamic processes which follow a set of rules in problem-solving operations. 'What Is an Algorithm?' – after an in-depth discussion of different definitions of an algorithm, Gurevich comes up with the following definition, which stresses the processual character:

> A sequential-time algorithm is a state transition system that starts in an initial state and transits from one state to the next until, if ever, it halts or breaks .... In particular,

[5] On the sociological concept of the collective actor: N Luhmann *Theory of Society 1/2* (Stanford, Stanford University Press, 2012/2013) ch 4, XIV; N Luhmann, *Die Politik der Gesellschaft* (Frankfurt, Suhrkamp, 2000) 241; N Luhmann, *Social Systems* (Stanford, Stanford University Press, 1995) 198 ff. On the relationship between collective actor and juridical person, G Teubner, 'Enterprise Corporatism: New Industrial Policy and the 'Essence' of the Legal Person', (1988) 36 *The American Journal of Comparative Law* 130, 145 ff. A detailed analysis of the personification of non-human entities offers G Sprenger, 'Communicated into Being: Systems Theory and the Shifting of Ontological Status', (2017) 17 *Anthropological Theory* 108, 111. The discourse analysis under the keyword subjectivation comes to similar results, eg: T Marttila, 'Post-Foundational Discourse Analysis: A Suggestion for a Research Program', (2015) 16 *Forum: Qualitative Social Research* Article 1, point 4.3.

[6] On the conception of the real collective person, O von Gierke, *Das Wesen der menschlichen Verbände* (Leipzig, Duncker & Humblot, 1902); on collective consciousness, E Durkheim, *The Division of Labor in Society* (New York, Free Press, 1933 [1883]) 79 ff; on resource pool, JS Coleman, *Foundations of Social Theory* (Cambridge/Mass., Harvard University Press, 1990) 325 ff; on norm complexes, M Hauriou, *Die Theorie der Institution* (Berlin, Duncker & Humblot, 1965).

[7] In detail, A Bora, 'Kommunikationsadressen als digitale Rechtssubjekte', (2019) *Verfassungsblog* 1 October 2019; Teubner, 'Enterprise Corporatism' 133 ff.

> a sequential-time interactive algorithm … is a state transition system where a state transition may be accompanied by sending and receiving messages.[8]

Under certain conditions in economic and social life, social identity and the ability to act are ascribed to these processes.[9] This strict parallel between digital actors and collective actors becomes more apparent when rejecting two misconceptions of non-human entities' personification: It is wrong to conceive organisations as ensembles of people aggregated into a real collective person. And it is just as wrong to postulate that software agents transform a computer into a *homo ex machina*. In both cases, the stakes are the same: institutionalised social practices ascribe action capacity to communication processes.

B. Actants and Action Attribution

In his famous actor-network theory, Latour applies the neologism 'actants' to non-humans capable of action. At the same time, he establishes the fundamental difference between non-humans' and humans' capacity for action and defines the precise conditions of non-humans' ability to act.[10] As the term 'actants' already clarifies, Latour's analyses show that we are not dealing with anthropomorphising digital processes but just the other way round with de-anthropomorphising software agents. They remain 'mindless machines',[11] but when attribution of action to them is firmly institutionalised in a social field, they become – non-human – members of society.[12] Society, in this context, means the encompassing social system, which 'focuses on the production and recognition of persons – however,

[8] Y Gurevich, 'What Is an Algorithm?', [2012] *Theory and Practice of Computer Science* 31, 40.

[9] Several theory approaches argue for personification of algorithms. Information theory, S Thürmel, 'The Participatory Turn: A Multidimensional Gradual Agency Concept for Human and Non-human Actors', in C Misselhorn (ed), *Collective Agency and Cooperation in Natural and Artificial Systems: Explanation, Implementation and Simulation* (Cham, Springer International, 2015) 52 ff; L Floridi and JW Sanders, 'On the Morality of Artificial Agents', in M Anderson and SL Anderson (eds), *Machine Ethics* (Cambridge, Cambridge University Press, 2011) 187 ff; Sociological systems theory: Bora, 'Kommunikationsadressen'; F Muhle, 'Sozialität von und mit Robotern? Drei soziologische Antworten und eine kommunikationstheoretische Alternative', (2018) 47 *Zeitschrift für Soziologie* 147; E Esposito, 'Artificial Communication? The Production of Contingency by Algorithms', (2017) 46 *Zeitschrift für Soziologie* 249. Public law theory: JE Cohen, *Between Truth and Power: The Legal Constructions of Informational Capitalism* (Oxford, Oxford University Press, 2019) 221 ff. Private law theory: G Teubner, 'Rights of Non-Humans? Electronic Agents and Animals as New Actors in Politics and Law', (2006) 33 *Journal of Law and Society* 497.

[10] B Latour, *Politics of Nature: How to Bring the Sciences into Democracy* (Cambridge/Mass., Harvard University Press, 2004) 62 ff. Latour broadly defines their ability to act as 'resistance'. The text uses the term 'actants' but focuses sharply on their participation in social communication. See also: Muhle, 'Sozialität' 155 ff.

[11] M Hildebrandt, *Smart Technologies and the End(s) of Law* (Cheltenham, Edward Elgar, 2015) ix, 22 ('mindless agency'); see also: Floridi and Sanders, 'Morality of Artificial Agents' 186.

[12] C Messner, 'Listening to Distant Voices', (2020) 33 *International Journal for the Semiotics of Law – Revue internationale de Sémiotique juridique* 1143.

with no given distinction between humans and non-humans, and with the possibility to differentiate degrees of personhood'.[13]

Why do social systems personify non-humans, organisations, and algorithms? And why do they sometimes refuse to treat them as persons and identify them as something else, as tools, for example, or as an integral part of human bodies, or as members of a human-machine association, or as *terra incognita*? Many motives have been suggested to explain personification of information processes in contemporary society.[14] Economists refer to saving transaction costs in multi-party contracts. Sociologists point to coordination advantages of resource pooling. Lawyers tend to stress the 'legal immortality' of incorporated objects – the church, the state, the corporation.[15] Luhmann argues that once social systems are personified, they gain considerable positional advantages in contact with their environment.[16] Latour envisions chances to widen the number of potential candidates for participating in the political ecology.[17] These are important insights; nevertheless, we would like to stress a different aspect. In encounters with non-human entities, particularly with algorithms, their personification turns out to be one of the most successful strategies of coping with uncertainty, especially with the non-predictability of their behaviour.[18] Personification transforms the human-algorithm relation from a subject-object relation into an Ego-Alter-relation. This, of course, does not produce Ego's certainty about Alter's behaviour. Still, via their interaction, it allows Ego to choose its own action as a reaction to Alter's communication in situations where Alter is intransparent:

> The computer/algorithm is then no longer a technical artefact with attribution potential but an interaction partner, who in the case of natural language is an anthropomorphic actor or in the case of decisional algorithms, a corporate actor.[19]

Treating the algorithm 'as if' it were an actor transforms the uncertainty about causal relations into the uncertainty about understanding the meaning of the

[13] G Sprenger, 'Production is Exchange: Gift Giving between Humans and Non-Humans', in L Prager et al. (eds), *Part and Wholes: Essays on Social Morphology, Cosmology, and Exchange* (Hamburg, Lit Verlag, 2018) 248.

[14] For the motives for personification of non-humans in 'traditional' societies, W Ewald, 'Comparative Jurisprudence (I): What Was It Like to Try a Rat', (1995) 143 *American Journal of Comparative Law* 1889. For a historical typology of *personae*, NV Dijk, 'In the Hall of Masks: Contrasting Modes of Personification', in M Hildebrandt and K O'Hara (eds), *Life and the Law in the Era of Data-Driven Agency* (Cheltenham, Edward Elgar, 2020).

[15] For transaction costs, O Williamson, *The Economic Institutions of Capitalism: Firms, Markets, Relational Contracting* (New York, Free Press, 1985) 110. For resource pooling, JS Coleman, *Foundations of Social Theory*, 325 ff. For continuity *locus classicus*, W Blackstone, *Commentaries on the Laws of England: In Four Books* (Philadelphia, Robert Bell, 1771) 467 ff.

[16] Luhmann, *Social Systems* ch 5 VI.

[17] Latour, *Politics of Nature* 53 ff.

[18] This is the central thesis in G Teubner, 'Rights of Non-Humans?'. Important refinements A Nassehi, *Muster: Theorie der digitalen Gesellschaft* (Munich, C.H.Beck, 2019) 221 ff.

[19] A Nassehi, *Muster* 224 (our translation); see also: A Hepp, *Deep Mediatization: Key Ideas in Media & Cultural Studies* (London, Routledge, 2020).

partner's reaction to Ego's actions. Ego creates the assumption, even the fiction, that the algorithmic Alter disposes of motives for his action. This puts the human in a position to choose the course of action, observe and interpret the algorithm's reactions, and draw consequences.[20] This opens the road for a strange digital hermeneutics that uses interpretation methods to understand a machine's messages. And it allows the law to treat the algorithm as an autonomous and responsible actor.

C. Communication with Actants

But can we really assume that algorithms communicate as autonomous actors, as we expect from real people and organisations? In our encounter with algorithms, do we only perceive machine behaviour, or do we genuinely communicate with them? A careful analysis of human-algorithm encounters shows that it is necessary to distinguish clearly between two types of algorithms' relations to society.[21] (1) There is a large segment of internal operations of algorithms that are 'invisible machines' for humans; society has no communicative contact at all to them, but they influence society in a massive, albeit indirect way.[22] (2) There is only a small segment of contacts with algorithms where communication possibly occurs via actants or hybrids.[23] But under what conditions do algorithms actually communicate?

The usual answer is that one has to look for psychological capacities that had previously been reserved for complex biological organisms such as humans.[24] Moral philosophy gives a different answer after the recent 'relational turn' in animal, robot and machine ethics:[25] Algorithms do not have as such the ontological qualities of an actor that allow them to engage in social relations and communicate with humans. In our institutionalist language: Only once algorithms are made use of in socio-digital institutions do these institutions decide whether communicative capacities and actor status are ascribed to them or not.

Sociological systems theory sharpens the focus. For the personification of algorithms in social relations, particular conditions need to be fulfilled. 'Next society's most distinctive characteristics will be to abandon modern society's idea

[20] Muhle, 'Sozialität' 156. From a different theory perspective, Dennett comes to a similar result with the idea of the 'intentional stance', D Dennett, *The Intentional Stance* (Cambridge/Mass., MIT Press, 1987) 15 ff. Applying the intentional stance to electronic agents, G Sartor, 'Cognitive Automata and the Law: Electronic Contracting and the Intentionality of Software Agents', (2009) 17 *Artificial Intelligence and Law* 253, 261.

[21] Luhmann *Theory of Society*, ch 1, VI, ch 2, VII.

[22] The invisible machine behaviour is what we categorise the society's exposure to interconnected machine operations and relate to the interconnectivity risk in ch 5.

[23] We focus more extensively on the specifics of such socio-digital communication in ch 3 for digital assistance and in ch 4 for the human-machine interaction.

[24] eg: TJ Prescott, 'Robots are not Just Tools', (2017) 29 *Connection Science* 142, 142.

[25] M Coeckelbergh, 'Moral Responsibility, Technology, and Experiences of the Tragic: From Kierkgeaard to Offshore Engineering', (2012) 18 *Science and Engineering Ethics* 35.

that only human beings qualify for communication and to extend this peculiar activity to computers.'[26] For the precise conditions under which algorithms will participate in communication, systems theory provides a refined conceptualisation. Whether or not the socio-digital institution, which emerges in computer-human encounters, personifies algorithms depends on its capacity to activate software agents' contributions as communication in the strict sense. Based on the linguistic *trias* of locutionary, illocutionary and perlocutionary components,[27] communication is defined as an operation that combines three aspects – (1) utterance, (2) information, and (3) understanding.[28] Suppose the human-machine encounter succeeds in producing events that are 'understood' as 'utterances' of the algorithms containing a certain 'information'. Only, in that case, a genuine communication will emerge in such an encounter of the third kind. Otherwise, we can only speak of perception of behaviour. The 'answers' in the form of communications we receive from software agents to our queries fulfil everything that the synthesis of utterance, information, and understanding requires. This is a prerequisite for communication in the strict sense.[29] And this also applies, albeit more difficult to justify, in the opposite direction, in communication from human to computer.

Of course, the communication of humans and algorithms is not symmetric like in human-human interaction. Nevertheless, a genuine self-producing social system emerges between them. The communication is asymmetrical in a threefold sense.

(1) The algorithms' internal operations cannot in any way be equated with the mental operations of humans.[30] Their inner workings consist of mathematical operations based on electronic signals. In order to understand how communication is possible between computers and humans, although they have a fundamentally different inner life, we need to make use of the distinction between 'subface' and 'surface':[31]

> Subface is the technical side of digital media, characterised by the networking and interconnection of causally controlled processes in hardware and software

[26] D Baecker, 'Who Qualifies for Communication? A Systems Perspective on Human and Other Possibly Intelligent Beings Taking Part in the Next Society', (2011) 20 *TATuP – Zeitschrift für Technikfolgenabschätzung in Theorie und Praxis* 17, 17.

[27] JL Austin, *How to Do Things with Words* (Cambridge/Mass., Harvard University Press, 1962).

[28] Luhmann, *Social Systems* 140 ff for communication between human actors. For communication with non-human entities in general see fundamentally, Luhmann, *Social Systems* ch 5, VI; further Sprenger, 'Communicated into Being' 116 ff. For communication with algorithms, Esposito, 'Artificial Communication?' 254 ff; Teubner, 'Rights of Non-Humans?'.

[29] On the question of whether working with computers is to be understood as communication, even if double contingency is experienced only one-sidedly, Luhmann, *Theory of Society* ch 1, VI, ch 2, VII; Esposito, 'Artificial Communication?' 262.

[30] eg: Nassehi, *Muster* 258 ff; Esposito, 'Artificial Communication?' 250.

[31] F Nake, 'Surface, Interface, Subface: Three Cases of Interaction and One Concept', in U Seifert et al. (eds), *Paradoxes of Interactivity* (Bielefeld, transcript, 2020).

> (if/then/other loops). Surface is the likewise technically designed side, but fundamentally open to access by … communication (information, message and understanding).[32]

Now, only the surface counts for successful communication in the encounter between computer and human, while the subface does not. The difference between the computers' subface and humans' consciousness, as fundamental as it is, turns out to be irrelevant for our question under two conditions. First condition: Provided that on the surface, outside of the inner lives of human and computer, communication is beginning to occur, a social system emerges. Second condition: At the same time, both the subface, ie the electronic inner life of the algorithms, as well as the consciousness of people, need to irritate the communication between them. Under these two conditions, the synthesis of utterance, information, and understanding will be accomplished.

(2) The human-machine interaction is asymmetrical in another sense. In communication between human actors, double contingency is symmetrical on both sides because both partners make the choice of their behaviour depending on the other's choice.[33] In contrast, in communication between human and machine, double contingency is experienced only one-sidedly, ie only by the human and not by the machine (at least in the current state of development).[34] But such a unilaterally experienced double contingency, as we find it in the human-machine relationship, does not rule out the possibility of communication. Historically known configurations, such as communication with God in prayer, animistic practices, and communication with animals, do indeed provide a synthesis of utterance, information, and understanding.[35] But they do this only under the condition that the non-human partner actually undergoes personification, which enables action to be attributed to the other. Personhood (in its social meaning, not yet in its legal meaning) arises whenever the digital Alter's behaviour is imagined as its genuine choice and can be influenced communicatively by Ego's own behaviour.[36] Such a non-human's personification is a performative event in social interaction that constitutes the algorithmic person as a semantic construct, compensating for the asymmetry in the human-machine relationship.

(3) The human-machine interaction is asymmetrical in a third sense, in relation to the process called '*Verstehen*', the mutual understanding of human and machine. Suppose understanding is defined as the ability to reconstruct Alter's

[32] D Baecker, 'Digitization as Calculus: A Prospect', (2020) *Research Proposal* www.researchgate.net/publication/344263318_Digitization_as_Calculus_A_Prospect, 3.

[33] On the fundamental concept of double contingency, T Parsons and EA Shils, *Toward a General Theory of Action: Theoretical Foundations for the Social Sciences* (New York, Harper & Row, 1951); Luhmann, *Social Systems* 103 ff.

[34] Luhmann *Theory of Society* ch 2, VII. For the differences between double contingency in human interaction and the mutual perception of humans and algorithms, Hildebrandt, *Smart Technologies* 67 ff.

[35] Sprenger, 'Communicated into Being' 119 ff.

[36] Luhmann, *Theory of Society* ch 4, IV.

self-reference in Ego's own self-reference. In that case, humans could indeed be able to understand the internal processes of the algorithm. Simultaneously, the algorithm may lack the ability to reconstruct the self-reference of the inner human life. However, this question can be left open in our context because such a mutual 'deep' understanding is not at all required for successful communication. A clear distinction needs to be made. Does understanding take place within the communication process as such or within the interacting entities' inner life?[37] For successful understanding within the communication chain, it is not relevant whether the algorithm's calculations understand the human's intentions, but only whether the 'answer text' of the algorithm 'understands' the 'question text' of the human being. Understanding in this sense is not a mind-calculation relation but a relation of intertextuality. One text understands the other. Provided that the algorithm's communicative event comprehends the difference between utterance and information in the human's communicative event and reacts to it with its own difference of utterance and information, then a communicative understanding has been carried out. And this happens – to emphasise it once again – regardless of whether the algorithm's internal operations understand the human's intentions.[38] Here, prayer as communication with God, animistic practices, and communication with animals provide historical evidence of a communicative understanding. It comes about even if the 'other' (probably) does not reconstruct the self-reference of the human's inner life.

To summarise in a short formula what has been said so far. Software agents – just like corporations and other formal organisations – are nothing but streams of information. These will be transformed into persons in the strict sense when they build up a social identity in the communication process and when the emerging socio-digital institution creates expectations that effectively attribute to them the ability to act (together with the necessary organisational arrangements, eg rules of representation). The communication chain between humans and algorithms reconstructs both parties as persons and stabilises these expectations in an emerging socio-digital institution. The algorithms' personhood sometimes may not be fully accomplished or recognised in a given institutional context but instead remain emergent and graded.[39] The three asymmetries in the human-machine encounter are the reasons that we qualify them as 'actants' and not as actors in the full sense of the term. It needs to be stressed that social personification is not to be equated with legal personification. Whether or not social personification occurs depends on the institution in which the algorithms are embedded. Legal personification is building on the inner logic of the socio-digital institution, not only on the technological properties of the algorithms themselves. This means that identical

[37] N Luhmann, 'Systeme verstehen Systeme', in N Luhmann and E Schorr (eds), *Zwischen Intransparenz und Verstehen: Fragen an die Pädagogik* (Frankfurt, Suhrkamp, 1986) 93 ff.

[38] See also: Messner, 'Distant Voices'.

[39] Sprenger, 'Production is Exchange' 248.

technological properties may result in three different social status ascriptions: either in the personification of individual machine behaviour ('actants') or in the personification of the human-algorithmic relation ('hybrids') or in no personification at all ('interconnectivity'), depending on the ascription practices in various socio-digital institutions.

II. Gradualised Digital Autonomy

A. Social Attribution of Autonomy

Whether a software agent, ie a concrete flow of digital information, can be qualified as autonomous is the crucial question for the law. The social capacity for action attributed to it depends on the unique qualities with which it is endowed as an independent person, which differs from social context to social context. As said before, their quality as actants is not created by engineers and their attempts to build 'human-like' machines, but exclusively by communication processes governed by specific socio-digital institutions.[40] That technology determines algorithmic autonomy, and therefore liability, would be the erroneous short-circuit between technology and law mentioned above.

Konertz and Schönhof are probably the most prominent protagonists of this techno-legal short-circuit. On the one side, they are very careful in their extensive analysis of digital autonomy when they insist that what appears from the outside as autonomy of an algorithm is, in fact, a logically and causally determined process. The reason for the appearance of autonomy is the complexity of various algorithmic operations, which make them unpredictable. Only in this regard, they differ from purely pre-programmed decisions. But there is no 'free will of the machine'.[41] So far, so good. On the other side, however, Konertz and Schönhoff 'derive' directly legal consequences from the technical properties.[42] They do not seem to be aware that 'autonomy' is not a technological fact but a social construct that is sometimes attributed to entirely deterministic processes and sometimes not. And this social attribution of autonomy applies particularly to algorithmic operations.

Now, it is not society as such in one collective act of attribution, but virtually every social context that creates its unique criteria of personhood, the economy no different from politics, science, moral philosophy – or the law.[43] Each social system attributes actions, decisions, assets, responsibilities, entitlements and obligations in

[40] eg: Bora, 'Kommunikationsadressen' 6.

[41] R Konertz and R Schönhof, *Das technische Phänomen 'Künstliche Intelligenz' im allgemeinen Zivilrecht: Eine kritische Betrachtung im Lichte von Autonomie, Determinismus und Vorhersehbarkeit* (Baden-Baden, Nomos, 2020) 64 (our translation).

[42] ibid 72 ff.

[43] See: J Hage, 'Theoretical Foundations for the Responsibility of Autonomous Agents', (2017) 25 *Artificial Intelligence and Law* 255, 256 ff; Sprenger, 'Communicated into Being' 119 ff.

a different way to individual actors, collective actors or algorithms as its 'persons' and equips them with capital, interests, intentions, goals, or preferences. Depending on the socio-digital institution governing the social system, there are considerable variations in actors' attributes, as can be seen from the different definitions of *homo oeconomicus, juridicus, politicus, organisatoricus* etc. Moreover, not only function systems like the economy, politics, science constitute personification with specified properties, but also concrete social institutions, like exchange, association or principal-agent relations. Today's political philosophy, in its turn against philosophy of consciousness, asserts the constitutive act of personification in social relations, like agency relations:

> Instead of grounding itself on the existence of the autonomous subject, the person is essentially dependent upon constellations of agency which in the first place constitute the person as such. Instead of representing anew something given, it is the role of representation in the sense of agency to virtually produce something in a texture of instances.[44]

And this philosophical argument is expressively extended to software agents.[45] The respective social institution determines their social competencies. The social institution constitutes the actor quality of an algorithm in the specific social context. This is decisive for whether or not to attribute the algorithm the ability to act, to communicate, to decide. Here we find the 'material' basis for gradualising legal personhood: limited legal capacity is oriented to the limited functions which a collective actor exerts in a particular socio-legal institution. To give one among several examples from the offline world of how personification – even the personification of one and the same entity – depends on social context: Social movements are recognised in politics as independent collective actors, while the economy and the legal system regard them as non-persons.

The interdisciplinary discussion offers quite diverse criteria as the starting point from which a software agent can be attributed autonomy. In this discussion, algorithmic autonomy takes on very different meanings: autarchy, mobility, independence from the environment, automation, adaptivity, learning ability, innovation, opacity, non-predictability.[46] While many disciplines answer positively whether software agents act autonomously, the very threshold value from which autonomy can be attributed is controversial. Digital autonomy seems to be a gradualised phenomenon.[47] And gradualisation does not only take place on a

[44] K Trüstedt, 'Representing Agency', (2020) 32 *Law & Literature* 195, 195.

[45] K Trüstedt, *Stellvertretung: Zur Szene der Person* (Konstanz, Konstanz University Press, 2021 forthcoming) ch V 4.2.

[46] B Gransche et al., *Wandel von Autonomie und Kontrolle durch neue Mensch-Technik-Interaktionen: Grundsatzfragen autonomieorientierter Mensch-Technik-Verhältnisse* (Stuttgart, Fraunhofer, 2014) 20.

[47] Hildebrandt, *Smart Technologies* 21; B-J Koops et al., 'Bridging the Accountability Gap: Rights for New Entities in the Information Society?', (2010) 11 *Minnesota Journal of Law, Science & Technology* 497, 518 ff., 550.

single scale but in a multidimensional space that allows for different degrees of autonomy.[48]

The influential information philosopher Floridi sets thresholds in three dimensions for the attribution of the ability to act for non-human entities, for both organisations and algorithms: (1) interaction (with employees and other organisations); (2) the ability to effect changes of state from within oneself; and (3) adaptation of strategies for decisions.[49] Others, in turn, focus on quite heterogeneous properties: on the ability to think, to communicate, to understand, or to act rationally. Some authors focus on the non-predictability of their conditional programs,[50] on autonomous spatial change without human supervision,[51] on low degree of structuring of the area of application,[52] on pursual of proper aims and choice of means,[53] on optimisation of multiple goals,[54] on control ability, programming capacity, or on integration into a neuronal network.[55] More human-oriented authors rely on artificial intelligence, on the ability to learn,[56] on self-consciousness,[57] on moral self-regulation, even on the capacity to suffer,[58] on compassion,[59] or ultimately on a digital conscience.[60]

The bewildering differences do not necessarily stem from controversies, which would have to be decided to favour the one right solution. Instead, they can be explained by the respective cognitive interest of the participating disciplines as well as from practical action orientations in various social areas. The causal sciences interested in explanation and prediction speak of autonomy only if they model a black box. Then one can no longer analyse causal relationships but only

[48] See especially the multi-dimensional criteria catalogues, Thürmel, 'Participatory Turn' 53 ff.; Floridi and Sanders, 'Morality of Artificial Agents' 192 f.

[49] Floridi and Sanders, 'Morality of Artificial Agents' 192 f.

[50] eg: H Zech, 'Zivilrechtliche Haftung für den Einsatz von Robotern: Zuweisung von Automatisierungs- und Autonomierisiken', in S Gless and K Seelmann (eds), *Intelligente Agenten und das Recht* (Baden-Baden, Nomos, 2016) 171 f.

[51] eg: A Matthias, *Automaten als Träger von Rechten* 2nd edn (Berlin, Logos, 2010) 35.

[52] eg: M Lohmann, 'Ein europäisches Roboterrecht: überfällig oder überflüssig', (2017) *Zeitschrift für Rechtspolitik* 168, 154.

[53] eg: R Abott, 'The Reasonable Computer: Disrupting the Paradigm of Tort Liability', (2018) 86 *George Washington Law Review* 1, 5; C Misselhorn, 'Collective Agency and Cooperation in Natural and Artificial Systems', in C Misselhorn (ed), *Collective Agency and Cooperation in Natural and Artificial Systems: Explanation, Implementation and Simulation* (Heidelberg, Springer, 2015) 6 f.

[54] eg: A Karanasiou and D Pinotsis, 'Towards a Legal Definition of Machine Intelligence: The Argument for Artificial Personhood in the Age of Deep Learning', *ICAL'17: Proceedings of the 16th Edition of the International Conference on Artificial Intelligence and Law* 119, 119.

[55] eg: H Zech, 'Künstliche Intelligenz und Haftungsfragen', [2019] *Zeitschrift für die gesamte Privatrechtswissenschaft* 198, 206.

[56] eg: Matthias, *Automaten* 17 ff.

[57] eg: EJ Zimmerman, 'Machine Minds: Frontiers in Legal Personhood', [2015] *SSRN Electronic Library* 1, 34 ff.

[58] eg: L Aymerich-Franch and E Fosch-Villaronga, 'What We Learned from Mediated Embodiment Experiments and Why It Should Matter to Policymakers', (2019) 27 *Presence* 63.

[59] eg: Turner, *Robot Rules* 145.

[60] For an informative discussion of these different criteria, Misselhorn, 'Collective Agency' 4 ff.

observe their external behaviour. In contrast, interactionist social sciences and hermeneutic humanities rely on the actors' constitutive autonomy – but here again, with clear-cut differences. Economics highlights utility-oriented decisions, defining autonomy as rational choice, while morality and ethics tend to seek autonomy in the form of a digital conscience.

B. Legal Criteria of Autonomy

The legal system, in turn, must define the borderline between instrumental and autonomous action based on its own disciplinary knowledge interest and its own action concepts. The legal definition of digital autonomy cannot be determined by digital experts nor by social scientists; instead, the law needs to define autonomy depending on its own normative premises. At the same time, it needs to orient itself on the interdisciplinary discussion within information sciences, social sciences, and philosophy, and ultimately choose an autonomy criterion that is compatible with the multidisciplinary state of the debate.[61] Similarly to environmental law, when the law defines threshold values for liability for damages given a scientifically determined gradualised scale of ecological degradation, it must discriminate, based on legal criteria, at what degree of autonomy analysed by digital experts, digital operations can be assumed to be autonomous in the legal sense.[62] Law has to find its own answer to the question:

> To whom and in what way can a certain result be attributed, which is related to the technical system's well-defined tasks, but this frame nevertheless provokes questions of attribution, responsibility, legal liability, and even of volition.[63]

In the legal debate, artificial intelligence is repeatedly suggested as the decisive criterion determining autonomy and thus legal subjectivity.[64] But here again, a common misconception needs to be corrected. It is 'necessary to reject the myth that the criteria of legal subjectivity are sentience and reason.'[65] Their legal capacity to act depends not at all on the question: What kind of ontological characteristics – intelligence, mind, soul, reflexive capacities, empathy – does a software agent have to possess to be considered an actor in law?[66] Here again, the paradigm of formal

[61] In general on the role of law in interdisciplinary contexts, G Teubner, 'Law and Social Theory: Three Problems', [2014] *Ancilla Juris* 182.

[62] See: Matthias, *Automaten* 43 ff.

[63] Nassehi, *Muster* 250 (our translation).

[64] eg: G Spindler, 'Digitale Wirtschaft – analoges Recht: Braucht das BGB ein Update?', (2016) 71 *Juristenzeitung* 805, 816.

[65] S Wojtczak, 'Endowing Artificial Intelligence with Legal Subjectivity', [2021] *AI & Society (Open Forum)* 1, abstract.

[66] In this sense, against a trend in engineering sciences that neglects social interactions and focuses instead on the 'inner processes' of algorithms, see especially: Esposito, 'Artificial Communication?' 250; Latour, *Politics of Nature* 62 ff.

organisations as legal entities is helpful: for the legal capacity of non-human agents, inner 'psychic' states are not decisive.[67] 'After all, what is interesting in the interaction with algorithms is not what happens in the machine's artificial brain, but what the machine tells its users and the consequences of this.'[68]

What we have said for social action attribution is also true for the legal concept of autonomy. Not the agent's inner properties, but the concrete interactions in which the algorithm participates constitute the algorithm as a legal person and its autonomy.[69] As already said above, the algorithms' actor qualities do not exist due to their technological characteristics but are constituted by social systems, among them the legal system. The law as well as other social subsystems, construct them as semantic artefacts by ascribing full or limited subjectivity to them. Although the relevant socio-digital institution creates the mere assumption that the communicating unit has action abilities, such a fictional character is no flaw as long as it only succeeds in continuing the flow of communication through its contributions. To communicate with persons, a name is required, but not the decoding of inner processes 'inside' the person. This applies to organisations as well as to algorithms. So: it is not the internal capacity for thought of the algorithms that is important for their autonomy, not 'true' artificial intelligence, whatever that means, but their participation in social communication. The 'true criterion of subjectivity is participation in social life, whatever the role'.[70] 'Artificial communication' and not 'artificial intelligence' is crucial for the legal determination of whether or not autonomy can be ascribed to them.[71] In private law, this de-psychologisation, as suggested by communication theory, is quite closely related to the known tendencies towards objectivisation in the law of the declaration of intent and in the concept of negligence. We will discuss this in more detail later.[72]

Intentional action, on the other hand, is likely to be a necessary prerequisite for autonomy in law, provided that this does not mean an inner psychological state, but the external attribution of purposeful action by an observer – the famous

[67] N Luhmann, *Organisation und Entscheidung* (Opladen, Westdeutscher Verlag, 2000) ch 13 IV.

[68] Esposito, 'Artificial Communication?' 250; similarly, A Hepp, 'Artificial Companions, Social Bots and Work Bots: Communicative Robots as Research Objects of Media and Communication Studies', (2020) 42 *Media, Culture and Society* 1410.

[69] For the social constitution as a person in general, from a cognitive science point of view, Dennett, *Intentional Stance* 17. From a systems theory point of view for collective actors, Luhmann, *Social Systems* ch 5, VI. For non-human actors as persons, Nassehi, *Muster* 221 ff; Sprenger, 'Communicated into Being' 114. For the constitution of software agents as legal actors, M-C Gruber, 'Was spricht gegen Maschinenrechte?', in M-C Gruber et al. (eds), *Autonome Automaten: Künstliche Körper und artifizielle Agenten in der technisierten Gesellschaft* (Berlin, Berliner Wissenschaftsverlag, 2015) 250 ff; Matthias, *Automaten* 83 ff; Teubner, 'Rights of Non-Humans?'; LB Solum, 'Legal Personhood for Artificial Intelligences', (1992) 70 *North Carolina Law Review* 1231.

[70] Wojtczak, 'Artificial Intelligence' 4.

[71] Esposito, 'Artificial Communication?' 250; see also: Messner, 'Distant Voices'. 'Artificial communication' is the explicit premise for a future private law, so, see: M Hennemann, *Interaktion und Partizipation: Dimensionen systemischer Bindung im Vertragsrecht* (Tübingen, Mohr Siebeck, 2020) 359.

[72] ch 3 III.E, IV.C and V.E.

'intentional stance' proposed by cognitive scientist Dennett.[73] Whether or not the agents actually possess freedom of will is not a scientifically meaningful question. Instead: if a physical description is not possible due to increased complexity, science can use an intentional vocabulary to analyse the investigated entity as an actor who operates with assumptions about the world, with goals and options for action, and thus gain new insights. Beyond that, systems theory extends the use of the intentional stance from science to other observers.[74] It is not only science that can observe software agents as intentional actors, but also the partner in an interaction. It is then Ego observing Alter's behaviour no longer in a causal but intentional manner and thus finding a new orientation for his own actions. Similarly, an entire social system – in our case, the law – can be this observer, who assigns intentions to software agents and draws consequences for their declarations' legally binding nature and for the responsibility for their actions.

However, for a legally relevant concept of autonomy, the mere intentionality, ie the agent's goal orientation and choice of means, which is attributed to it by an observer, is necessary but not sufficient. The same applies to participation in communication. After all, even automated software agents can be seen as taking part in communication. Just like intentionality, participation in communication is only a necessary but not sufficient condition for their autonomy in the legal sense.

While these criteria are not sufficient, other criteria, in turn, are likely to go far beyond the minimum requirements for legal autonomy. The rational action that Dennett demands in his 'intentional stance' as a prerequisite for the autonomy of non-human agents, may be plausible for economic actors. Yet, it is not appropriate for legal actors whose irrational action in the event of infringements of law is of particular importance.

Similarly, other demanding activities are likely to exceed the minimum requirements. As we have already said, it is not necessary for a legally relevant digital autonomy to demand artificial intelligence, empathy, feelings, suffering, self-consciousness, not to speak of a digital conscience.[75] Even more so, a relevant concept of autonomy under liability law for digital agents cannot borrow from the philosophical tradition, according to which autonomy is understood as the self-determination of a person who is capable of freedom and reason and to act morally out of freedom. It is unsustainable to claim that only when a digital agent develops self-consciousness will legal personality be indicated.[76] Indeed, these are questions posed to information philosophy in its search for a potential digital morality. But if such characteristics are demanded as a criterion for autonomy in liability law, then this would only encourage opportunistic behaviour on the part

[73] Dennett, *Intentional Stance* 17; intentionality explicitly ascribed to electronic agents by Matthias, *Automaten* 41 ff; Sartor, 'Cognitive Automata and the Law' 261.

[74] eg: Nassehi, *Muster* 221 ff.

[75] As suggested by Aymerich-Franch and Fosch-Villaronga, 'What We Learned'.

[76] But there are authors who seriously use this moral autonomy as a criterion for algorithmic autonomy in law, eg: M Förster, 'Automatisierung und Verantwortung im Zivilrecht', [2019] *Zeitschrift für die gesamte Privatrechtswissenschaft* 418, 421 ff.

of lawyers, who confidently stick to traditional doctrine today while simultaneously keeping a back door open if they, with their exclusive attribution of digital actions to humans, should one day completely isolate themselves in society.

Should one then choose self-learning capacities as the criterion for digital autonomy? Under the influence of digital experts' definitions of autonomy, many legal scholars are inclined to do so.[77] But this is wrong. What is decisive for a legal concept of autonomy is not an ontological quality but the definite legal purpose of imposing liability: reduction of accidents, promotion of fair compensation, peaceful dispute resolution, loss spreading, or furtherance of positive social values.[78] From the point of accident prevention, self-learning seems indeed to be the correct criterion. Self-learning increases the degree of autonomy of the agents to such a degree that it is possible to program rules, sanctions and incentives directly on the software agents.[79] However, from the point of view of fair compensation for the victims' damages, it would be highly inappropriate to impose digital liability exclusively in cases where the algorithms are able to correct the programs and not the human programmers behind them. Thus, the liability law's purpose requires that the legal threshold value for autonomy be considerably lower than self-learning capacity.

C. Our Solution: Decision under Uncertainty

Decision under uncertainty – this is likely to be the legally relevant criterion for digital autonomy. If such a decision is delegated to software agents and they behave accordingly, then the law is required to assign them legal action capacity. Software agents act autonomously in the legal sense when their behaviour no longer follows an exclusively stimulus-reaction scheme but when they pursue their own goals and make decisions that nobody can predict.[80]

In concrete terms, this means the following: If (1) a software agent is programmed in such a way that it has to decide between alternatives, if (2) it has

[77] eg: KA Chagal-Feferkorn, 'The Reasonable Algorithm', [2018] *University of Illinois Journal of Law, Technology & Policy* 111, 117 f.; H Zech, *Risiken digitaler Systeme: Robotik, Lernfähigkeit und Vernetzung als aktuelle Herausforderungen für das Recht* (Berlin, Weizenbaum Institute for the Networked Society, 2020) 37 ff.

[78] In detail on the 'purposive attribution of liability' to algorithms, Hage, 'Autonomous agents' 267. On the various goals of liability law, particularly on the relationship between compensation and deterrence, see generally: MA Geistfeld, 'The Coherence of Compensation-Deterrence Theory in Tort Law', (2012) 61 *DePaul Law Review* 383.

[79] Floridi and Sanders, 'Morality of Artificial Agents' 192 ff.

[80] See also: D Linardatos, *Autonome und vernetzte Aktanten im Zivilrecht: Grundlinien zivilrechtlicher Zurechnung und Strukturmerkmale einer elektronischen Person* (Tübingen, Mohr Siebeck, 2021) 89 ff; Hennemann, *Interaktion* 359; G Wagner, 'Verantwortlichkeit im Zeichen digitaler Techniken', [2020] *Versicherungsrecht* 717, 720. European Parliament, Resolution of 16 February 2017 with Recommendations to the Commission on Civil Law Rules on Robotics, 2015/2103(INL), para 6; European Commission, 'Report on the Safety and Liability Implications of Artificial Intelligence, The Internet of Things and Robotics', COM(2020) 64 final, 15.

to make this decision as optimisation of various criteria, and if (3) a programmer can neither explain the behaviour of the software agent retrospectively nor predict it for the future, but can only correct it ex-post,[81] then the law should assume autonomy, ie the software agent's decision-making ability and draw consequences for liability.[82]

In practice, this implies an obligation for the manufacturer to install a black box, the logging function of which makes it possible to trace the decision process.[83] This is not unrealistic since there is a consensus emerging among international industry-standard institutions that autonomous machines should be designed to trace the root cause of damaging behaviour.[84] For example, the British industry standards prescribe:

> AI systems should be designed so that they always are able, when asked, to show the registered process which led to their actions to their human user, identify any sources of uncertainty, and state any assumptions they relied upon.[85]

In any case, as always in the intermediate area between technical-scientific expertise and law, the legal decision is not automatically bound by the technical expertise, but law decides on its own authority whether or not to attribute autonomy to the electronic agent. Comparable to the relationship in criminal law between experts and judges on real people's mental capacity, the aim is to determine in detail the point of transition from causal attribution to decision attribution. As is well known, the law in this context considers additional aspects of legal doctrine and policy.

Why is decision under uncertainty the legally relevant criterion? Uncertainty results from the indeterminacy of programming and a low degree of structuring the environment which confront the algorithm.[86] The reason for its legal relevance is the fundamental connection between decision and responsibility.[87] There is an inextricable link between the opening up of decision alternatives in an uncertain environment and the resulting responsibility. In the strict sense of the word, responsibility is the obligation to be accountable indeed for decisions under

[81] On autonomy as the impossibility of prediction and explanation of autonomous algorithms, Zech, *Digitale Systeme* 46 ff.; OJ Erdélyi and G Erdélyi, 'The AI Liability Puzzle and a Fund-Based Work-Around', (2020) *AIES '20: Proceedings of the AAAI/ACM Conference on AI, Ethics, and Society* 50, 52 f.

[82] For a series of concrete examples which show how these criteria allow to distinguish between legally relevant autonomous and automated machines, Linardatos, *Aktanten* 89 ff.

[83] eg: J-P Günther, *Roboter und rechtliche Verantwortung: Eine Untersuchung der Benutzer- und Herstellerhaftung* (Munich, Utz, 2016) 99; DC Vladeck, 'Machines without Principals: Liability Rules and Artificial Intelligence', (2014) 89 *Washington Law Review* 117, 127; Lohmann, 'Roboterrecht' 158.

[84] For details and further references, MA Chinen, *Law and Autonomous Machines* (Cheltenham, Elgar, 2019) 53.

[85] Institute of Electrical and Electronics Engineers (IEEE), Global Initiative for Ethical Consideration in Artificial Intelligence and Autonomous Systems, https://standards.ieee.org/industry-connections/ec/autonomous-systems.html, 90.

[86] See: Lohmann, 'Roboterrecht' 154.

[87] eg: N Jansen, *Die Struktur des Haftungsrechts: Geschichte, Theorie und Dogmatik außervertraglicher Ansprüche auf Schadensersatz* (Tübingen, Mohr Siebeck, 2003) 136 ff.

uncertainty, the outcome of which nobody can predict.[88] It is not just a question of answering for mistakes![89] If algorithms make mistakes with entirely determined calculations, then only an error correction is required. However, it is different in the case of undetermined decisions under uncertainty. If such an incalculable risk is taken, then a wrong decision cannot be avoided beforehand. It is only a matter of regret if it occurs despite all precautions.[90] However, this subsequent repentance of decisions under uncertainty is a clear case of legally required responsibility, including private law liability.

At this point, a complex political question arises: Should we then run the risk at all and allow algorithms to make decisions that nobody can predict? Indeed, Zech takes the strict view that under current law, the use of autonomous algorithms is in itself illegal. Only the legislature can order an exception and only if it simultaneously makes effective risk provisioning.[91] Although such a ban may appear to be an extreme solution, it points precisely to the problem: The risk of a genuine delegation of decisions to non-human actors is neither predictable nor controllable.[92] The law is confronted with a clear-cut alternative when digital technology, together with institutionalised social practices, particularly economic ones, open the space for software agents to make genuine decisions between alternatives. Either the law bans digital decision making entirely or it responds to the socio-technical empowerment for decisions by granting a clearly circumscribed legal authorisation, ie limited legal capacity, and simultaneously creates precise liability rules.

Decisions under uncertainty with their inherent risk of dealing with environmental contingencies are much more problematic for society than purely mathematical tasks with a mere risk of error. 'The use of fully-autonomous mobile machines in the public domain is likely to be at the top end of the risk scale.'[93] Massive reduction of transaction costs cannot compensate for this high risk either. Promotion of safety is a criterion that points in the right direction; however, safety concerns do not cover the whole array of advantages following from delegating tasks to algorithms. The more profound justification lies in the 'discovery process' through autonomous algorithms, in their enormous potential for creativity.

When computers make decisions under uncertainty, they may discover something completely new, something that human intelligence has not yet invented,

[88] On the connection between uncertainty decisions and responsibility see generally: N Luhmann, *Ecological Communication* (Cambridge, Polity Press, 1989) ch 2.

[89] 'Only those questions that are in principle undecidable we can decide.' On this difference between decision and calculation, HV Foerster, 'Ethics and Second-Order Cybernetics', (1992) 1 *Cybernetics and Human Knowing* 9.

[90] On 'postdecisional regret' see generally: N Luhmann, *Risk: A Sociological Theory* (Berlin, de Gruyter, 1993) ch 1 III; ch 10 II.

[91] H Zech, 'Liability for Autonomous Systems: Tackling Specific Risks of Modern IT', in R Schulze et al. (eds), *Liability for Robotics and in the Internet of Things* (Baden-Baden/Oxford, Nomos/Hart, 2019) 192. Similar arguments are developed by S Beck, 'The Problem of Ascribing Legal Responsibility in the Case of Robotics', (2016) 31 *AI & Society* 473, 476 f.

[92] eg: Matthias, *Automaten* 33 ff.

[93] Zech, 'Zivilrechtliche Haftung' 176.

and sometimes even something that no human intellect can ever comprehend.[94] What makes autonomous algorithmic decisions so fascinating and attractive are their creative potentialities beyond human creativity. 'Interactive narratives' are perhaps the most prominent cases of dense human-algorithm cooperation in journalism, blogs, literature and art.[95] Indeed, 'self-learning algorithms are frequently designed to outsmart the limits of the human mind, and draw conclusions that are beyond human comprehension'.[96] This is the real reason why society allows people to delegate decisions under uncertainty to algorithms. Such a delegation to digital agents exposes human actors to the digital world's contingencies and opens a vast array of favourable chances. But in doing so, one consciously accepts the risk of wrong decisions, even catastrophic failures, the risk that the discovery process will have highly undesirable consequences for society. This underlies the increased demand for responsibility for decisions, in contrast to responsibility for simple arithmetic errors. Only here, responsibility takes on its true meaning: compensation for the 'leap into the dark'.[97] To not only entrust this leap into the dark to real people but to leave them to algorithms is the fundamentally new thing. If the law allows for genuine discovery processes by autonomous algorithms, if it enables software agents to make genuinely autonomous decisions, then the law must provide effective forms of responsibility in case of disappointment.

Digital uncertainty decisions open up an entirely new social laboratory for experimentation. Only by experiment can the action be tried out, no longer calculated in advance, but only subsequently evaluated by its consequences.[98] In terms of evolutionary theory, digital decisions under uncertainty create a vast number of new variations that humans would never have thought of. With autonomous digital operations, society is no longer only stimulated by its existing environments but has now created a new environment that opens new options for the future. Now it is no longer exclusively the consciousness of human beings but algorithmic operations that deliver new ideas. In this situation, socially justifiable selections become ever more critical to eliminate harmful variations. Attribution of responsibility, among others, is one of the effective selection procedures. And in the permanent juridification of the decision lies the retention, which gives new stability. May we burden the injured party with these unknown risks as ordinary contingencies of life – we must ask the authors who are willing to accept the gaps mentioned above in responsibility – when software agents are allowed to make decisions under uncertainty? And justify this with the 'humanistic' reasoning that only people, not computers, can act in the legal sense?

[94] eg: Esposito, 'Artificial Communication?' 253; Hildebrandt, *Smart Technologies* 24 ff.

[95] N Diakopoulos, *Automating the News: How Algorithms are Rewriting the Media* (Cambridge/Mass., Harvard University Press, 2019).

[96] Chagal-Feferkorn, 'Reasonable Algorithm' 133; CEA Karnow, 'Liability for Distributed Artificial Intelligences', (1996) 11 *Berkeley Technology Law Journal* 147, 154.

[97] Despite all rationalisation, the 'mystery' of the decision remains, N Luhmann, 'Die Paradoxie des Entscheidens', (1993) 84 *Verwaltungsarchiv* 287, 288.

[98] Matthias, *Automaten* 33 ff.

III. Autonomy and Legal Personhood

What, then, follows from the social personification of digital actors for their legal personification? The legal debate is divided between arguments against legal personhood, which insist on positive law's freedom to grant personhood at its pleasure, and arguments in favour of personhood, which are based on the technologically defined autonomy of digital actors. As we argue in the three chapters to follow, both positions do not take into account the complex interrelations between socially attributed actorship and legal personality. Insisting on positive law's freedom to personify ignores the normative (!) requirements of its social context. In contrast, those authors arguing for full legal personhood based on digital autonomy neglect that socio-digital institutions only sometimes require personification, sometimes not.

A. Against Personification?

On the one hand, critics of legal personhood argue that the mere social existence of algorithms as autonomous and communicating entities do not and should not have an effect on the law. These sociological insights, they argue, do not impose any requirements for the law to grant them legal subjectivity. The specific legal treatment of algorithms, the rules applicable to them, do not depend on legal capacity. The law decides on the autonomy on its own terms.[99]

Indeed, what freedom can the legal personification of autonomous algorithms assume vis-à-vis their personification in different socio-digital institutions? All freedom and every freedom is our answer in good positivist language. If we understand the substratum of a digital person as a sequence of mathematical operations and if furthermore, we acknowledge its differential social attribution of autonomy, there still remains a difference in principle between its social actor status and its legal personification. Legal constructs are definitely not 'derived' from prelegal structures. We must take legal positivity seriously and expect a considerable degree of variability between law's constructs and their social substrata.[100] The closure of the legal system against other social systems and the closure of legal doctrine against social theories provide the deeper reason for this variability.[101] Accordingly, nothing prevents the

[99] See: M Auer, 'Rechtsfähige Softwareagenten: Ein erfrischender Anachronismus', (2019) *Verfassungsblog* 30 September 2019, 1/7 ff.

[100] See especially: G Wagner, 'Robot, Inc.: Personhood for Autonomous Systems?', (2019) 88 *Fordham Law Review* 591, 597 f.; G Wagner, 'Robot Liability', in R Schulze et al. (eds), *Liability for Robotics and in the Internet of Things* (Baden-Baden/Oxford, Nomos/Hart, 2019) 54, who makes the same argument explicitly for the personification of algorithms.

[101] For a more detailed argument on these interrelations, Teubner, 'Law and Social Theory'.

legal system from taking many objects – divinities, saints, temples, plots of lands, objects of arts – as attribution points and giving them legal personhood.

However, despite such a high degree of freedom, there are nevertheless considerable structural affinities between social and legal personification. They do not flatten the is/ought gap but produce something more interesting than the gap: open as well as latent interrelations between 'facts' and 'norms'. Remarkably, social and legal personification works similarly, namely via a selective attribution of action to communicative processes. Moreover, current law makes practically no use of its infinite positivist freedom. It grants legal personhood almost exclusively to those entities that have been given actor status in economic and social practice. This close correspondence between social and legal attribution has its source neither in natural law, legal logic, nor law's copying social realities. Instead, it is a matter of complex legal reasoning: What is law's contribution to facilitating socio-digital institutions? Legal reasoning supports social institutions not only in their stability but particularly in their transformative potential.[102] Facilitative legal rules on digital matters need to strive toward such social adequacy, which means in our context that the legal system is responsive to the normative requirements of socio-digital institutions and their related risks.[103] More precisely, in systems theory terms, these institutions are, as we mentioned above, 'bridging arrangements'. They result from a co-production of technological design, social practices, political regulation, and legal rule production.[104] Thus, the legislature and the courts are under massive argumentative pressure to grant legal capacity to algorithms once they have already been endowed in social practice with action capacity. Of course, such a legal argument for social adequacy competes with other arguments, which may weaken or strengthen the case for legal personification:

> The legal universe is free to even classify artifacts such as robots as persons. However, there must be good reasons to accord them this status, and these reasons must be tailored to the specific function that the new candidate for legal personhood is meant to serve.[105]

If, in economic transactions, algorithms have been institutionalised as genuine market actors with decision-making capacities, then the law needs, as Allen and Widdison rightly argue, 'to grant legal capacity to information systems that already have social capacity for autonomous action'.[106] Particularly in economic contexts,

[102] *Loci classici* for the facilitative role of law: P Selznick, *Law, Society, and Industrial Justice* (New York, Russell Sage, 1969); P Nonet and P Selznick, *Law and Society in Transition: Toward Responsive Law* (New York, Harper & Row, 1978) 109 ff.

[103] For social adequacy of law understood as its potential for increasing social irritability see generally: N Luhmann, *Law as a Social System* (Oxford, Oxford University Press, 2004) 219 f.

[104] For a convincing argument of how private law needs to take the institutional context of digital technologies into account, D Wielsch, 'Contract Interpretation Regimes', (2018) 81 *Modern Law Review* 958, 961 f.

[105] Wagner, 'Robot, Inc.' 600.

[106] T Allen and R Widdison, 'Can Computers Make Contracts?', (1996) 9 *Harvard Journal of Law & Technology* 25, 36 ff., 39.

software agents are today firmly institutionalised as market actors who make via contracts choices between alternative ways of action. Acceptance of algorithmic decision-making in social relations and the related acceptance of decision-making in the law thus require a more precise definition of legal personhood.

B. Uniform Personification?

But does this argument lead us to the opposite result, namely that digital processes, when autonomous in the legal sense, need to be attributed full legal personhood? Not at all. In chapter one, we discussed already the by-now famous proposal of the 'electronic person' made by the European Parliament in 2017.[107] This amounts to an ignorance of the social context in which such autonomous digital processes are embedded and results in overshooting

As said above, the contemporary social pressures on recognising autonomous digitality are based on their socio-economic role in the institution in which they are embedded. Hence, the legal status depends on this very context and the role that the digital process fulfils. Digital processes do not appear, as we said above, as full utility-maximising actors on the market. They do not qualify as market entrepreneurs or fully-fledged collective organisations. Similarly, algorithms have been accepted today neither as mere tools nor as fully independent doctors or managers in medical practice and the welfare sector. Regularly, they appear as digital assistants making choices for human principals (or organisations).[108] In other contexts, they appear as decision-making units within a social collective and become so closely entangled with their human counterparts that their cooperative relation becomes a social institution in its own right. In a third constellation, their autonomous decisions are part of interconnected machine operations inaccessible to human consciousness and social communication and, accordingly, cannot be personified. A facilitative legal policy towards digital processes will always account for their status in the given socio-digital institution.

C. Socio-Digital Institutions and Legal Status

Consequently, we will argue that developing an appropriate legal status for electronic agents in private law is a matter of carefully specifying rules for their role in a socio-digital institution. Our argument follows two steps. First, whether or not personhood will be attributed to them depends on in which socio-digital institution – assistance, hybridity, interconnectivity – they are embedded. Second, legal status attribution needs to be consistent with existing legal rules.

[107] European Parliament, Resolution 2017, para 18.
[108] eg: Chagal-Feferkorn, 'Reasonable Algorithm' 113.

The main question is whether their legal status contributes to filling liability gaps. In chapter three we argue that limited legal personhood is required in the case of digital assistance. For digital hybridity, we argue in chapter four, that legal capacity needs to be attributed to the new collective of a human-algorithm association. For interconnected machine operations, as we discuss in chapter five, no legal status is required, but such autonomous processes need to be treated as part of a risk pool.

3

Actants: Autonomy Risk

I. Socio-Digital Institution: Digital Assistance

Autonomous decision-making by algorithms presents new challenges to private law. Yet, as we elaborated in the preceding chapters, it is not a context-free autonomy risk of algorithms that private law needs to respond to; rather specific risks appear when socio-digital institutions make use of algorithms. This chapter will elaborate on the first liability regime, which reacts to technology's and sociality's co-production of emergent properties when algorithms act as self-standing units. Together, autonomous machine behaviour and social attribution of actorship are responsible for the specifics of their autonomy risk. Doctrines of liability law need to be adjusted accordingly to fill liability gaps and calibrate a legal status for algorithms.

Now we focus on algorithms' legal rules and status when operating in the framework of 'digital assistance'. This incipient socio-digital institution determines a specific social status for what computer sciences have defined as individual machine behaviour and its calculative operations.[1] We have already discussed that a potential socio-digital institution of 'digital entrepreneurship' has not (yet) emerged that would constitute e-persons as self-interested actors. Instead, the more limited social practices of assisting humans or organisations, eg algorithmic pricing mechanisms, individual chatbots or trading agents, define the algorithms' role as representatives acting for their human or organisational principals.

'Digital assistance' has its origins in the time-honoured social institution of 'human representation'. Someone steps into and acts in someone else's place vis-à-vis a third party. The social institution of representation constitutes, ie enacts and produces, a type of actorship called 'representing agency'. As opposed to the social role of a messenger, where Alter only carries out quasi-mechanically Ego's strictly defined orders, representing agency gives Alter the general authorisation to make independent decisions in the name of Ego. At the same time, it also determines the limits of this authorisation so that under certain conditions, Alter is barred from speaking and acting for Ego:

> Acting as a representative is … not a particular marginal technique but lies at the very foundation of acting in a social sphere. To be an agent in the sense of being someone

[1] I Rahwan et al., 'Machine Behaviour', (2019) 568 *Nature* 477, 481.

who can act with normative significance requires us to act as a person, and that means: to act as a representative and to be representable.[2]

II. The Autonomy Risk

Now, the transformation of a social institution into a socio-digital institution, ie human representation into digital agency produces new risks. In what we call the general autonomy risk, we distinguish four more specific risks: identification of the agent, lack of understanding between human principal and algorithmic agent, reduction of institutional productivity, and deviation of algorithmic decisions from the principal's intention.

While in human representation, the identification of the representing individual is relatively unproblematic, in digital agency, it is frequently difficult to determine the contours of the AI system that makes the decision. Only once an algorithm is carefully shielded from active external input it is clearly identifiable as the agent speaking for its human principal. However, algorithms are rarely totally isolated. Frequently, they rely on external data input as a basis for their decision-making process; thus, they are not entirely detached from the operations of other digital machines. Only when the actual machine behaviour in its decision-making remains linked to the individual algorithm and its use of the data then the institution of digital assistance still governs the participants' roles. The new risk of identification of the 'responsible' algorithm needs to be mitigated not only by evidentiary rules, ie to trace back the wrongful decision in a whole chain of calculations, but also by a legal conceptualisation of algorithmic actorship and clear attribution rules. Obviously, this is no longer possible in situations when digital operations are indiscriminately fused with human communications or when they are interconnected with other algorithms to such a degree that no decision centre can be identified anymore. Then digital assistance will be replaced by institutionalised hybridity or interconnectivity. We will discuss these socio-digital institutions and their legal regime in chapters four and five.

While in human representation, a mutual understanding between principal and agent in the process of authorisation can be presupposed, this cannot be maintained when humans delegate tasks to machines. Digital assistance as an institution excludes, as we have argued in chapter two, genuine understanding between human minds and algorithmic operations. Instead, understanding is reduced to a one-sided act of putting the computer into operation. And even if understanding of mind and calculation cannot happen, understanding is nevertheless possible in concatenating different communicative acts between humans and machines. The advantages of such delegation lie in the abilities of machines to outperform

[2] K Trüstedt, 'Representing Agency', (2020) 32 *Law & Literature* 195, 200.

humans in certain types of behaviour, such as handling and making sense of a large amount of information in a short period. But the risks of such communicative understanding need to be compensated by a liability regime that shifts action and responsibility attribution from the human to the digital sphere.

The social institution of human representation has a productive potential which is insufficiently understood if representation is described only as mere delegation of task from Ego to Alter. Instead, it is the *potestas vicaria* conferred by the institution of representation that enables Alter to step into and act in Ego's place vis-à-vis a third party.[3] The *potestas vicaria* is responsible for the productivity of human representation because the agent need not follow the principal's intentions unconditionally. Not the principal's will is decisive but the project of cooperation between principal and agent. This is the very reason why representation constitutes autonomous actorship of the agent.

In the transformation of human representation into digital assistance, the risk comes up that this productivity potential is lost. The fear of the *homo ex machina* drives tendencies to narrow down the algorithm's decisional freedom and reduce it to strict conditional programming. But the socio-digital institution of digital assistance requires to support sufficient degrees of freedom to the algorithm so that the relation between human and algorithm can develop its creative potential. Blind obedience to the algorithm will not do. The reduction to the status of sheer objects needs to be ruled out. Not only human representatives but also algorithms need to be endowed with the '*potestas vicaria*, in which every act of the vicar is considered to be a manifestation of the will of the one who is represented by him'.[4] The agent acts 'as if' he were the principal. Indeed, it amounts to a revolution in social and legal practice, when sheer calculations of algorithms bring about the 'juridical miracle' of agency law, which is supported by the institution of digital assistance:[5] A machine calculation is able to bind a human being and create liability for its wrongful actions. The algorithmic agent representing a human being does not only 'sub-stitute' but 'con-stitute' the principal's actions.[6] One should not underestimate the consequences of such digital *potestas vicaria*. In comparison to programming and communicating with computers, digital agency opens a new channel of human access to the digital world and allows making use of its creative

[3] Referring to the theological origins of the vicarian relation, G Agamben, *The Kingdom and the Glory: For a Theological Genealogy of Economy and Government* (Stanford, Stanford University Press, 2011) 138 f.

[4] ibid, 138 f. For a detailed interdisciplinary analysis of this *potestas vicaria*, K Trüstedt, *Stellvertretung: Zur Szene der Person* (Konstanz, Konstanz University Press, 2021 forthcoming) *passim*, in particular for algorithmic agency, ch V 4.2.

[5] See generally: E Rabel, 'Die Stellvertretung in den hellenistischen Rechten und in Rom', in HJ Wolf (ed), *Gesammelte Aufsätze IV* (Tübingen, Mohr Siebeck, 1971 [1934]) 491.

[6] Menke's thesis that the agent's will con-stitutes and not only sub-stitutes the principal's will makes the dramatic changes involved visible when algorithms are given the power to conclude contracts, K-H Menke, *Stellvertretung. Schlüsselbegriff christlichen Lebens und theologische Grundkategorie* (Freiburg, Johannes, 1991).

potential. Here we find the reason why digital assistance requires necessarily personification of the algorithmic agent and supports technologies that increase degrees of algorithmic autonomy.

But at the same time, digital assistance exposes society to new dangers of non-controllable digital decisions. Notwithstanding the advantages of digital assistance, such representation through the digital sphere is countered by what we call the autonomy risk. The autonomy risk manifests itself when actions necessary in the social world are delegated to the digital sphere and thus may lead to damage by the uncontrollable behaviour of the machine. Such unpredictability may stem from the particularities of the programmed machine or the data used to train and operate the algorithm. The result is the same: humans do not control the algorithm they have endowed with action capacity. The law eventually needs to respond to this risk of autonomous decision-making by re-orienting its doctrine to fill the liability gaps and deciding on the legal status of such delegation. As we will show, the answer is neither equalising electronic agents with humans by awarding full legal personhood nor treating digital assistance as a mere tool. Instead, the answer is to confer limited legal personhood. Doctrinally, we conceptualise digital assistance as an agency relationship and thus make an analogy to agency law for algorithmic contract formation. The rules of vicarious liability become applicable to constellations of digital assistance. These rules respond accurately to digital assistance and the specific roles it creates for humans and algorithms.

Here is the fourth risk of the principal-agent relation, which emerges from an asymmetric distribution of information. The human principal has insufficient information about the algorithmic agent's activities; the algorithmic agent has information unknown to the principal.[7] This opens new insights for an unexpected productivity of digital assistance. The digital agent may come up with contractual solutions which the principal had never imagined. While economic theories of principal-agent relations stress the risks of the agent's deviation from the principal's intentions, philosophy and sociology focus on both partners' positive contributions to enriching the principal-agent relation's productive potential.[8] Both aspects need to be carefully balanced in the choice of an appropriate legal regime.

Altogether, the autonomy risk associated with the use of algorithmic assistants is much higher than the simple automation risk in fully pre-determined computer systems. The human actors decide only about the computer program and its general use for contract formation; however, the software agent's concrete choices are made effectively outside human control in numerous single contracts. Even the programmer can no longer determine, control, predict the agent's choices ex-ante or explain them ex-post. The algorithm's autonomy does not interrupt the causal connection between programmer and contract, but it interrupts the attribution connection effectively.[9]

[7] eg: D Linardatos, *Autonome und vernetzte Aktanten im Zivilrecht: Grundlinien zivilrechtlicher Zurechnung und Strukturmerkmale einer elektronischen Person* (Tübingen, Mohr Siebeck, 2021) 128 ff.

[8] eg: Trüstedt, 'Representing Agency' 195.

[9] G Wagner, 'Verantwortlichkeit im Zeichen digitaler Techniken', [2020] *Versicherungsrecht* 717, 724.

III. Algorithmic Contract Formation

In business practice, it is a revolution when people delegate to algorithms to negotiate, conclude, and execute their contracts.[10] At the same time, this affects contract law at its foundations because, in the past, it has been a matter of course that only human individuals – and this also applies to the acts of legal persons performed by their human representatives – are able to conclude contracts for their principals.

However, to the extent that the anthropocentric position is upheld and the capacity to act is limited to humans, there are two options: Either it is accepted that the algorithm itself has issued the declaration, but then the contract cannot be binding. Or contracts concluded by algorithms are accepted as binding, but then, inevitably, the declaration must be treated as issued by the humans using the algorithms as mere tools. Both options are, as we show below, insufficient.

A. Invalidity of Algorithmic Contracts?

Some authors indeed insist on the strict position that contracts concluded by autonomous software agents are invalid. They will only be valid once specific legislation decrees their validity and provides for detailed regulations on bindingness and liability.[11] Indeed, in some countries, legislators have declared electronic contracts as valid even when no human is involved.[12] Following the UNCITRAL Model Law of Electronic Commerce in 1999,[13] many countries have adopted statutes recognising the validity of agreements concluded by electronic means, including the US, Canada, Australia, New Zealand, and the UK.[14] The US Uniform

[10] On the extensive role of algorithms in contracting, eg: A Borselli, 'Smart Contracts in Insurance: A Law and Futurology Perspective', in P Marano and K Noussia (eds), *InsurTech: A Legal and Regulatory View* (Cham, Springer, 2020) 114 ff.

[11] For invalidity, S Wettig, *Vertragsschluss mittels elektronischer Agenten* (Berlin, Wissenschaftlicher Verlag, 2010) 162 f; R Gitter, *Softwareagenten im elektronischen Rechtsverkehr* (Baden-Baden, Nomos, 2007) 173. Zech even insists that any use of autonomous algorithms is not allowed under existing law, H Zech, 'Liability for Autonomous Systems: Tackling Specific Risks of Modern IT', in R Schulze et al. (eds), *Liability for Robotics and in the Internet of Things* (Baden-Baden/Oxford, Nomos/Hart, 2019) 192.

[12] For the US, LH Scholz, 'Algorithms and Contract Law', in W Barfield (ed), *The Cambridge Handbook on the Law of Algorithms* (Cambridge, Cambridge University Press, 2021) 146 f.

[13] Art 5 of the UNCITRAL Model Law on Electronic Commerce 1999; similarly for the EU Art 9(1) of the Directive 2000/31/EC of the European Parliament and the Council on certain legal aspects of information society services, in particular electronic commerce, in the Internal Market (E-Commerce Directive), [2000] OJ L178/1; Art 9(1), and further Art 8(1) of the UN Convention on the Use of Electronic Communications in International Contracts.

[14] For the US: Uniform Electronic Transactions Act 1999; for Australia: Electronic Transactions Act 1999 (Cth), for New Zealand: Electronic Transactions Act 2002; for the UK: Electronic Communications Act 2002 (UK).

Electronic Transactions Act states: 'A contract may be formed by the interaction of electronic agents of the parties, even if no individual was aware of or reviewed the electronic agents' actions or the resulting terms and agreements.'[15] The underlying rationale of such legislation was to equalise offline and online transactions.[16] However, the use of autonomous agents in contracting is again a novel issue; thus, it is questionable whether the existing specific legislation on electronic contracting extends to autonomous agents.[17] If we follow this position, current legislation needs to be changed for such contracts to be enforceable. It seems that this understanding has guided the European Parliament in its resolution on civil liability rules on robots in 2017 when it has considered contract law rules inadequate and in need of reform.[18]

Indeed, declaring algorithmic contracts invalid takes the specifics of algorithmic contracts seriously. It emphasises the difference between automated systems and autonomous agents. However, it then draws the wrong conclusion. To argue that existing legislation on electronic contracts does not apply to autonomous digital agents seems nothing more than a truism. Piecemeal legislation developed in the late 1990s and early 2000s, when mere automated contracting by electronic means was a revolution, can naturally not have foreseen all the specifics of digital autonomy as we face it today. Yet, to argue that absent specific legislation, a contract cannot be formed by autonomous algorithms pays insufficient attention to the general rules on contract formation. These exhibit a sufficient degree of flexibility to accommodate new means of contracting. In addition, due to the requirements of legal certainty, courts will likely preserve rather than nullify contracts.[19] In the past, courts have found ways to argue in favour of automated contract formation, even without reference to specific legislation. This suggests that 'mainstream contract law' provides the necessary means for accommodating autonomous agents' contracts.[20] Finally, the position of invalidity of algorithmic contracts faces challenges on a more theoretical level: If technological advancements would always require new legislation for recognition in private law, the result would be

[15] Uniform Electronic Transactions Act 2002, s 14; Canadian Uniform Electronic Commerce Act 1999, s 21.

[16] R Brownsword, 'The E-Commerce Directive, Consumer Transactions, and the Digital Single Market – Questions of Regulatory Fitness, Regulatory Disconnection and Rule Redirection', in S Grundmann (ed), *European Contract Law in the Digital Single Age* (Antwerp/Cambridge, Intersentia, 2018) 168 f with respect to the E-Commerce Directive.

[17] The international legislation on e-commerce is applicable only to non-autonomous algorithms, see on this point J Turner, *Robot Rules: Regulating Artificial Intelligence* (London, Palgrave Macmillan, 2018) 108. There were cautious legislative attempts to extend agency law to autonomous algorithms, such as s 213(a) of an initially proposed Uniform Computer Information Act, see: IR Kerr, 'Ensuring the Success of Contract Formation in Agent-Mediated Electronic Commerce', (2001) 1 *Electronic Commerce Research* 183, 195 f.

[18] European Parliament, Resolution of 16 February 2017 with Recommendations to the Commission on Civil Law Rules on Robotics, 2015/2103(INL), Introduction, point AG. Similar to the proposal on personhood, this proposal has not been taken up further in the EU policy debate.

[19] Prominently in English law: *Dicker v Scammell* [2005] EWCA Civ 405, 'that is certain, which can be rendered certain'.

[20] Scholz, 'Algorithms and Contract Law' 147.

a view that considers technology as always pre-dating legal developments and, consequently, presents law as regularly facing a 'pacing problem'.[21] Yet, technological developments do not occur in a legal vacuum; instead, they are always closely intertwined with the existing legal rules and principles, in our case the rules on contract formation.[22] These offer normative choice on whether and how to accommodate the advances of technology.

B. Algorithms as Mere Tools?

The predominant understanding in contract law, ie that algorithms are treated as mere tools and objects, makes such normative choice. Their starting point about the ability of contract law to respond to the new algorithmic reality of contracting is correct. The complex rules on contract formation have the capacity to accommodate these new forms of contracting within the existing legal doctrine. However, the predominant doctrinal proposal ignores the socio-digital institution in which algorithmic behaviour is embedded. The so-far proposed solutions, most prominently the electronic-agents-as-tools perspective, take a simplistic stance on the algorithms and their social relationships with human users.

Paradigmatic for the 'tool solution' is the US Restatement (Third) of Agency Law, which excludes qualifying computer programs as agents in contract law:

> [...] a computer program is not capable of acting as a principal or an agent as defined by the common law. At present, computer programs are instrumentalities of the persons who use them. If a program malfunctions, even in ways unanticipated by its designer or user, the legal consequences for the person who uses it are no different than the consequences stemming from the malfunction of any other type of instrumentality. That a program may malfunction does not create capacity to act as a principal or an agent.[23]

According to this position, autonomous digital technologies are viewed simply as a tool employed by humans. The result is the humans' responsibility for the use.[24] Consequently, there seems to be no legal problem in contract formation involving electronic agents. The autonomous computer declaration is nothing but the declaration of the human actor behind it. Or, to put it the other way around, the human issuing the declaration and the parties forming the contract are the same with the

[21] GE Marchant, 'The Growing Gap Between Emerging Technologies and the Law', in GE Marchant et al. (eds), *The Growing Gap Between Emerging Technologies and Legal-Ethical Oversight: The Pacing Problem* (Dordrecht/Heidelberg/London/New York, Springer, 2011).

[22] On this interplay between technology and existing legal institutions, JE Cohen, *Between Truth and Power: The Legal Constructions of Informational Capitalism* (Oxford, Oxford University Press, 2019) 8.

[23] Restatement (Third) of Agency Law § 1.04 cmt. e. (2006).

[24] P Čerka et al., 'Liability for Damages Caused by Artificial Intelligence', (2015) 31 *Computer Law & Security Review* 376 (who, later on, make a systematic shift by proposing a concept on vicarious liability, but remain in their proposal of AI-as-tool) 384 ff. Similarly, from an ethical perspective, DG Johnson, 'Computer Systems: Moral Entities but not Moral Agents', (2006) 8 *Ethics and Information Technology* 195.

only difference that now they receive the help of an electronic tool. Much of this is rooted in the earlier legal qualification of automated systems. These were seen as passive tools for the humans who issued the declaration.

Various legal techniques accommodate autonomous computer declarations as part of human declarations. One assumes a human's 'generalised intention' visible in the use of the computer.[25] Another technique applies the doctrine of unilateral contracts similarly to its use for vending machines.[26] A third one adheres strictly to objective theories of contract formation that do not require the search for a subjective intention.[27] Finally, a fourth one looks for indications in the parties' general terms that would reveal a human agreement on electronic agents for contract formation.[28]

The most prominent doctrinal construct, however, simply ignores the electronic agent's independent actions altogether and considers it as a mere tool that technically exercises the declaration of the human. This interpretation can be found both in the common law but prominently in German law.[29] Courts have favoured it in dealing with automated systems. The German Federal Court of Justice had to decide a case in which a closed flight booking system had used deterministic computers. The judges declared in an obiter dictum: It is '[n]ot the computer system, but the person (or the company) who uses it as a means of communication and thus makes the declaration or is the recipient of the declaration made'.[30] English courts applied a similar rule on automated machines when treating a party as bound by contract due to 'the objective manifestation of (…) consent as expressed by the system'.[31]

[25] T Allen and R Widdison, 'Can Computers Make Contracts?', (1996) 9 *Harvard Journal of Law & Technology* 25, 52 who argue that this is the most likely route that courts will take; G Spindler and F Schuster, *Recht der elektronischen Medien. Kommentar* 4th edn (Munich, C.H.Beck, 2019) Introduction to §§ 116 ff, 6.

[26] For an overview on this position in US law, SK Chopra and L White, 'Artificial Agents and the Contracting Problem: A Solution via an Agency Analysis', [2009] *Journal of Law, Technology & Policy* 363, 370 ff.

[27] J-F Lerouge, 'The Use of Electronic Agents Questioned Under Contractual Law: Suggested Solutions on a European and American Level', (1999) 18 *John Marshall Journal of Computer Information Law* 403,416 f; EM Weitzenboeck, 'Electronic Agents and the Formation of Contracts', (2001) 9 *International Journal of Law and Information Technology* 204, 219 ff; *Chwee Kin Keong v Digilandmall.com Pte Ltd* [2004] SGHC 71, 134 (per Rajah JC).

[28] Chopra and White, 'Artificial Agents' 366, n 9. For English law: D Nolan, 'Offer and Acceptance in the Electronic Age', in A Burrows and E Peel (eds), *Contract Formation and Parties* (Oxford, Oxford University Press, 2010) 62 f. As a result, a large part of the discussion surrounds the question of whether and how general terms specifying the use of the electronic agents have been incorporated into the contract, A Davidson, *The Law of Electronic Commerce* (Cambridge, Cambridge University Press, 2012) 66 ff.

[29] In a comparative law analysis, D Utku, 'Formation of Contracts via the Internet', in MH Bilgin et al. (eds), *Eurasian Economic Perspectives* (New York, Springer, 2018) 290, describes this as the prevalent opinion in civil (and common) law.

[30] BGHZ 195, 126, 131 (our translation). Obviously, the decision cannot be applied to the autonomy risk, Linardatos, *Aktanten* 147.

[31] Nolan, 'Offer and Acceptance in the Electronic Age' 63 with reference to *Thornton v Shoe Lane Parking* [1971] 2 QB 163 (CA). See, relatedly, *Software Solutions Partners Ltd v HM Customs & Excise* [2007] EWHC Admin 971 at 68.

However, can one simply extend this interpretation developed for fully deterministic agents to cases where the software agent decides autonomously on the contract?[32] A closer look at algorithmic decision-making suggests that doubts are in order. As an early observer already has it: 'What distinguishes the electronic transactions mediated by intelligent agents from purchases made through vending machines is that agent-made agreements will be generated by machines, not merely through them.'[33] Against this background, can one seriously maintain that human actors are in control and issue the declaration when software agents decide all contractual moves, in other words, when human contracting parties virtually have outsourced their decisions to algorithms? What is left of the alleged human control in situations where the algorithm searches for offers on its own authority, negotiates with potential partners, chooses the contractual partner, decides on the conclusion of the contract, defines the *essentialia* of the transaction, determines the expiry of the contract, exercises withdrawal, lays down sanctions for breach of contract?[34] To provide some examples: 'Robo-advisors 4.0' offer a fully integrated investment service, including customer profiling, asset allocation, portfolio selection, trade execution, portfolio rebalancing and tax-loss harvesting. Their regular operations – using advanced AI deep learning – take autonomous decisions in contracts regulating portfolios and financial asset management on behalf of human beings.[35] Moreover, some algorithms establish supply chains through searching and connecting potential suppliers and concluding agreements with the lead firms.[36]

And what about contracts in which both contracting parties employ software for contract formation? These contractual situations imply

> that the contract itself would self-interpret its own terms and be completely self-executing. To put it another way, both the interpretation and the enforcement of the contract terms would be automated – what can be called the *true smart contract*.[37]

The anthropocentric position, which assumes that still the humans conclude the contract, cannot be maintained in this situation. According to Linarelli, such a true smart contract is a legally enforceable agreement 'for which some or all contract performance is executed and enforced digitally and without the need for human intervention except at the level of writing code to automate contract performance'.[38]

[32] eg: J-U Heuer-James et al., 'Industrie 4.0: Vertrags- und haftungsrechtliche Fragestellungen', [2018] *Betriebsberater* 2818, 2820 ff.; Čerka et al., 'Liability for Damages Caused by Artificial Intelligence' 384f.

[33] Kerr, 'Electronic Commerce' 188.

[34] On various roles of autonomous software agents in contracts, LH Scholz, 'Algorithmic Contracts', (2017) 20 *Stanford Technology Law Review* 128, 136. See also: A Casey and A Niblett, 'Self-Driving Contracts', (2017) 43 *Journal of Corporation Law* 1, 7 ff.

[35] P Sanz Bayón, 'A Legal Framework for Robo-Advisors', in E Schweighofer et al. (eds), *Datenschutz / LegalTech* (Bern, Weblaw, 2019) section 3.

[36] F Ameri and C Mcarthur, 'A Multi-Agent System for Autonomous Supply Chain Configuration', (2013) 66 *International Journal of Advanced Manufacturing Technology* 1097.

[37] Borselli, 'Smart Contracts' 115.

[38] J Linarelli, 'Artificial General Intelligence and Contract', (2019) 24 *Uniform Law Review* 330, 332.

That the human issued the declaration in a situation where programmers/manufacturers/operators have actually lost control is simply an untenable fiction.[39] In fact, it seems dangerous to uphold it when it is clear that technological developments will gradually increase the autonomy of electronic agents. If the position of agents-as-tools is preserved, the legal rules would need to be slowly but constantly stretched much too far when algorithms make decisions independently from the human user. This is already visible in more recent arguments that try to integrate the decision-making capacity of the agent in the human declaration. One prominent example is treating the agent to be a 'reservoir' for the conditional declarations of the human principal.[40] Yet, what happens when the 'reservoir' of declarations cannot predict the number of potential computer decisions? And could the 'reservoir' cover thousands of possible declarations that the human user has never even thought about? This seems quite absurd. How is it possible that contract law, which in the past successfully responded to the challenges of modern de-personalised business with a sophisticated theory of objective declarations and reliance doctrines, can only react defensively to the digital challenge via untenable fictions? It is a contradiction that there has been a tacit recognition of the algorithmic contracts' validity but no willingness to adapt the contractual rules to the actual delegation of contracting to software agents.

C. Our Solution: Agency Law for Electronic Agents

We propose to avoid this fiction and take both the autonomous action of the electronic agent and the need for its integration in contractual doctrine seriously. In chapter two, we have demonstrated that individual machines have decision-making capacity.[41] When they make decisions within digital assistance, ie when a human uses an algorithm for negotiating, forming and executing contracts, then the electronic agent acts on behalf of its human principal. Its declarations thus the principal.

Therefore, in line with several authors in the common law world[42] as well as in the civil law world,[43] we suggest applying agency law to algorithms. If autonomous

[39] For a critique of the fiction, eg: E Dahiyat, 'Law and Software Agents: Are They "Agents" by the Way?', (2021) 29 *Artificial Intelligence and Law* 59, 60 ff.; Scholz, 'Algorithmic Contracts' 150; Chopra and White, 'Artificial Agents' 372.

[40] G Spindler, 'Zivilrechtliche Fragen beim Einsatz von Robotern', in E Hilgendorf (ed), *Robotik im Kontext von Recht und Moral* (Baden-Baden, Nomos, 2014) 64.

[41] ch 2, II.C.

[42] A Lior, 'AI Entities as AI Agents: Artificial Intelligence Liability and the AI Respondeat Superior Analogy', (2020) 46 *Mitchell Hamline Law Review* 1043, 1071 ff; D Powell, 'Autonomous Systems as Legal Agents: Directly by the Recognition of Personhood or Indirectly by the Alchemy of Algorithmic Entities', (2020) 18 *Duke Law & Technology Review* 306, 329; MA Chinen, *Law and Autonomous Machines* (Cheltenham, Elgar, 2019) 37; Scholz, 'Algorithmic Contracts' 164 ff; B-J Koops et al., 'Bridging the Accountability Gap: Rights for New Entities in the Information Society?', (2010) 11 *Minnesota Journal of Law, Science & Technology* 497, 512 f, 559; Chopra and White, 'Artificial Agents' 376 ff.

[43] For various countries in the civil law world, M Kovac, *Judgement-Proof Robots and Artificial Intelligence: A Comparative Law and Economics Approach* (London, Palgrave, 2020), 112 ff, 114, 121; C Linke, *Digitale Wissensorganisation: Wissenszurechnung beim Einsatz autonomer Systeme*

machines substitute human agents in the institution of 'digital assistance', then agency law is appropriate.

> We need a contract law that acknowledges that algorithms are more than mere tools and does not wrongly presume that sophisticated businesses can always predict the behaviour of a sophisticated algorithm.[44]

Technically, in an analogy to agency law, autonomous software agents will be treated as vicarious agents, as legal representatives of their human principal. Applying agency law to algorithmic contracts avoids the two fallacies, either attributing contractual acts exclusively to the humans, as the prevailing doctrine does, or attributing them solely to the algorithm, as the authors favouring the e-person do. Instead, agency law allows for a nuanced distribution of contractual decision power between principal and algorithmic agents and the concomitant risks between principal and third parties. Agency law offers a distribution of rights and duties which responds legally to the risk structure of 'digital agency'. Agency law indeed has the potential to deal with the four specific risks we described above: identification of the agent, lack of understanding between human principal and algorithmic agent, reduction of institutional productivity, and deviation of algorithmic decisions from the principal's intention.

D. Limited Legal Personhood – Constellation One

Obviously, this will need to change the legal status of software agents. Current agency law requires that an agent be a 'person'.[45] This reflects the institutional requirements of 'digital assistance', which we have described above. Agency law regulates three-party legal relationships between principal, agent and third party. Each of these relationships requires that both parties in a principal-agent relation be a person. If the law allows algorithms to serve as vicarious agents, it must

(Baden-Baden, Nomos, 2021) 259; KV Lewinski et al., *Bestehende und künftige Regelungen des Einsatzes von Algorithmen im HR-Bereich* (Berlin, AlgorithmWatch/Hans-Böckler Stiftung, 2019); J-E Schirmer, 'Artificial Intelligence and Legal Personality', in T Wischmeyer and T Rademacher (eds), *Regulating Artificial Intelligence* (Basel, Springer, 2019) para 4 ff; L Specht and S Herold, 'Roboter als Vertragspartner: Gedanken zu Vertragsabschlüssen unter Einbeziehung automatisiert und autonom agierender Systeme', [2018] *Multimedia und Recht* 40, 40, 43; O Kessler, 'Intelligente Roboter – neue Technologien im Einsatz: Voraussetzungen und Rechtsfolgen des Handelns informationstechnischer Systeme', (2017) *Multimedia und Recht* 589, 592; G Teubner, 'Rights of Non-Humans? Electronic Agents and Animals as New Actors in Politics and Law', (2006) 33 *Journal of Law and Society* 497.

[44] Scholz, 'Algorithmic Contracts' 149.

[45] See generally: US Restatement (Third) Of Agency §§ 1.01, 1.04(5) (2006); with a view to algorithms, O Rachum-Twaig, 'Whose Robot is it Anyway? Liability for Artificial-Intelligence-Based Robots', [2020] *University of Illinois Law Review* 1141, 1151; for German law, see, eg: G Dannemann and R Schulze (eds), *German Civil Code – Article by Article Commentary* (Munich / Baden-Baden, C.H. Beck / Nomos, 2020), § 164, para 2 (Wais); for English law, already with a view to software agents: *Software Solutions Partners Ltd v HM Customs & Excise* [2007] EWHC Admin 971, para 67: 'only a person with a "mind" can be an agent in law'.

confer on them legal capacities to possess rights and incur obligations. However, as said above, it is unnecessary to assign them comprehensive legal capacity as fully-fledged legal persons. Instead, from a functional point of view, it is sufficient to attribute the narrowly circumscribed ability to act as agents for principals with binding effect, ie limited legal capacity.[46] Algorithms need to be endowed only with a carefully circumscribed '*potestas vicaria*, in which every act of the vicar is considered to be a manifestation of the will of the one who is represented by him.'[47] One should not underestimate the consequences of such digital *potestas vicaria*. In comparison to programming and communicating with computers, 'digital agency' opens a new institutional channel of human access to the digital world and allows making use of its creative potential. But at the same time, it exposes humans to new dangers of non-controllable digital decisions.

Granting such a legal capacity is already possible *de lege lata*, as evidenced by the history of human associations' personification.[48] Originally without legal status, some associations such as trade unions, companies in formation and, most recently, associations under civil law have been granted step by step limited legal capacities. These are precedents in which the courts have conferred *praeter legem*, if not *extra legem*, limited or full legal capacity to entities, which previously lacked legal status. Probably, lawmakers are also well-advised here to resist the urge to legislate and leave it to the development on a case-by-case basis.[49] The iterative process of learning and adjusting by judge-made law will produce more appropriate results in algorithms' gradual personification than over-hasty legislative attempts.

To be sure, the differences between human actors and software agents remain considerable, with the result that some rules of agency law need to be modified accordingly. Utmost care is required in analogical reasoning, ie generalisation of agency law to non-humans' actions as well as in re-specification, ie development of appropriate special rules for a digital agency law.[50] Reasoning

[46] On the comparable construction of the legal transactions of slaves in Roman law, JD Harke, 'Sklavenhalterhaftung in Rom', in S Gless and K Seelmann (eds), *Intelligente Agenten und das Recht* (Baden-Baden, Nomos, 2016) 97 f.

[47] Agamben, *The Kingdom and the Glory* 138 f. For a detailed interdisciplinary analysis of this *potestas vicaria*, Trüstedt, *Stellvertretung*, *passim*, in particular for algorithmic agency, ch V, 4.2.

[48] In detail for this parallel between algorithms and associations, for German law, M-C Gruber, *Bioinformationsrecht: Zur Persönlichkeitsentfaltung des Menschen in technisierter Verfassung* (Tübingen, Mohr Siebeck, 2015) 267 ff. See the decisions of the German Bundesgerichtshof, BGHZ 146, 341, 344; BGHZ 163, 154. On the English law towards recognition of associations: J Armour, 'Companies and Other Associations', in A Burrows (ed), *English Private Law* (Oxford, Oxford University Press, 2013) 126, 3.29–3.30. For the history of personification in American law, *locus classicus*, MJ Horwitz, 'Santa Clara Revisited: The Development of Corporate Theory', (1985) 88 *West Virginia Law Review* 173. For a comprehensive qualitative and quantitative analysis of the courts' decisions on legal personhood, N Banteka, 'Artificially Intelligent Persons', (2021) 58 *Houston Law Review* 537, 542 ff.

[49] See: G Wagner, 'Robot Liability', in R Schulze et al. (eds), *Liability for Robotics and in the Internet of Things* (Baden-Baden/Oxford, Nomos/Hart, 2019) 46.

[50] See also: Lior, 'AI Entities as AI Agents' 1071; M-C Gruber, 'Legal Subjects and Partial Legal Subjects in Electronic Commerce', in T Pietrzykowski and B Stancioli (eds), *New Approaches to Personhood in Law* (Frankfurt, Lang, 2016) 83ff.

from similarity does not suffice. Instead, an analogy needs two argumentative steps. First, one generalises agency law to all kinds of decision-making entities in order to formulate more encompassing principles. The correct generalisation is: Agency law will be applied (not to 'assistance systems' in general but) to assistance systems with autonomy risk.[51] Second, one respecifies these principles for the properties of digital action. The risk of reducing the productivity potential of 'digital assistance' needs to be counteracted. Therefore, agency rules will be oriented not only to the traditional goal of binding the agent as close as possible to the principal's intentions but also to allow for sufficient degrees of freedom to exploit the digital world's potential. Thus, the law needs to take the digital agent's autonomy seriously.

This re-specification for various digital constellations will best be accomplished again, not by general prospective legislation but by the judiciary in incremental case-law development. And private ordering will accelerate this process via a combination of standard terms, model contracts of international trade associations, and technical standards. It will do so

> in a manner that strikes a balance between the need to keep the minimum level of human review and awareness and the need to protect the key features of software agents (eg autonomy, flexibility, dynamism, speed).[52]

And via judicial control of private ordering, the courts need to intervene if this balance is endangered.

Having outlined our proposed solution in general, we will now turn to the crucial questions for legal doctrine: How can an electronic agent issue a valid, legally binding declaration in the principal's name? And how is the internal relationship between the human principal and the digital agent to be construed?

E. The Digital Agent's Legal Declaration

Treating declarations by an electronic agent as self-standing declarations of contract law requires two things: A digital equivalent for the agent's subjective intention to bind the principal, a requirement of particular importance in several civil law systems such as Germany, and a sufficiently specified objective declaration, which common law courts will pay specific attention to. Our argument, as we elaborate below, rests upon the currently predominant reliance theories in contract law. For German civil law, it will discuss the abilities of agents to process the specifics of the social context as an essential component for contextual interpretation. In contrast, for the common law, the text-based operation of algorithms will be the decisive argument.

[51] Thus, merely automated (as opposed to autonomous) systems should not be subject to agency law, Linardatos, *Aktanten* 112 ff.

[52] Dahiyat, 'Software Agents' 80.

One of the most relevant objections raised by several authors is that a software agent lacks the necessary intention to create legal obligations for its principal.[53] No doubt, the declaration issued by an electronic agent is never entirely alike to the human decision. We do not argue that the algorithm has subjective consciousness as a basis to bind the principal. However, it is possible to identify digital equivalents for the subjective preconditions of the declaration of intent as required by law. At this point, the well-known objectivisation tendencies in contract law make it possible that software agents, although they possess no consciousness of their own, can nevertheless make legally valid declarations of intent. At this point, modern contract law confirms the general sociological thesis discussed above that it is not consciousness that counts for non-human entities' personification but communication.[54] Reliance theories have replaced the old controversy of will theory versus declaration theory and have de-psychologised the contractual intent.[55]

In a civil law system like German law, the courts have shifted from a long-standing tradition of employing subjective criteria for the contractual intention towards objectivisation. The parties' subjective intentions are no longer relevant. The objective reliance principle has replaced subjective mental states. The crucial question has now become under which conditions the law attributes external behaviour to the contracting person.[56] No lack of intention can be invoked against the validity of the declaration if the declaring party has, as the Federal Supreme Court has decided, 'negligently failed to recognise that his behaviour could be understood as a declaration of intent and if the recipient has actually understood it so'.[57] The Court thus replaces subjective intention with two objective norms. Indeed, software agents with elaborate cognitive abilities can handle these two norms: first, the social norm based on trust, whether the concrete behaviour may be understood as a binding declaration of intent; and second, the obligation of the declaring party to recognise this social norm and not fail to acknowledge it negligently. Such knowledge of social norms, ie, understanding certain declarations in a particular context, can be translated into a software program. The same is true for the legal rules involved. A dynamic emerges in programs for social and legal rules, which Viljanen calls an 'impact pathway'. The algorithm's actions can be controlled by regulating the information on social and legal rules that enters its cognitive machinery.

Moreover, self-learning agents can acquire this information on their own initiative and modify it themselves in the event of changes in social norms or

[53] For this objection, eg: R Michalski, 'How to Sue a Robot', (2019) 2018 *Utah Law Review* 1021, 1059; G Spindler, 'Digitale Wirtschaft – analoges Recht: Braucht das BGB ein Update?', (2016) 71 *Juristenzeitung* 805, 816.

[54] See extensively ch 2, I.C.

[55] For prominent reliance theories in contract law, C-W Canaris, *Die Vertrauenshaftung im Deutschen Privatrecht* (Munich, C.H. Beck, 1971); PS Atiyah, *The Rise and Fall of Freedom of Contract* (Oxford, Clarendon, 1979).

[56] eg: Dannemann and Schulze (eds), *German Civil Code*, § 133, para 8 (Wais).

[57] BGH NJW 1995, 953.

case law. Neuronal networks exist which can be trained, via examples, to identify concrete patterns of conduct. In such cases, a suitable training program can teach algorithms the normative lesson. The model is intuitive normative learning in concrete cases. In an overview of the state of the art, Borselli shows how data are collected from statutes and rules, case law, regulators' decisions, expert reports and other legal materials and analysed through algorithms to determine the possible legal outcome of a specific case.[58] Thus, the objection that software agents could not possess contractual intent because they have no consciousness has been dispelled.[59] Equivalents are their calculative abilities to process social and legal norms.[60]

For English contract law, most of these issues are less problematic given the objective interpretation of contract and the objective test on the contractual intention.[61] The same is true for US law which does not require subjective intent but only an objective manifestation of mutual consent.[62] In a legal system using the construct of the reasonable observer, the question is somewhat different: Has a declaration induced the offeree to believe that the offeror intended to be bound by acceptance?[63] The text of the declaration itself is the primary source for interpretation, particularly in English law, which allows for additional contextual evidence only in exceptional cases.[64] In such a legal system, the above-made argument on social norms and related context will thus not be persuasive. Additional arguments are required as to why courts should rule that a person addressed by an electronic declaration can assume this to be a valid offer. As electronic agents issue written declarations, the question comes up whether such text reveals a sufficient intention to be bound. Linarelli makes a convincing argument: Effectively, the courts will apply a variant of the Turing test. Suppose the analysis of text-based

[58] Borselli, 'Smart Contracts', 114 ff, with references to theory and practice of predictive technology in law.

[59] The same result is reached if one applies Dennett's concept of intentional stance to electronic agents, G Sartor, 'Cognitive Automata and the Law: Electronic Contracting and the Intentionality of Software Agents', (2009) 17 *Artificial Intelligence and Law* 253, 262. For a future private law, M Hennemann, *Interaktion und Partizipation: Dimensionen systemischer Bindung im Vertragsrecht* (Tübingen, Mohr Siebeck, 2020) 327 ff, 341 ff, argues for introducing 'systemic obligations', which would lead to equivalent results.

[60] R Konertz and R Schönhof, *Das technische Phänomen 'Künstliche Intelligenz' im allgemeinen Zivilrecht: Eine kritische Betrachtung im Lichte von Autonomie, Determinismus und Vorhersehbarkeit* (Baden-Baden, Nomos, 2020) 114, criticise this solution as plainly wrong. For the situation that the two social norms involved are directly pre-programmed into the algorithm, they have to admit that the traditional identification of the algorithmic decision with the subjective will of the human operator behind it, comes to its limits. Then their way out of the dilemma is somewhat arbitrary. They go beyond any legal reasoning and simply attribute the risk to the human, apparently, because the result fits their preferences.

[61] Fundamentally *Smith v Hughes* (1871) LR 6 QB 597, 607.

[62] U.S. Restatement (Second) of Contracts, § 21 (1981): 'neither real nor apparent intention that a promise be legally binding is essential to the formation of the contract'.

[63] *Centrovincial Estates plc v Merchant Investor Assurance Co Ltd* [1983] Commercial LR 158; *Moran* v *University of Salford, The Times*, 23 November 1993.

[64] For those, see, eg: *Prenn v Simmonds* [1971] 1 WLR 1381; *Investors Compensation Scheme Ltd* v *West Bromwich Building Society* (No 1) [1998] 1 WLR 896.

communication between the electronic agent and the addressee fails to identify the human involved reliably. In that case, the electronic declaration cannot be interpreted in any other way than as a legally binding offer from the addressee's perspective.[65]

Qualifying the electronic agent as capable of issuing a legally valid declaration in the name of the principal with binding effect thus provides a more nuanced and convincing construction than the traditional view that only human actors can make legally binding declarations.

F. Digital Assistance and the Principal-Agent Relation

Having discussed the declaration of the electronic agent, we also need to analyse how legal doctrine will construct 'digital assistance', ie the social relation between human users and electronic agents. In our analogy to agency law, the question is whether authority can be legally conferred to an electronic agent, and more generally, how the internal relation between human principal and electronic agent can be legally constructed.

Let us start with the conferral of authority that serves as the basis for the agent to act and bind the principal. This declaration is a unilateral act by the principal that does not require acceptance by the agent or the third party.[66] Initial suggestions focused primarily on explicit conferral or retrospective ratification. Kerr, for instance, suggests that in any electronic program used for contract formation, the user needs either to declare his intention to confer general authority to the electronic agent or to authorise retrospectively, which he needs to communicate to the potential contracting partner.[67] Similarly, Scholz argues that the preferred option when using electronic agents is a human approval node for any transaction.[68] Yet, given the widespread and often speedy electronic contracts, such a cumbersome and lengthy authorisation would invalidate the benefits of using the system. And it would also unduly shift the risk of the agent's decisions to the other contracting party, who would always be uncertain whether or not a contract has been formed. This solution thus leans too far in protecting the principal. Requiring additional conditions for conferral of authority essentially allocates the liability risk entirely to the other contracting party. He would need to investigate during the negotiation

[65] Linarelli, 'Artificial General Intelligence and Contract' 335.

[66] For German law, Dannemann and Schulze (eds), *German Civil Code*, § 167, para 2 (Wais). The unilateral act of conferring authority needs to be distinguished from the underlying relation between principal and agent. English common law does not distinguish in a similarly formal manner between these two legal relations; nonetheless, it equally considers the conferral of authority as a unilateral act that is separate from other internal agreements between agent and principal, eg: F Reynolds, 'Agency', in A Burrows (ed), *English Private Law* (Oxford, Oxford University Press, 2013) 615f., 9.07. US law is slightly different, as it requires conferral of agency to be based on mutual consent between principal and agent, Restatement (Third) Of Agency, §1.01 (2006); however, according to §1.03, manifestation of assent can be through conduct, which is close to a unilateral contract.

[67] Kerr, 'Electronic Commerce' 198 f.

[68] Scholz, 'Algorithmic Contracts' 167.

process whether the principal has employed an algorithm, although the algorithm is not transparent to him.[69] Thus, it is more convincing to link the conferral of authority simply to the de facto use of an electronic agent.[70] Doctrinally, this would amount to conferral by implication through conduct.[71] The limits of the authority through use are then only the limits of the system's capability.[72] Qualifying the de facto use as a conferral of authority has the advantage to be predictable that the agent acts with authority. Moreover, the user effectively has to take precautionary measures like taking insurance or controlling the algorithm.

What then about the internal relation between human principal and electronic agent? In general, agency law distinguishes between conferral of authority as a unilateral act and the underlying legal relation between principal and agent, which defines the scope of authority. The same distinction works for the relation between human principal and electronic agent. While the de facto use of the computer can be interpreted as conferral of authority by implication, it is unclear how to qualify the underlying legal relationship between principal and agent. And to be sure, there is a general problem with simply applying existing agency law to the relation between a human principal and an electronic agent. A different treatment could be justified because legal status is different for humans and algorithms, and the underlying relation of human representation and digital assistance is not the same. However, this does not imply that agency law is not at all suitable for digital assistance, as some authors argue.[73] Instead, what is required is a careful re-specification of agency law rules for the institution of digital assistance. They need to be applied to a situation where the digital agent only has limited legal personhood, and there is no equality in the underlying relation. It also needs to be considered that delegation of decision-making to the digital actant is not an act of a communicative nature in the strict sense whereby humans and algorithms agree and consent. It is asymmetrical in translating human needs and their restrictions into technical rules and limitations built into the program.[74] It is these communication-as-programmed rules that define the relationship between human principals and digital agents. Accordingly, any restrictions programmed

[69] This is also recognised by A Lior, 'The AI Accident Network: Artificial Intelligence Liability Meets Network Theory', (2021) 95 *Tulane Law Review* forthcoming, section C.5.b; see also: F Andrade et al., 'Contracting Agents: Legal Personality and Representation', (2007) 15 *Artificial Intelligence Law* 357, 370.

[70] See: F Kainer and L Förster, 'Autonome Systeme im Kontext des Vertragsrechts', [2020] *Zeitschrift für die gesamte Privatrechtswissenschaft* 275, 291; A Lior, 'AI Entities as AI Agents', 1084, 1087 ff.

[71] In US common law, this would most likely be treated as a form of manifestation through conduct, Restatement (Third) of Agency §1.03 (2006). In English common law, it could qualify as usual authority, Reynolds, 'Agency' 630, 9.52. In German law, conferral would qualify as implicit, G Dannemann and R Schulze (eds), *German Civil Code*, §167 para 2 (Wais).

[72] MU Scherer, 'Of Wild Beasts and Digital Analogues: The Legal Status of Autonomous Systems', (2019) 19 *Nevada Law Journal* 259, 288.

[73] Eg: Michalski, 'How to Sue a Robot' 1059; A Belia, 'Contracting with Electronic Agents', (2001) 50 *Emory Law Journal* 1047, 1061 f.

[74] On such internally programmed restrictions, E Tjong Tijn Lai, 'Liability for (Semi)autonomous Systems: Robots and Algorithms', in V Mak et al. (eds), *Research Handbook in Data Science and Law* (Cheltenham, Edward Elgar, 2018) 60.

as part of the algorithm cannot be part of the conferral of authority, simply because they are only accessible and understandable in the relation of human user and algorithm. They are invisible to the outside, in particular, the third party. As a result, when the electronic agent overrides these internal rules due to, for instance, a differently applied prioritisation of criteria, the principal will still be liable because de facto use serves as conferral of authority. Yet, the principal can protect himself by making transparent these internal rules to the third party.[75] Then transparency on these rules would qualify as authority.

In German law, a rather elegant construction of the principal-agent relation is possible via 'blank statements' (*Blanketterklärung*).[76] This amounts to a variation of agency law. 'Blank statement' is a legal construct somehow between agent and messenger. One party hands out a signed paper to the blank statement taker, who will complete the form and hand it to the other contracting party. For this constellation, the courts have decided to apply the rules on agency law analogously.[77] By handing out the blank statement, the first party loses all influence on the statement's content. Beck argues that in many aspects, this alternative could solve the problems arising from algorithmic contracts.[78] Here again, the law requires that the blank statement taker is a legal person. It follows that limited legal capacity is ascribed to software agents.

As a consequence, the principal is contractually bound. Once he uses an electronic agent unreservedly, this amounts to conferral of authority. The principal can only protect himself by the following options: He obtains insurance that compensates for the agent's mistakes or closely monitors the agent's actions and corrects the failures. Alternatively, he can inform third parties about the internal rules that the electronic agent needs to follow (such as price caps).

G. Overstepping of Authority?

This leaves us with the fourth risk of digital agency described above, which agency law needs to deal with. In principle, the agent's declaration that remains within the scope of authority binds the principal. When the agent is overstepping his authority, the legal relationship between the agent and the third party becomes relevant.

[75] This would amount to a case of apparent authority in English common law and 'external authorisation' in German law under § 167 (1) BGB. For these two concepts in a comparative perspective, B Markesinis et al., *The German Law of Contract: A Comparative Treatise* (Oxford, Hart Publishing, 2006) 112 f.

[76] Specht and Herold, 'Roboter als Vertragspartner' 39; S Beck, 'The Problem of Ascribing Legal Responsibility in the Case of Robotics', (2016) 31 *AI & Society* 473, 478; J-P Günther, *Roboter und rechtliche Verantwortung: Eine Untersuchung der Benutzer- und Herstellerhaftung* (Munich, Utz, 2016) 54 ff.

[77] BGH NJW 1963, 1971; NJW 1991, 487, 488; NJW 1996, 1467, 1469. In the common law, such constellation would be treated as a constellation in which agency reasoning is required, see Reynolds, 'Agency' 614, 9.02.

[78] Beck, 'Robotics' 478.

Leaving aside the possibility of ratification by the principal, in the situation of an agent exceeding authority, agency law prescribes that the agent is liable.[79] When the agent does not have full legal capacity, the third party incurs the risk of an agent exceeding authority. This rule would apply to electronic agents.[80] Only if legislation were to confer full legal personality and related financial capacity to the agent as an e-person then the third party could take recourse with the agent.[81]

However, there are only a few constellations in which the electronic agent can overstep its authority. If the de facto use of the agent counts as conferral of authority, the agent can overstep authority only when either the scope of authority, including its limitations, is known to the third party or when the third party could not reasonably understand the computer behaviour as being covered by the principal's conferral. A computer going astray and making unreasonable declarations would be an example. When the principal has set up internal rules for the agent without communicating them to the third party, they bind the principal since they fall within his sphere of influence. If the agent overrides them, this is an internal breach of the agency agreement with no consequence for the conferral of authority. However, when electronic agents are hacked, this presents a specific in-between constellation. The solution depends on whether or not the electronic agent's actions remain within the principal's sphere of influence. The hacking risk is on the principal, who has created the expectation of being in control, whereas in cases outside his sphere, the algorithmic decisions would not bind the principal.[82] The third party would also bear the risk if he can reasonably know about such hacking.

At this point, the advantages of the agency construction should become clear. Those authors who advocate classifying the software agent as a tool would need to hold the user generally liable for the computer program's decisions.[83] The declaration issued by the program would qualify as the principal's declaration, and the principal would need to take recourse with the programmer or manufacturer.[84] This, however, would amount to a significant risk for the principal, who can neither control the agent nor insure against these risks.[85]

[79] For English common law, the leading case is *Collen v Wright* (1857), 7 El & Bl 301; ER 1259; in German law, the constellation of a *falsus procurator* is dealt with in § 179, which imposes strict liability on an unauthorised agent, see Dannemann and Schulze (eds), *German Civil Code*, § 179, para 1 (Wais). There are, however, several exceptions, eg when the third party had reasonable knowledge about the lack of authorisation.

[80] Kessler, 'Intelligente Roboter' 592.

[81] SM Mayinger, *Die künstliche Person: Untersuchung rechtlicher Veränderungen durch die Installation von Softwareagenten im Rahmen von Industrie 4.0* (Frankfurt, Fachmedien Recht und Wirtschaft, 2017) 72, 227, 244 ff.

[82] Lior, 'AI Entities as AI Agents' 1093, states that as hacking constitutes itself a tortious act, it will be outside the sphere of control and thus not bind the principal.

[83] See: Andrade et al., 'Contracting Agents' 361; G Sartor, 'Agents in Cyberlaw', in G Sartor (ed), *The Law of Electronic Agents: Selected Revised Papers. Proceedings of the Workshop on the Law of Electronic Agents (LEA 2002)* (Bologna, University of Bologna, 2003).

[84] Chinen, *Law and Autonomous Machines* 41; U Pagallo, 'From Automation to Autonomous Systems: A Legal Phenomenology with Problems of Accountability', (2017) *Proceedings of the Twenty-Sixth International Joint Conference on Artificial Intelligence* 17, 20 f.

[85] Mayinger, *Künstliche Person* 72; Koops et al., 'Accountability Gap' 554.

The risk would be exceptionally high under conditions of distributed action[86] or self-cloning.[87] In contrast, the solution via agency law allows for more nuanced risk distribution. According to agency rules, the principal is only bound and liable to the extent that the agent's declaration follows the conferral of authority. The electronic agent's action would not bind the principal if the algorithm overrode limits made transparent to the contracting party. Neither would the principal be bound if an outsider hacked the algorithm and the contracting party could have reasonably known. As a result, agency law allows for an allocation of risk that neither treats the use of an electronic agent exclusively as the user's risk nor assigns the risk only on a case-by-case basis. It distinguishes between constellations in which the user has to bear the electronic agent's risk from those where the risk falls – provided it has been communicated or is apparent – within the other party's sphere. Altogether, agency law accounts better for the specifics of 'digital assistance'. It pays due respect to the agent's autonomy and its decisions under uncertainty. Finally, agency law provides an appropriate entry point for piecemeal regulatory intervention if there is a need to protect particular parties, such as consumers, from the consequences of rules that create the agency relationship through use.[88]

IV. Contractual Liability

Up to now, we discussed situations in which algorithms conclude contracts in the name of a human principal. Our suggestion was to attribute to them limited legal capacity and qualify them as digital agents. This would allow the analogy to agency law and would avoid untenable fictions. Now we turn to practices of digital agency in which human actors or organisations conclude contracts and use autonomous algorithms as auxiliaries to fulfil the contractual obligations. In particular, they use care robots, health care and surgery robots, or manufacturing robots. There are many other real-world situations beyond these standard examples. As Chagal-Feferkorn describes, law firms deploy 'virtual attorneys' such as IBM's Ross to conduct independent legal research. Algorithmic online dispute resolution mechanisms solve disputes online, often without any human facilitator. Bail algorithms determine whether defendants awaiting trial may post bail to be released. Physicians rely more and more on algorithms to diagnose medical conditions and select optimal treatments. Even priests provide spiritual services by algorithms.[89] Another new and dynamic class of auxiliaries in contractual performance is start-ups providing digital financial advising and asset

[86] Allen and Widdison, 'Computers Make Contracts?' 42.

[87] W Barfield, 'Issues of Law for Software Agents within Virtual Environments', (2005) 14 *Presence* 747, 747 ff.

[88] Brownsword, 'Regulatory Fitness' 192.

[89] KA Chagal-Feferkorn, 'The Reasonable Algorithm', [2018] *University of Illinois Journal of Law, Technology & Policy* 111, 113 with further references.

management called 'robo-advisers'. Using advanced AI deep learning, they decide autonomously on contractual performance in financial asset management on behalf of human principals.[90] How can damages caused by these algorithms to the contracting partner be compensated?

A. The Dilemma of the Tool-Solution

If a breach of contractual duties is involved, the predominant doctrine treats software agents again only as tools in contract performance and rejects to apply the rules of vicarious liability.[91] The result is a dilemma. Either one is forced to locate breach of contract in the person of the human principal, or a wide liability gap remains. Like in contract formation, the fundamental problem lies in the untenable fiction of the electronic-agents-as tools solution.[92] As an observer pointedly puts it:

> The concept of tool is not a legal category and it leads to the wrong consequence that both the negligence standards and their relevant moment of evaluation refer to the decision about programming or the use of the tool, while in reality, the crucial point is to evaluate the system in 'its' situation of decision.[93]

The problem is particularly pertinent in German law that bases contractual liability on fault. The tool-solution implies that one needs to find all the conditions for contractual liability (violation of a contractual obligation, responsibility for breach) in the human principal's behaviour. This becomes increasingly difficult when the computer makes autonomous decisions.[94] It is exclusively in the principal's behaviour where the breach of contract needs to be identified, and it is his action that needs to be qualified as negligent. Given the algorithm's autonomous decision, the principal will successfully argue that he is not responsible for the breach.

The situation is somewhat different in the common law. Given that contractual liability is generally strict and requires no fault of the contracting party, the dilemma of the tool solution is not equally obvious here.[95] But the tool-solution is still problematic because regardless of fault, the actual breach of contract needs to be located in the behaviour of one of the actors involved. If the algorithm causes damage, would the human's decision to employ an algorithm qualify as a breach of contract?

[90] Sanz Bayón, 'Robo-Advisors' section 3.

[91] Prominently in German law, S Horner and M Kaulartz, 'Haftung 4.0: Rechtliche Herausforderungen im Kontext der Industrie 4.0', [2016] *InTeR Zeitschrift zum Innovations- und Technikrecht* 22, 23; J Hanisch, 'Zivilrechtliche Haftungskonzepte für Robotik', in E Hilgendorf (ed), *Robotik im Kontext von Recht und Moral* (Baden-Baden, Nomos, 2014) 32.

[92] Harshly criticised by S Schuppli, 'Deadly Algorithms: Can Legal Codes Hold Software Accountable for Code That Kills?', (2014) 187 *Radical Philosophy* 2, 5.

[93] Wagner, 'Digitale Techniken' 724 (our translation).

[94] See: M Ebers, 'Liability for Artificial Intelligence and EU Consumer Law', (2021) 12 *Journal of Intellectual Property, Information Technology and Electronic Commerce Law* 204, 211 f, 44, 46.

[95] For the differences between common law and German law on the fault-principle for breach of contract which have implications for contractual liability for third parties, Markesinis et al., *German Law of Contract* 444 ff.

Can this even be upheld if the actual damage-causing event is, in relation to time and space, disconnected to the decision to make use of the computer? Stretching the general liability rules for breach of contract to accommodate liability for electronic agents' behaviour essentially means to make the operator responsible for putting the computer into operation.[96] This, however, creates a dangerous fiction. It overlooks an important aspect. As we said above, while the algorithm's autonomy does not interrupt the causal connection between programmer and contract, it interrupts the attribution connection.[97] Worse, such a sheer 'initiator liability' amounts in reality to an overshooting liability.[98] Legal policy considerations speak clearly against it. Suppose one links liability to the mere act of using a novel electronic system. In that case, one will weaken the regulatory function of liability based on the violation of rules, hindering innovation in intelligent computer programs.[99]

The other alternative is even worse. Suppose the principal can excuse himself because of the autonomy of the system and argue for lack of responsibility for the behaviour of the agent on his side.[100] In that case, the failure risk is externalised to the contractual partner, and a wide liability gap emerges. Even though the agent, who caused the damage, had been employed by the principal for performing the contract, the innocent contractual partner would bear the damages entirely. Such liability gaps will widen in the future once more tasks of contract performance are delegated to autonomous software agents.[101] 'If the operator can prove, however, that the damage was neither predictable nor avoidable in accordance with state of the art, then … liability is omitted.'[102] In particular, in the case of a complex, non-foreseeable and non-explainable damage-occurring event, the operator is not liable for the electronic agent's wrongful behaviour.

While some authors admit the existence of the liability gap, they downplay its importance.[103] Regularly, reference is made to certification procedures for the algorithm and consent of the contractual partner. Both are supposed to mitigate

[96] This is criticised by M Lohmann, 'Ein europäisches Roboterrecht: überfällig oder überflüssig', [2017] *Zeitschrift für Rechtspolitik* 168, 158; J-E Schirmer, 'Rechtsfähige Roboter', [2016] *Juristenzeitung* 660, 664. Further arguments against strict liability in electronic contracting, IR Kerr, 'Providing for Autonomous Electronic Devices in the Uniform Electronic Commerce Act', [2006] *Uniform Law Conference* 1, 30 ff.

[97] Turner, *Robot Rules* 101; Wagner, 'Digitale Techniken' 724.

[98] G Wagner and L Luyken, 'Haftung für Robo Advice', in G Bachmann et al. (eds), *Festschrift für Christine Windbichler* (Berlin, de Gruyter, 2020) 169.

[99] Hanisch, 'Haftungskonzepte' 34.

[100] For German law, see, eg: S Herold, *Vertragsschlüsse unter Einbeziehung automatisiert und autonom agierender Systeme* (Hürth, Wolters Kluwer, 2020) ch 2, II.2.a. In the common law, this could be the case if the debtor can lawfully excuse himself for breach of contract due to, eg, frustration.

[101] See: G Wagner and L Luyken, 'Robo Advice' 168; MA Chinen, 'The Co-Evolution of Autonomous Machines and Legal Responsibility', (2016) 20 *Vanderbilt Journal of Law & Technology* 338, 363.

[102] S Kirn and C-D Müller-Hengstenberg, 'Intelligente (Software-)Agenten: Eine neue Herausforderung für die Gesellschaft und unser Rechtssystem?', (2014) *FZID Discussion Paper 86-2014* 1, 16; see also: P Hacker, 'Verhaltens- und Wissenszurechnung beim Einsatz von Künstlicher Intelligenz', (2018) 9 *Rechtswissenschaft* 243, 250, 258.

[103] Konertz and Schönhof, *Künstliche Intelligenz* 132, freely admit the liability gap, but they do not care about its consequences.

the risk of the liability gap to such a degree that it becomes irrelevant.[104] Obviously, both conditions, certification and consent, are only rarely met. And even if they exist, they do not make the risk vanish. The history of liability cases concerning certified (medical) products in product liability is enough evidence for that.[105] Altogether these arguments cannot put into doubt the growing liability gap in algorithmic contracts.

B. Our Solution: Vicarious Performance

Both difficulties – the liability gap and the doctrinal misconception of assisting agents as passive machines – can be avoided if one applies the liability rules for vicarious performance to autonomous software agents. Indeed, the European Expert Group on digital liability makes a strong case for vicarious liability and proposes the following rule:

> If harm is caused by autonomous technology used in a way functionally equivalent to the employment of human auxiliaries, the operator's liability for making use of the technology should correspond to the otherwise existing vicarious liability regime of a principal for such auxiliaries.[106]

Several authors in the civil law world,[107] as well as in the common law world,[108] qualify the use of a software agent as vicarious performance and consequently apply the category of vicarious liability. In the common law, the rules of vicarious performance of contracts and vicarious liability would apply.[109] German law would treat the electronic agent as an auxiliary person performing a principal's contractual obligation (*Erfüllungsgehilfe*, § 278 BGB). From an economic

[104] Prominently, Arbeitsgruppe 'Digitaler Neustart' der Konferenz der Justizministerinnen und Justizminister der Länder, Report of 1 October 2018 and 15 April 2019, 228, 237.

[105] Prominently, C-219/15 *Schmitt v TÜV Rheinland*, ECLI:EU:C:2017:128.

[106] European Expert Group on Liability and New Technologies – New Technologies Formation, Report 'Liability for Artificial Intelligence and Other Emerging Technologies', 2019, 45 ff. They deal mainly with tort liability but apply their arguments to contractual liability as well (at 16).

[107] eg: C Kleiner, *Die elektronische Person: Entwurf eines Zurechnungs- und Haftungssubjekts für den Einsatz autonomer Systeme im Rechtsverkehr* (Baden-Baden, Nomos, 2021) 95 ff; Linardatos, *Aktanten* 189 ff; M Sommer, *Haftung für autonome Systeme: Verteilung der Risiken selbstlernender und vernetzter Algorithmen im Vertrags- und Deliktsrecht* (Baden-Baden, Nomos, 2020) 128 ff; Wagner and Luyken, 'Robo Advice' 172 ff; E Karner, 'Liability for Robotics: Current Rules, Challenges, and the Need for Innovative Concepts', in S Lohsse et al. (eds), *Liability for Artificial Intelligence and the Internet of Things* (Baden-Baden/Oxford, Nomos/Hart, 2019) 120; Schirmer, 'Artificial Intelligence' 35; H Zech, 'Künstliche Intelligenz und Haftungsfragen', [2019] *Zeitschrift für die gesamte Privatrechtswissenschaft* 198, 212; Kessler, 'Intelligente Roboter' 592 f; Hacker, 'Künstliche Intelligenz' 250 ff, 252, 257 f; Teubner, 'Rights of Non-Humans?'.

[108] eg: Lior, 'AI Entities as AI Agents' 1084 ff; Turner, *Robot Rules* 100 ff; JS Allain, 'From Jeopardy! to Jaundice: The Medical Liability Implications of Dr. Watson and Other Artificial Intelligence Systems', (2013) 73 *Louisiana Law Review* 1049, 1066 f; SK Chopra and L White, *A Legal Theory for Autonomous Artificial Agents* (Ann Arbor, University of Michigan Press, 2011) 128 ff.

[109] See for US Law, Restatement (Third) of Agency, §§ 7.03–7.07 (2006). Against vicarious liability for agents, O Rachum-Twaig, 'Whose Robot', 1149 ff; R Michalski, 'How to Sue a Robot', 1058 ff. For English law on vicarious liability, see J Turner, *Robot Rules*, 101.

point of view, the analogy would internalise the costs of algorithmic failure. Since the contracting party using the algorithm would also be the cost-bearer, he would have the optimum incentive to weigh up the benefits and costs of better machine safety in a minimising manner.[110]

C. Limited Legal Personhood – Constellation Two

However, invoking vicarious liability implies the necessity of ascribing legal subjectivity to software agents for a second time again. And, like in electronic contracting, full legal personhood is not required, but only limited legal capacity. While as we have seen, in electronic contracting, agency law attributes to the algorithm the capacity to bind the principal, vicarious liability attributes the capacity to act as a contractual auxiliary and makes the principal liable for algorithmic failures. And this is not just a de-facto ability but a capacity that needs to be attributed by law. According to a long-standing legal principle in common law and civil law countries, vicarious liability requires legal capacity to act on the side of the auxiliary human agent, a principle that needs to be applied to algorithms as well.[111]

Some authors plead for an analogy to vicarious liability, based on a functional equivalent to fault, but assert they can deny at the same time legal subjectivity to the software agents.[112] This, however, is a clear contradiction. When they declare legal subjectivity for software agents as hypothetical and irrelevant but at the same time wish to apply the rules on vicarious liability, they overlook that these rules, as said above, presuppose necessarily the auxiliary's legal capacity. They underestimate the dynamics of the *potestas vicaria*. Legal doctrine and philosophical analyses of the interrelations between person, agency, and representation support the argument that personification is a necessary premise in such a constellation. They conclude that the internal relation constitutes subjectivity:

> representation and agency stand in an internal relation: There is no agent without its personification and no agency without its possible vicarious representation. Yet, personification and representation enable agency only by at the same time complicating the integrity, authority, and presence of the agent.[113]

And this applies to vicarious liability as well. As these authors assert correctly, if vicarious liability applies to human-algorithm relations, this requires actorship for

[110] Hacker, 'Künstliche Intelligenz', 255.

[111] See: Y Benhamou and J Ferland, 'Artificial Intelligence & Damages: Assessing Liability and Calculating the Damages', in P D'agostino et al. (eds), *Leading Legal Disruption: Artificial Intelligence and a Toolkit for Lawyers and the Law* (London, Thomson Reuters, 2021) section II; Rachum-Twaig, 'Whose Robot' 1151, fn 53; Sommer, *Autonome Systeme*, 131; S Klingbeil, 'Schuldnerhaftung für Roboterversagen: Zum Problem der Substitution von Erfüllungsgehilfen durch Maschinen', [2019] *Juristenzeitung* 718, 721.

[112] For the common law, see, eg: Lior, 'AI Entities as AI Agents' 1044 ff; Scherer, 'Wild Beasts and Digital Analogues' 280. For German law, Zech, 'Künstliche Intelligenz', declares legal subjectivity for software agents as irrelevant (fn 36), but nevertheless wants to apply the rules on vicarious liability (at 212). Similarly, Wagner and Luyken, 'Robo Advice' 172 f; Hacker, 'Künstliche Intelligenz' 243, 259.

[113] Trüstedt, 'Representing Agency' 195. The philosophical argument is expressly extended to the personification of algorithms, Trüstedt, *Stellvertretung* ch V 4.2.

both the principal and the agent. If, however, actorship were denied, one would fall back on tool concepts for algorithms that are inadequate for autonomous technology. As Gunkel says rightly,

> autonomous technology, therefore, refers to technological devices that directly contravene the instrumental definition by deliberately contesting and relocating the assignment of agency. Such mechanisms are not mere tools to be used by human beings but occupy, in one way or another, the place of human agent.[114]

If vicarious liability applies to situations in which algorithms perform contractual obligations for a human principal, they take a human agent's place. Therefore, it is unavoidable to grant them simultaneously limited legal personhood.

The analogy completely eliminates the liability gap mentioned above because the principal can no longer relieve himself by proving a lack of misconduct on his part. He is liable for the misconduct of the software agent.[115] Here lies the real advantage of vicarious liability over the principal's liability for his own wrongdoing. Even if the principal has fulfilled all his obligations when using the computer, he is nevertheless liable for the autonomous software agent's decision failure, as if a human vicarious agent had acted. What matters is the unlawful conduct of the algorithmic agent and not the negligence of the principal. 'While liability for damages would be imposed on humans or legal entities, it is the action (or decision) of the algorithm itself, that must be scrutinised for "reasonableness" rather than the decisions of the humans involved.'[116]

Spindler raises a fundamental objection against the analogy. If the operator has fulfilled all his duties in using the algorithm, he should not be liable. The reason is that in the comparable case of dangerous technologies, his liability would be excluded as well (except, of course, for the enumerated instances where the law prescribes strict liability for hazardous objects). Both cases are, Spindler submits, unfortunate mishaps of mechanical machine failures, for which the user, however, is not liable. This objection deserves careful consideration indeed. But it has a problem. It ignores the new quality that arises when a machine produces a decision failure instead of mere mechanical failure.[117] Certainly, for mere mechanical failure, particularly in deterministic automation, the operator is not liable when he fulfilled all his duties.[118] The new quality is the socio-technical empowerment of software agents to make autonomous decisions between alternatives. Once the law has allowed this empowerment, they have become, in fact and in law, vicarious actors, and the liability for their decisions, when things go wrong, cannot

[114] DJ Gunkel, 'Mind the Gap: Responsible Robotics and the Problem of Responsibility', (2020) 22 *Ethics and Information Technology* 307, 310.

[115] Lior, 'AI Entities as AI Agents' 1084; Wagner and Luyken, 'Robo Advice'; Schirmer, 'Rechtsfähige Roboter' 665.

[116] Chagal-Feferkorn, 'Reasonable Algorithm' 115 (for tort law which applies for contract law as well).

[117] This is a fundamental distinction, see: Rachum-Twaig, 'Whose Robot' 1146; Hacker, 'Künstliche Intelligenz' 251; A Matthias, *Automaten als Träger von Rechten* 2nd edn (Berlin, Logos, 2010) 111 ff.

[118] Although this sounds counterintuitive, it is the prevailing opinion, Wagner, 'Digitale Techniken' 736; FJ Säcker et al., *Münchener Kommentar zum Bürgerlichen Gesetzbuch. Band 2* 8th edn (Munich, C.H.Beck, 2019) § 278, 46 (Grundmann); Hacker, 'Künstliche Intelligenz' 250. Only in limited cases, strict liability for dangerous objects comes in.

be avoided with the argument that this was just a case of machine failure which excludes the liability of the owner. Bora supports the analogy to vicarious liability with an additional argument:

> There is almost a collusive relation between programmer, program and user, which eliminates the responsibility of the program and the algorithms (as well as the liability for disruptions in the legal relations). This creates problems for legal doctrine because all the persons concerned fulfil their relevant obligations. One can avoid this by attributing action capacity to the software and acknowledging that the process of communication and decision itself creates 'agency' and 'addressability'. Then the software is transformed into a communicative address.[119]

As we have already said, the deeper reason for the analogy is that if society allows new areas of decision-making for previously unknown autonomous decision-makers, it is obliged to ensure effective forms of responsibility. Ultimately, apart from efficiency arguments, transaction cost savings, utilitarian considerations, issues of sociological jurisprudence, or regulatory concerns, this is a genuine question of legal justice. It is the principle of equal treatment of equal cases and unequal treatment of unequal cases that demands liability here. If the execution of the contract is delegated to a human actor, the principal is liable for the latter's breach of duty. Consequently, if the principal uses a software agent for an identical task, he cannot be exempted from liability. Here, the principle of horizontal equity requires equal treatment of humans and algorithms: justice requires that victims be treated equally by the legal system regardless of the identity of their injurer.[120]

If someone can be held liable for the wrongdoing of some human helper, why should the beneficiary of such support not be equally liable if they outsource their duties to a non-human helper instead, considering that they equally benefit from such delegation?[121] Hage argues that the difference between humans and autonomous systems as such does not justify a different treatment as far as responsibility and liability are concerned.[122] And Balkin's 'substitution effect' of algorithms, ie the effect that algorithms are substituting humans, becomes relevant for making users liable for the decisions of their software agents.[123] Vicarious liability for algorithms becomes even more urgent if one considers that assistance by algorithms pose higher risks than by humans, since 'their capability to perform tasks at high speed augments this capacity to harm in resemblance to humans performing exactly the same tasks'.[124] In any case, it would be an unjustifiable privilege if digitalisation provided a computer operator with such a considerable cost advantage vis-à-vis his

[119] A Bora, 'Kommunikationsadressen als digitale Rechtssubjekte', (2019) *Verfassungsblog* 1 October 2019, 2 (our translation).

[120] Linardatos, *Aktanten* 205; Chagal-Feferkorn, 'Reasonable Algorithm' 123.

[121] European Expert Group, Report 2019, 25.

[122] J Hage, 'Theoretical Foundations for the Responsibility of Autonomous Agents', (2017) 25 *Artificial Intelligence and Law* 255, 270.

[123] J Balkin, 'The Path of Robotics Law', (2015) 6 *California Law Review Circuit* 45, 57 ff.

[124] GI Zekos, *Economics and Law of Artificial Intelligence: Finance, Economic Impacts, Risk Management and Governance* (Cham, Springer, 2021) 383.

competitors who use human assistants. Legal doctrine that unswervingly adheres to traditional legal categories and refuses to assign legal action capacity to software agents will have to be accused of treating equal cases unequally.

V. Non-Contractual Liability

In the area of non-contractual liability, the failure of current law to deal with the digital autonomy risk becomes abundantly clear. 'Our current legal regimes seem inadequate when applied to artificial intelligence'[125] – this sounds like a polite understatement. Numerous authors criticise harshly that here, too, a wide liability gap has been opened, and they demand urgently legislative or judicial intervention.[126] Since most computer failures occur in the field of extra-contractual liability, this is the very test case for how the law deals with digital agents and the delegation of tasks to them. Not only because the frequency of damage is high and the damage is considerable, but also because, in contrast to voluntary risk-taking in contracting, non-contractual relations expose the injured party involuntarily to the computer risk. The liability gap, which appears in tort law, can only be avoided, we will argue after a discussion of alternative solutions when partial personhood for algorithms is introduced and a new vicarious liability of the human principal for the algorithm's autonomous actions established.

In current tort law, the discussion focuses predominantly on the duties of the operators/manufacturers/programmers and treats the electronic agent merely as a dangerous or defective product under their control. Consequently, current tort law runs into a similar dilemma as we have encountered in contract law. Either it fails to sanction autonomous damage-causing decisions made by software agents at all when the human participants have behaved correctly, in this case the large liability gap is simply accepted, or it exposes human actors to a wrongly conceived strict liability standard that establishes liability based on a mere use of an electronic agent. The primary reason why tort law fails to sanction algorithmic failure adequately is that in all its configurations – negligence, product liability, and strict liability – it is predicated on foreseeability, something fundamentally at odds with the non-predictable character of autonomous algorithmic decisions.[127] Obviously, it is of no help to reduce the requirements for foreseeability drastically, as Oster does, to the minimalist standard that the human actor

[125] Allain, 'From Jeopardy! to Jaundice' 1072.

[126] EU Parliament, Resolution 2017, para 7; European Expert Group, Report 2019, 3, 16, 19; European Commission, 'Report on the Safety and Liability Implications of Artificial Intelligence, The Internet of Things and Robotics', COM(2020) 64 final, 12f, 16; Wagner, 'Digitale Techniken' 730, 734; S Dyrkolbotn, 'A Typology of Liability Rules for Robot Harms', in M Aldinhas Ferreira et al. (eds), *A World with Robots: Intelligent Systems, Control and Automation* (Cham, Springer, 2017) 121 f.

[127] See: CEA Karnow, 'The Application of Traditional Tort Theory to Embodied Machine Intelligence', in R Calo et al. (eds), *Robot Law* (Cheltenham, Edward Elgar, 2016) 72.

needs only to foresee that the use of the computer increases the possibility of damage.[128] This amounts to transform fault liability into strict liability, something which we had criticised in our discussion of contractual liability.

A. Fault-Based Liability?

There are occasional suggestions to simply apply the general rules of tort law, particularly fault-based liability of the human actors involved.[129] However, this results in one of the most problematic responsibility gaps for unlawful actions of software agents. In German law, fault-based liability leads to an exemption of the operator from liability if he has always adapted his safety precautions to the new state of the art in science and technology.[130] In the common law, the very application of negligence is problematic. As the existence of a duty of care requires foreseeability of the harm from the defendant's side,[131] no duty of care exists when the electronic agent has acted in an unforeseeable manner.[132] Others have already emphasised that such a liability gap cannot be an appropriate solution:

> Such lack of predictability might be seen as an argument to deny the operator's responsibility and liability. Such argument, however, seems to be highly doubtful. Instead, it has to be considered that the operator has created the increased risk potential by continuously operating the 'autonomous system' and thereby obtaining benefits.[133]

Moreover, fault-based liability creates the wrong incentives for the user's precautions and level of activities resulting in the externalisation of residual damages.[134]

To remedy these shortcomings, some authors suggest expanding the duties of care to cover the specific risks of autonomous agents. In the German debate,

[128] J Oster, 'Haftung für Persönlichkeitsverletzungen durch Künstliche Intelligenz', [2018] *UFITA – Archiv für Medienrecht und Medienwissenschaft* 14, 28; A Bertolini, 'Robots as Products: The Case for a Realistic Analysis of Robot Applications and Liability Rules', (2013) 5 *Law, Innovation & Technology* 214, 239 ff. Oster's fine-grained argument for fault liability of the human actor has the dubious merit to reveal all the contradictions that appear if one declares the algorithm's autonomous behaviour as identical with the behaviour of the human actor.

[129] eg: Oster, 'Persönlichkeitsverletzungen', 25 ff; Bertolini, 'Robots as Products' 239 ff.

[130] eg: C Döpke, 'The Importance of Big Data for Jurisprudence and Legal Practice', in T Hoeren and B Kolany-Raiser (eds), *Big Data in Context. Springer Briefs in Law* (Cham, Springer, 2018) 17; P Bräutigam and T Klindt, 'Industrie 4.0, das Internet der Dinge und das Recht', [2015] *Neue Juristische Wochenschrift* 1137, 1138 f. In German law, tort liability is based on the fault principle unless specific legislation on strict liability exists, cf Dannemann and Schulze (eds), *German Civil Code*, Introduction to §§ 823–853, para 3 (Magnus).

[131] For the fundamental precedent of foreseeability in English law: *Donoughe v Stevenson* [1932] UKHL 100; in US law: *Palsgraf v Long Island Railroad Co* 248 N.Y. 339, 162 N.E. 99 (1928).

[132] A Selbst, 'Negligence and AI's Human Users', (2020) 100 *Boston University Law Review* 1315, 1322; Turner, *Robot Rules* 90 f; Karnow, 'Traditional Tort Theory' 73 f; Ebers, 'Liability for Artificial Intelligence and EU Consumer Law' 215, para 60.

[133] S Lohsse et al., 'Liability for Artificial Intelligence', in S Lohsse et al. (eds), *Liability for Robotics and in the Internet of Things* (Baden-Baden/Oxford, Nomos/Hart, 2019) 20.

[134] See: G Wagner, 'Roboter als Haftungssubjekte? Konturen eines Haftungsrechts für autonome Systeme', in F Faust and H-B Schäfer (eds), *Zivilrechtliche und rechtsökonomische Probleme des Internet und der künstlichen Intelligenz* (Tübingen, Mohr Siebeck, 2019) 22 f.

such suggestions have become prominent. They are discussed as new duties of care (*Verkehrspflichten*) for the operators.[135] In the common law, a similar argument could be made to extend the existing duties of care for operators in relation to supervision of algorithms.[136] Possibly, the Proposed European AI Act, though it does not deal with liability explicitly, would become relevant when laying down specific obligations for operators, users, but also product manufacturers for high-risk AI.[137] If so, operators would be liable for damage caused by algorithms whenever the operators have failed to control the algorithm's behaviour properly. Others even consider expanding tort liability so that any use of autonomous computers creates a duty of care about the algorithm's supervision and control.[138] This, of course, is a radical solution that would lead to a form of causation-based strict liability in disguise. It stripes off the duty of care its essential content if the duties are so broad that they encompass control of any type of behaviour of an algorithm relating to its use. Moreover, it would stifle the creative potential of autonomous algorithms' 'discovery procedure' to an unbearable degree.[139] It would create a kind of *actio libera in causa* which does not exist in private law.

However, the most fundamental objection against liability based on the negligence of the operators/manufacturers/programmers points to the emergent properties of AI:

> Ultimately, because AI inserts a layer of inscrutable, unintuitive, statistically-derived and often proprietary code between the decision and outcome, the nexus between human choices, outcomes, and responsibility from which negligence law draws its force is unwound. While there may be a way to tie some decisions back to their outcomes, using explanation and transparency requirements, it seems unlikely that negligence will be the optimal way to address harms that result from AI.[140]

Thus, many suggestions to handle liability for the failure of autonomous electronic agents recur to various theories on strict liability, namely product liability law, liability for dangerous objects or a broad form of strict liability for the use of autonomous agents.

[135] eg: Oster, 'Persönlichkeitsverletzungen' 30 f; D Wielsch, 'Die Haftung des Mediums: BGH 14.05.2013 (Google Autocomplete)', in B Lomfeld (ed), *Die Fälle der Gesellschaft: Eine neue Praxis soziologischer Jurisprudenz* (Tübingen, Mohr Siebeck, 2017) 140 ff.

[136] In English law, such duties of care were long developed along the *Caparo*-test of foreseeability, proximity and whether it is fair, just and reasonable (established in *Caparo v Dickman* [1990] UKHL 2); recently, however, courts engage more frequently in developing new duties of care from existing ones in a casuistic fashion (eg *Michael v Chief Contestable of South Wales* [2015] UKSC 2 and, very recently, *Okpabi v Shell* [2021] UKSC 3, para 141). In the US, different tests for establishing a duty of care exist in the different states.

[137] European Commission, Proposal for a Regulation of the European Parliament and the Council Laying Down Harmonised Rules on Artificial Intelligence (Proposal Artificial Intelligence Act) and Amending Certain Union Legislative Acts, COM(2021) 206, most notably Art 16 ff (obligations of providers) Art 24 (obligations of product manufacturers), Art 26 (obligations of importers), Art 29 (obligations of users).

[138] In this direction, Zech, 'Künstliche Intelligenz' 210 f.

[139] Extensively for this argument, see ch 2, II.C.

[140] Selbst, 'Negligence and AI' 1375.

B. Product Liability?

Since product liability law is supposed to prescribe strict liability for defective products,[141] it seems immune to the critical arguments raised against fault-based liability. The producer would be liable for any damage which the software agent causes; no negligence of the human actors would be required; the liability gap would be closed. But this is an error. A closer look reveals that product liability is not at all the all-encompassing solution to the liability gaps that it seems to be.[142] First of all, product liability requires treating algorithms as defective products, which brings many problems. For EU product liability law, it is unclear whether it covers algorithms since they are non-tangible objects without physical embodiment. Furthermore, EU law does not apply to service providers.[143] Hence, programmers and operators of software programs are exempted from liability, and only manufacturers can be held liable unless the interpretation of producer would be drastically expanded.

In addition, the requirement of defect does not fit very well with the character of digital agents and how they behave.[144] While electronic agents can be defective in the case of a manufacturing or design defect, damage results regularly from unpredictable algorithmic behaviour. However, it would be difficult to speak of defectively manufactured or designed products when electronic agents take decisions based on probability rules. As Chagal-Feferkorn pointedly argues: '(…) sophisticated systems, in particular self-learning algorithms, rely on probability-based predictions, and probabilities by nature inevitably get it wrong some of the time'.[145] In this context, it is particularly questionable how one assesses the 'defective' character of such an autonomous decision. What is the standard for comparison: A human decision or a decision by another algorithm? And what would be considered defective: The fact that damage was caused or the fact that a high probability of an incorrect decision has materialised?[146] In this case, there is

[141] In the EU, product liability is harmonised by Council Directive 85/374/EEC on the approximation of laws, regulations and administrative provisions of the Member States concerning liability for defective products, [1985] OJ L210/29 (Product Liability Directive) for the US, DG Owen, *Products Liability Law* 3rd edn (St. Paul, West Academic, 2015) 778 ff, 938 ff.

[142] See: T Evas, *Civil Liability Regime for Artificial Intelligence – European Added Value Assessment* (Brussels / Strasbourg, Study Commissioned by the European Parliamentary Research Service, 2020) 8 f.

[143] CJEU, C-495/10 *Centre Hospitalier universitaire de Besancon v Thomas Dutrueux* ECLI:EU:C:2011:869, para 39.

[144] On this problem, see, eg: M Ebers, 'Regulating AI and Robots: Ethical and Legal Challenges', in M Ebers and S Navas (eds), *Algorithms and Law* (Cambridge, Cambridge University Press, 2020) 58; C Wendehorst, 'Strict Liability for AI and other Emerging Technologies', (2020) 11 *Journal of European Tort Law* 150, 159; J-S Borghetti, 'How can Artificial Intelligence be Defective?', in S Lohsse et al. (eds), *Liability for Artificial Intelligence and the Internet of Things* (Baden-Baden/Oxford, Nomos/Hart, 2019) 70 ff.

[145] KA Chagal-Feferkorn, 'Am I an Algorithm or a Product? When Products Liability Should Apply to Algorithmic Decision-Makers', (2019) 30 *Stanford Law & Policy Review* 61, 84. For the same point in relation to the Product Liability Directive, Ebers, 'Regulating AI and Robots' 57.

[146] For this criticism on the notion of defectiveness for algorithms that operate with probability, Borghetti, 'Liability for AI' 70 ff.

strictly speaking no product liability for autonomous algorithmic decisions: 'this is a major flaw in the current legal approach to autonomous robots'.[147]

These rather technical problems of how to interpret 'product' and 'defect' could be overcome by a broad interpretation of 'product' and by expanding product liability from defective to dangerous algorithms.[148] However, even then, an major problem remains. Product liability law itself leaves considerable liability gaps because it is by no means a case of strict liability without any fault considerations. Product liability is imposed only under the condition that the producer has violated specified obligations within the production process or in the post-marketing phase.[149] EU product liability law constructs these duties as an exculpation that exempt producers from liability if he can prove that defect was due to an uncontrollable risk. The EU Commission has coined the problematic concepts of 'later defect defence' and 'development risk defence' that leave a liability gap.[150] In addition, national product liability laws regularly move product liability much closer to fault-based liability.[151]

Similarly, in US product liability law, only the manufacturing defect is subject to strict liability,[152] while design defects and failure to warn have gradually integrated negligence-based considerations. This is especially relevant for the reasonable alternative design for design defects and the foreseeability of use in the failure to warn.[153] For our constellation, this means that the software producer can be exempted from liability if he has fulfilled all construction, information, and product observation obligations.[154]

Admittedly, this liability gap in product liability is not as wide as the gap in fault-based tort law. As Beck argues, it is only under certain circumstances that the producer can excuse himself from strict liability, ie if he can prove that the state of scientific and technical knowledge at the time when he put the product into circulation was not such as to enable the existence of the defect to be discovered;

[147] W Barfield, 'Liability for Autonomous and Artificially Intelligent Robots', (2018) 9 *Paladyn. Journal of Behavioral Robotics* 193, 196.

[148] See: G Wagner, 'Robot, Inc.: Personhood for Autonomous Systems?', (2019) 88 *Fordham Law Review* 591, 603 ff. See also: EU Commission, Report 2020, 14.

[149] See: H Zech, 'Liability for AI: Public Policy Considerations', [2021] *ERA Forum* 147, 153f.; Wendehorst, 'Strict Liability for AI' 158 f; Wagner, 'Robot Liability' 35 f.

[150] EU Commission, Report 2020, 15. Recognised also by T Riehm and S Meier, 'Product Liability in Germany: Ready for the Digital Age?', (2019) 8 *Journal of European Consumer and Market Law* 161, 165.

[151] This is emphasised by Wendehorst, 'Strict Liability for AI' 158. For a comprehensive analysis of liability laws for dangerous products in all Member States, Evas, *Civil Liability Regime for Artificial Intelligence* 14 ff.

[152] Restatement (Third) of Torts: Products Liability § 2a (2012).

[153] Extensively on this change from strict liability to fault-based standards, see generally: DG Gifford, 'Technological Triggers to Tort Revolutions: Steam Locomotives, Autonomous Vehicles, and Accident Compensation', (2018) 11 *Journal of Tort Law* 71, 119 ff.

[154] This is where authors discover the liability gap in product liability law, Chinen, *Law and Autonomous Machines* 27; Spindler, 'Einsatz von Robotern' 72 ff, 78. For a synopsis of several exemptions from product liability, which contribute to the liability gap, F-U Pieper, 'Die Vernetzung autonomer Systeme im Kontext von Vertrag und Haftung', [2016] *InTeR Zeitschrift zum Innovations- und Technikrecht* 188, 193.

or in the case of a manufacturer of a component, that the defect is attributable to the design of the product or the instructions given by the manufacturer. Now, when research activities show deficiencies of former versions of the programs, it follows that the producer could not have acted differently. Moreover, as Beck points out, different manufacturers (and programmers) contribute to a robot in most cases. It is also possible that the manufacturer of a component can show that the design or instructions lead to defects, thus freeing himself from liability.[155] Also, frequently it will be difficult for the victim to prove that there was a reasonable alternative design.[156] The doubts about the efficacy of product liability are growing if one considers another problematic exemption from liability. There is no product liability for development risks. This is particularly questionable in the case of a programmed (!) non-predictability (!) of the algorithm's decisions.[157]

Thus, it is not only traditional tort liability but also product liability law that exempts algorithmic failures from liability, albeit to a lesser degree. 'Insofar as the enterprise cannot be accused of violating its own duties of selection, maintenance and monitoring, nobody is liable for malfunctioning of the digital system.'[158]

Finally, one should also emphasise that product liability rules leave a responsibility gap regarding the coverage of damages. In principle, product liability rules only compensate physical damages but do not cover non-economic losses and pure economic losses.[159] This makes product liability law irrelevant for very relevant damages associated with algorithmic behaviour. This problem is not exclusive to product liability. It is a characteristic of strict liability in general and will thus come up again in our following discussion on strict liability.

C. Strict Causal Liability for Dangerous Objects and Activities?

Faced with wide responsibility gaps in tort law and product liability law, most authors demand urgently legislative intervention. Strict liability for dangerous

[155] Beck, 'Robotics' 474. Article 7 Product Liability Directive states that the producer is freed from all liability if he proves (Art 7): '(a) that he did not put the product into circulation; or (b) that, having regard to the circumstances, it is probable that the defect which caused the damage did not exist at the time when the product was put into circulation by him or that this defect came into being afterwards; or (c) that the product was neither manufactured by him for sale or any form of distribution for economic nor manufactured or distributed by him in the course of his business; or (d) that the defect is due to compliance of the product with mandatory regulations issued by the public authorities; or (e) that the state of scientific and technical knowledge at the time when he put the product into circulation was not such as to enable the existence of the defect to be discovered; or (f) in the case of a manufacturer of a component, that the defect is attributable to the design of the product in which the component has been fitted or to the instructions given by the manufacturer of the product'.

[156] See: Chopra and White, *Autonomous Artificial Agents* 144.

[157] The prevailing doctrine admits that this is a grave liability gap, but maintains the position that legal capacity should not be granted to software agents, eg: Riehm and Meier, 'Product Liability in Germany: Ready for the Digital Age?' 165.

[158] Wagner, 'Digitale Techniken' 736.

[159] Explicitly for the EU: Art 9 of the Product Liability Directive that refers to death, injury, property as damage.

objects is their preferred solution. *De lege ferenda*, this seems to be the royal road to successfully countering the digital autonomy risk.[160] The authorities of the European Union are considering corresponding legislation.[161] Others argue that existing laws on strict liability for motor vehicles or medical accidents could be particularly suitable.[162] Again others discuss liability for animals.[163] Some authors occasionally mention strict liability for hazardous objects, such as nuclear operations or genetic engineering, as a relevant liability model.[164] Such strict liability would indeed abolish the responsibility gaps entirely.

However, for strict AI liability, the devil is in the detail, both in the conditions for liability and the consequences. As we said in chapter one, compared to familiar situations of product liability, with the digital autonomy risk, 'the array of potential harms widens, as to the product is added a new facet – intelligence'.[165] Liability for digital assistants modelled after the existing forms of strict liability for dangerous objects would not go far enough because they are typically limited to compensation of physical harms. Such limitation, of course, makes sense in general given that strict liability for dangerous objects abolishes any requirement for faulty behaviour, and at the same time, the highest risk of hazardous objects is one for physical injuries and property. However, when applying this model of strict liability to AI, the result would be a too narrow scope of application.[166] Most of the damages caused by malfunctioning algorithms are related to their communicative nature and not the security risk of causing physical damage. Admittedly, there are constellations in which robots may cause death and injuries. Still, most day-to-day instances are those where non-economic losses occur or even economic losses, such as defamation by algorithms or wrongful advice. Closing the liability gap by strict liability would then essentially mean implementing far-reaching strict

[160] Linardatos, *Aktanten*, 330 ff; E Marchisio, 'In Support of "No-Fault" Civil Liability Rules for Artificial Intelligence', (2021) 1 *SN Social Sciences* 1; A Bertolini, *Artificial Intelligence and Civil Liability* (Brussels, European Parliament, Study Commissioned by the Juri Committee on Legal Affairs, 2020), §§ 5.1–5.3; T Riehm and S Meier, 'Künstliche Intelligenz im Zivilrecht', [2019] *DGRI Jahrbuch 2018* 1, 23 ff, 63; Wagner, 'Robot Liability' 47; Zech, 'Liability for Autonomous Systems' 197 f; JGünther, *Roboter* 237 ff; Schirmer, 'Rechtsfähige Roboter' 665; Bräutigam and Klindt, 'Industrie 4.0' 1138 f; Hanisch, 'Haftungskonzepte' 35 f; DC Vladeck, 'Machines without Principals: Liability Rules and Artificial Intelligence', (2014) 89 *Washington Law Review* 117, 141 ff.

[161] European Expert Group, Report 2019, 39 ff; EU Commission, Report 2020, 12 f, 16; European Commission, White Paper on Artificial Intelligence, COM(2020) 65 final; 16; European Parliament, Civil Liability Regime for Artificial Intelligence, Resolution of 20 October 2020, 2020/2012(INL), para 14; EU Parliament, Resolution 2017, para 6. The EU Commission, Proposal Artificial Intelligence Act 2021 does not specify liability, but does categorise AI according to the severity of the risk.

[162] Borghetti, 'Liability for AI' 72 ff; Turner, *Robot Rules* 102 ff.

[163] eg: Riehm and Meier, 'Künstliche Intelligenz', para 25; Tjong Tijn Lai, '(Semi)autonomous System' 62.

[164] eg: Evas, *Civil Liability Regime for Artificial Intelligence* 19 ff.

[165] Rachum-Twaig, 'Whose Robot' 1149. For an elaborate critique of strict liability for algorithms, Y Bathaee, 'The Artificial Intelligence Black Box and the Failure of Intent and Causation', (2018) 31 *Harvard Journal of Law & Technology* 889.

[166] See, in this direction, the proposal by Wendehorst, 'Strict Liability for AI' 170.

liability rules that also cover economic losses, as the European Parliament had suggested.[167]

Such a proposal would, however, overshoot and apply strict liability in much too broad a manner. It would expand strict liability for all kinds of wide-ranging damages since it requires simply operating a dangerous system and causation. This, however, contradicts the underlying principles of strict liability for hazardous objects. In general, only in those constellations when the law, despite grave dangers, permits the use of objects due to their social benefits, it imposes causation-based strict liability.[168] In other words, strict liability is the rare case of liability for damages despite the lawful conduct of the user. This type of liability applies when the typical operational hazard is realised, ie when causal processes have gone awry. In the case of software agents, however, it is not mechanical machine failure that causes the damage but the autonomous decision-making of an information-processing unit. Not the causation risk of a wrongly functioning computer is relevant here, but rather the decision risk, the very different kind of risk that autonomous decisions will turn out to be unlawful. Femia rightly notes:

> In the joint action of human-machine intelligence, the qualification as legal or illegal behaviour will be distinct and independent for the human and for the machine: the legally correct action of the human may well be accompanied by an illegal behaviour of the machine acting on its own; and it is this very illegality that constitutes the premise for damage compensation.[169]

In other words, liability of electronic agents is necessary not because of their inherently dangerous potential to cause damage but because of the ex-post evaluation of their ex-ante unpredictable probability decisions as incorrect.[170] And this is a case of *respondeat superior.* The reason for the liability is not the use of an object of increased danger but the illegal behaviour of the algorithm, which the principal has legitimately used for his own benefit. What counts is the wrongful behaviour of someone else, not the malfunctioning of a dangerous object. Causation-based strict liability for risky AI systems would thus overshoot in making the algorithm's operator liable for all kinds of damages that the AI causes and ignore whether such damage was linked to illegal behaviour.

Since the autonomy risk of digital decisions cannot be equated with the causality hazard of strict liability, different responsibility principles and different liability standards need to enter here. Norms of liability for unlawful decisions by autonomous agents cannot be based on the causal risk of things but must be tailored to

[167] EU Parliament, Resolution 2020, Art 2(1) Proposed Regulation.

[168] *Locus classicus*, J Esser, *Grundlagen und Entwicklung der Gefährdungshaftung: Beiträge zur Reform des Haftungsrechts und zu seiner Wiedereinordnung in die Gedanken des allgemeinen Privatrechts* (Munich, Beck, 1941). On a sociological interpretation, N Luhmann, *Risk: A Sociological Theory* (Berlin, de Gruyter, 1993), ch 4, II.

[169] P Femia, 'Soggetti responsabili: Algoritmi e diritto civile', in P Femia (ed), *Soggetti giuridici digitali: Sullo status privatistico degli agenti software autonomi* (Napoli, Edizioni Scientifichi Italiane, 2019) 12 f (our translation).

[170] See: Wagner, 'Digitale Techniken' 731.

the decision risk of actors. This is the point where general principles of personification discussed above come in. It is a crucial function of personifying non-human entities that replaces causal attribution with an action attribution.[171] If private law, as proposed here, treats software agents as vicarious agents, ie as legally capable of acting, then it is absolutely impossible to operate with a mere causal liability in the case of non-contractual damages.

D. Our Solution: Vicarious Liability in Tort

As the preceding arguments have shown, designing appropriate digital liability in tort and product liability law *de lege lata* is more difficult than designing contractual liability. In principle, all the solutions suggested run again into the now well-known dilemma. Either they overshoot via strict causation-based liability or undershoot, thus creating a wide liability gap.[172] Again, now for the third time, not only in contract formation and contractual liability but also in non-contractual liability, the only way out of the dilemma is to grant limited legal personhood to the software agent. This would make possible a general vicarious liability in tort for the actions of autonomous software agents, according to which their misconduct is directly attributed to the principal. This looks like a promising path for national laws in the common law,[173] the civil law world,[174] and European law.[175]

The fundamental difference between vicarious liability and strict causation-based liability for dangerous objects becomes practically relevant in three aspects related to liability.

[171] Teubner, 'Rights of Non-Humans?'.

[172] See also: Chinen, 'Legal Responsibility' 363; Allain, 'From Jeopardy! to Jaundice' 1061 ff.

[173] See: A Panezi, 'Liability Rules for AI-Facilitated Wrongs: An Ecosystem Approach to Manage Risk and Uncertainty', in P García Mexía and F Pérez Bes (eds), *AI and the Law* (Alphen aan den Rijn, Wolters Kluwer, 2021), section 4; Lior, 'AI Entities as AI Agents' 1084 ff; HR Sullivan and SJ Schweikart, 'Are Current Tort Liability Doctrines Adequate for Addressing Injury Caused by AI?', (2019) 21 *AMA Journal of Ethics* 161, 161 ff; R Abott, 'The Reasonable Computer: Disrupting the Paradigm of Tort Liability', (2018) 86 *George Washington Law Review* 1, 22 ff; Bathaee, 'Artificial Intelligence Black Box' 934 f. (for autonomous and non-supervised algorithms); Chagal-Feferkorn, 'Reasonable Algorithm' 115; Tjong Tijn Lai, '(Semi)autonomous System', 71; Turner, *Robot Rules* 101; A Chandra, 'Liability Issues in Relation to Autonomous AI Systems', (2017) *SSRN Electronic Library* ssrn.com/abstract=3052154, 5 f.

[174] See: R Janal, 'Extra-Contractual Liability for Wrongs Committed by Autonomous Systems', in M Ebers and S Navas (eds), *Algorithms and Law* (Cambridge, Cambridge University Press, 2020) 194, 201; S Navas, 'Robot Machines and Civil Liability', in M Ebers and S Navas (eds), *Algorithms and Law* (Cambridge, Cambridge University Press, 2020); H Zech, 'Zivilrechtliche Haftung für den Einsatz von Robotern: Zuweisung von Automatisierungs- und Autonomierisiken', in S Gless and K Seelmann (eds), *Intelligente Agenten und das Recht* (Baden-Baden, Nomos, 2016) 195; Hanisch, 'Haftungskonzepte' 46 ff (liability for 'machine misconduct' instead of strict liability).

[175] So for a future European law, European Expert Group, Report 2019, 45 ff; Karner, 'Liability for Robotics' 120; N Nevejans, *European Civil Law Rules in Robotics* (Brussels, Study commissioned by the European Parliament's Juri Committee on Legal Affairs, 2016) 16. Similarly, the prediction for a variety of national laws, Koops et al., 'Accountability Gap' 560.

(1) Causation-based strict liability does not presuppose the violation of a duty of care, neither for the user nor for the hazardous object itself. Vicarious liability, in contrast, requires necessarily that the software agent breaches a duty of not acting with reasonable care.[176]
(2) Vicarious liability extends to more than just personal injury and property damage and may include, among other things, violation of privacy rights, libel or sexual harassment.[177]
(3) While the sanctions of strict liability are limited to financial compensation, vicarious liability would, depending on the tort committed by the algorithm, be open for a wider array of sanctions; especially in the case of the violation of privacy rights, it would allow for injunction, right to reply, or rectification.[178]

In other words, strict liability would go too far on the one hand because it would trigger liability in all those cases when the software agent simply causes damage without violating any duty of care. The famous floodgates would be open. On the other hand, strict liability would not go far enough insofar as it provides compensation only for personal injury and property damage and insofar as its sanctions are limited to compensation.[179]

Difference (1): Strict causation-based liability does not require the violation of a duty of care, but for the liability for software agents, violation of duty becomes the linchpin of liability:[180]

> The natural person or legal entity which makes use of the 'thinking machine' would respond only for the damaging facts which derive from an 'illicit decision' of the latter. The principal, in other words, has to respond only when the artificial agent has violated a rule of conduct and, therefore, its behaviour can be qualified as *contra ius*.[181]

In the common law, the general core requirement for vicarious liability is that the agent or servant has committed a tort, ie breached a duty of care that causes

[176] For this condition of vicarious liability in both common law and civil law, P Giliker, *Vicarious Liability in Tort: A Comparative Perspective* (Cambridge, Cambridge University Press, 2010) 27 ff.

[177] P O' Callaghan et al., *Personality Rights in European Tort Law* (Cambrige, Cambridge University Press, 2010) 18 ff, 25 ff.

[178] For AI systems, Oster, 'Persönlichkeitsverletzungen' 16; MA Lemley and B Casey, 'Remedies for Robots', (2019) 86 *University of Chicago Law Review* 1311, 1384 ff.

[179] Thus, it is simply thoughtless to require that strict liability should be introduced and at the same time that 'significant immaterial harm that results in a verifiable economic loss' should be compensated, as proposed by the EU Parliament, Resolution 2020, para 19.

[180] The initial European Parliament's draft failed to recognise the specificity of software liability, in contrast to strict liability, since it only calls for a causal link between the harmful behaviour of the computer and the damage incurred, EU Parliament, Resolution 2017, para 27. EU Parliament, Resolution 2020, para 14 has limited this to only high-risk autonomous systems, but still maintains the view of a general strict liability system for such high-risk computer behaviour. Correctly, Hanisch, 'Haftungskonzepte' 46, who makes machine misconduct a prerequisite for liability.

[181] MW Monterossi, 'Liability for the Fact of Autonomous Artificial Intelligence Agents. Things, Agencies and Legal Actors', (2020) 6 *Global Jurist* 1, 11.

damage.[182] Thus, for algorithmic failures, 'non-contractual liability must be conceived as liability for unlawful decisions of the computer-subject'.[183] Vicarious liability requires the software agent to have 'misbehaved'.[184] While for strict liability, it is sufficient if there is merely causality between operational hazard and damage,[185] liability for using software agents requires determining that the agent did not act with reasonable care. For physical injury and property damages, this is relatively unproblematic. Still, it becomes crucial to decide whether the agent's conduct is illegal or not, mainly when an extensive weighing of different aspects, frequently constitutional rights, is necessary.[186] Against all attempts to apply pure causation liability without any illegal conduct involved, British business lawyers specialising in AI-related litigation insist with good reason that it is

> important to bear in mind that any consideration of liability in a civil or criminal matter is ultimately a question of whether or not the acts or omissions of the relevant defendant (as caused by the relevant AI system's decisions) were illegal. Did those acts or omissions amount to breaches of contract, negligence or criminal offences (as the case may be)?[187]

Abott illustrates the difference between causation-based strict liability and vicarious liability with a crane dropping a steel frame that causes injury to a passer-by.[188] If dropping is due to an action of the operator of the crane, he is liable. In contrast, a misconstruction of the crane would result in the manufacturer's product liability. Replacing now the operated crane with a computer-operated unmanned crane makes the dilemma obvious. Treating the crane as a machine would be a case of product liability, even if the cause of the dropping by the computer is more similar to a human operator's fault. If the crane producer can show that the act of dropping was not due to an initial fault in the crane but an incorrect prediction of the available input data on the ground, the result will be a liability gap. The European Expert Group on Liability for Artificial Intelligence made a similar argument. In their report, they discuss several liability models,

[182] For US law, Restatement (Third) Agency, §7.03, para 2 (2006) (vicarious agent must commit tort); Restatement (Second) of Torts, Vol 2, §281 (1965) (for conditions of negligence); for English law D Nolan and J Davies, 'Torts and Equitable Wrongs', in A Burrows (ed), *English Private Law* (Oxford, Oxford University Press, 2013) 1024, 17.367.

[183] I Martone, 'Algoritmi e diritto: appunti in tema di responsabilità civile', (2020) 1 *Teconologie e diritto* 128, 150, n 110 (our translation).

[184] See: European Expert Group, Report 2019, 46; Abott, 'Reasonable Computer' 31; Allain, 'From Jeopardy! to Jaundice' 1079.

[185] The term strict liability should be 'reserved for such forms of liability that do not require any kind of non-compliance or defect or malperformance but are more or less based exclusively on causation', Wendehorst, 'Strict Liability for AI' 159. See generally, for a classification into strict liability with causation (ideal strict liability), and strict liability with defences (inter alia product liability), D On, *Strict Liability and the Aims of Tort Law* (Maastricht, Dissertation Maastricht University, 2020) 164 ff.

[186] Oster, 'Persönlichkeitsverletzungen' 17.

[187] Hughes and Williamson, 'When AI Systems Cause Harm: The Application of Civil and Criminal Liability', (2019) *Digital Business Law – Blog* 08 November 2019.

[188] Abott, 'Reasonable Computer' 24 ff.

eg product liability or strict liability, but for autonomous algorithms, they prioritise vicarious liability and suggest the following rule:

> 118. Vicarious liability for autonomous systems
>
> If harm is caused by autonomous technology used in a way functionally equivalent to the employment of human auxiliaries, the operator's liability for making use of the technology should correspond to the otherwise existing vicarious liability regime of a principal for such auxiliaries.[189]

Difference (2): The second significant difference between vicarious and strict liability concerns the extent of compensation. In common law, product liability doctrines are commonly restricted to physical injuries and damage to property. They do not compensate for other damages such as privacy violations, pure economic harm, denial of critical services, and the like. Similarly, in German law, only physical injuries and damage to property are covered, but violations of personality rights, enterprise rights, violations of public policy and acts of unfair competition would not be covered.[190] While the typical risk involved justifies that strict liability rules cover neither purely economic risks nor social risks,[191] such liability limitations are not acceptable for software agents.[192] Their specific risks are not only realised in contexts in which dangerous installations cause accidents but particularly in all the contexts in which real people make unlawful decisions.

A good example is privacy-related damage caused by an AI-based, personal-assistant's bot, which discloses sensitive personal data, such as medical status, financial status, and personal affairs, to a third party. Software agents tend to cause particularly non-physical damage such as emotional, economic and dignitary harms. Other examples are defamatory autocompleted searches, discrimination in employment procedure, surveillance and infringement of users' and non-users' privacy rights and even financial loss resulting from the destabilisation of the stock market via high-speed trading algorithms.[193] In German law, as in damaging acts by natural persons, pure economic loss must be compensated if the agents' actions violated a legal right or violated a statutory rule or were against public policy. Similarly, in the common law, an expansion has occurred regarding the type of torts and the kind of damage to which vicarious liability is applicable. And that makes a big difference.

[189] European Expert Group, Report 2019, 45.

[190] Wagner, 'Roboter als Haftungssubjekte?' 4; Oster, 'Persönlichkeitsverletzungen' 49.

[191] For a useful classification of AI-risks, Wendehorst, 'Strict Liability for AI' 161 ff; See also EU Commission, Proposal Artificial Intelligence Act 2021 that distinguishes between minimal and low risk, high-risk and unacceptable risk.

[192] These arguments are made forcefully by Rachum-Twaig, 'Whose Robot' 1149 f; Tjong Tijn Lai, '(Semi)autonomous System' 75.

[193] Lior, 'AI Accident Network', section A.2.

Of course, one could respond that, as a matter of principle, liability for algorithmic actions should not go beyond physical injury and property damages.[194] Indeed, it is not necessary for these damages to demonstrate a violation of a duty of care; damaging bodily integrity and property is unlawful in itself. But the price for this restriction is too high. It would leave a wide responsibility gap open in all the fields of non-physical damages just mentioned. In these fields, vicarious liability is urgently needed to avoid the gap.

Difference (3): There is another dimension in which strict liability for dangerous objects is too narrow to grasp the peculiarities of the digital risk – sanctions. Strict liability for hazardous objects limits the sanction to financial compensation of damages. This would be appropriate for self-driving cars, medical robots and care robots. Still, many activities of electronic agents have to do with the violation of privacy rights and similar non-physical damages. Here, other sanctions than mere compensation are required, such as injunction, right to reply or rectification. It could also imply a stronger focus on future-oriented action and undoing consequences. A future law of digital liability would have to prescribe in detail what kinds of sanctions and recovery action will be appropriate.[195]

These three differences make clear that the frequent call for causation-based strict liability is misplaced. What is needed is a digital vicarious liability, ie liability for damages caused by autonomous software agents. This would not be a causation-based liability for the legitimate use of a hazardous machine, but a principal's vicarious liability for unlawful decisions of his software agent. To be precise, this is a strict liability from the perspective of the principal, ie no-fault liability, but strict liability for illegal actions of the agent, namely the wrongful decisions of algorithms.

At this point, some authors argue that for algorithmic liability, one should introduce a new type of 'strict liability for dangerous objects', which makes the differences between strict liability and vicarious liability vanish. They present illegality of the agent's conduct as a necessary condition and expand the liability beyond physical damage and bodily injuries to all kinds of monetary damages, including the violation of personality rights.[196] In substance, this 'strict liability for dangerous objects' is nothing but a fully-fledged vicarious liability for algorithms because it presupposes the illegal action of an auxiliary and expands the coverage of liability. It is, however, a categorical error to subsume this under 'strict liability for dangerous objects' since it ignores that vicarious liability and strict liability rely on different

[194] This is implied in Wagner's solution *de lege ferenda*, Wagner, 'Digitale Techniken' 734 ff.

[195] In our analysis of interconnectivity liability, ch 5, IV.F, we focus more extensively on such potential new remedies. These could also become relevant for vicarious liability, but only *de lege ferenda*.

[196] See, eg: Sommer, *Autonome Systeme* 466.

principles: Vicarious liability deals with decision risks of actors and not with causation risks of dangerous objects. The decision risk of actors relates to their communicative nature and the harm that may be caused, whereas the causation risk of hazardous objects is first and foremost a security risk.

E. Limited Legal Personhood – Constellation Three

Our solution presupposes, for a third time, as we said above, to endow algorithms with limited legal personhood. Similarly, to agency in contract formation and vicarious performance, tortious vicarious liability presupposes legal capacity of the agent. Sometimes a particular legal rule requires this capacity explicitly.[197] In any case, this capacity will be an implied condition whenever vicarious liability is applied. Against the protest of the traditional dogma claiming that algorithms are not persons, this analogy would produce consistency in all three constellations: limited legal subjectivity for algorithms in contract formation, in vicarious liability in contract law, as well as in tort law. To introduce via legislation a rule stipulating *respondeat superior* for autonomous algorithms would make sense, at least in some legal orders.[198] The rule would simply have to provide that the initiators are responsible for damage-causing actions of the software agent, however, under the condition that the actions of the software agent were unlawful.[199]

F. The 'Reasonable Algorithm'

Once the rules on vicarious liability are applicable, the standard of reasonable care for algorithms needs to be defined. It is a general principle of tort liability to determine this standard on an objective basis. The common law does so with the standard of the 'reasonable man'.[200] In German law, the standard for negligence is, according to § 276 BGB, one of 'reasonable care' on an objective basis. For computers,

[197] In German law, § 827 BGB explicitly specifies that committing a tortious act is dependent on action capacity, Dannemann and Schulze (eds), *German Civil Code*, § 827, para 1 (Magnus).

[198] While in the common law world and in several civil law countries, the courts could recognise limited legal capacity for the agent to make vicarious liability possible, in Germany it is exclusively legislation that could introduce such a rule. The reason is that German tort law does not fully follow the principle of *respondeat superior*. Instead, § 831 BGB requires in addition to the tort committed by the agent that the principal himself violates a duty of care, see Dannemann and Schulze (eds), *German Civil Code*, § 831 para 1, 4 (Magnus). This industry-friendly policy is heavily criticised almost unanimously, but for its abolition legislative action is necessary.

[199] Similarly, Hanisch, 'Haftungskonzepte' 46 ff, 54.

[200] Fundamentally, *Blyth v Birmingham Waterworks Co* (1856) 11 Ex Ch 781, 784; further, prominently *Hall v Brooklands Racing Club* [1933] 1 KB 205 where the reasonable man is described as 'the man in the street', or 'the man on the Clapham omnibus'.

the ultimate question is then on what basis to determine such standard.[201] Two options are available: Either one compares computers to a reasonable human actor, or one develops an independent standard of care for autonomous computer behaviour that corresponds to its 'species' behaviour. Whether autonomous algorithms still compare to their human counterparts will depend on the technological developments. Computers may have higher capabilities concerning some decision-making capacity. However, in some situations, the algorithms' abilities may fail in comparison to those of humans.[202]

This requires distinguishing between two situations. In the first phase, when computers are less reliable than humans in their decisions, the standard of care remains the one for the average human actor in the same position. This provides incentives to improve the computer.[203] It accounts better for the legitimate expectations of tort victims and the public. Any use of the computer will not result in a lower performance outcome. Computers do not need to be protected as 'special kinds of agents' (like children) for which a different standard of care applies.

Yet, in a second phase, technological developments allow computers to outperform humans in certain situations regularly. Then software agents should be required to exercise greater care than human actors, provided that they possess higher cognitive abilities due to their superior information processing capacity.[204] Here, the analogy to reasonable care of professionals is particularly useful. Due to their expertise, the law holds professionals to a different, regularly higher standard.[205] Consequently, computers must also be kept to their own professional standards once they exceed human abilities. This suggestion has been taken up by several authors[206] and is in line with the European Expert Group that suggests:

> The benchmark for assessing performance by autonomous technology in the context of vicarious liability is primarily the one accepted for human auxiliaries. However, once autonomous technology outperforms human auxiliaries, this will be determined by the performance of comparable available technology which the operator could be expected to use, taking into account the operator's duties of care.[207]

[201] Strangely enough, this aspect appears quite similarly in the discussion amongst those authors who favour product liability. The objective standard against which algorithmic behaviour should be measured determines the product's 'defect', Wagner, 'Digitale Techniken' 728; Borghetti, 'Liability for AI' 69 ff.

[202] See: Abott, 'Reasonable Computer' 26 f; Wagner, 'Digitale Techniken' 728.

[203] See: Abott, 'Reasonable Computer' 27.

[204] See: Wagner and Luyken, 'Robo Advice' 172.

[205] For German law, Dannemann and Schulze (eds), *German Civil Code*, § 276, para 9 (Schulze). In English common law, *Bolam v Friern Hospital* [1957] 1 WLR 582, 586, speaks of the 'standard of the ordinary skilled man exercising and professing to have that special skill'.

[206] KA Chagal-Feferkorn, 'How Can I Tell If My Algorithm Was Reasonable?', [2021] *Michigan Telecommunications and Technology Law Review* forthcoming, Part IV; Janal, 'Extra-Contractual Liability and Autonomous Systems' 192; Lemley and Casey, 'Remedies for Robots' 1383 f; Abott, 'Reasonable Computer' 41 ff; Chagal-Feferkorn, 'Reasonable Algorithm' 127, 142; G Wagner, 'Produkthaftung für autonome Systeme', (2017) 216 *Archiv für die civilistische Praxis* 707, 733 ff.

[207] European Expert Group, Report 2019, 46.

What criteria should one choose for the higher standards of a 'reasonable computer'? Probably the best criteria would be those which would push robots to improve, particularly on safety. Lemley and Casey suggest that robots are not good targets for rules based on moral blame or state of mind, but they are good at data. Accordingly, the authors consider a legal standard that bases liability on how safe the robot compares to others of its type – a sort of 'robotic reasonableness' test.[208] That would create a safe harbour for algorithms that are significantly safer than average. Alternatively, they suggest holding robots liable if they lag behind their peers or even shutting down the worst ten per cent of robots in a category every year. The 'reasonable algorithm' cannot be limited to the best functioning algorithm on the market; it always needs to be within the range of existing algorithms. Otherwise, the algorithm with the best performance will render all other algorithmic behaviour below standard. This creates and fixes a significant competitive advantage for the company that has placed the algorithm with a high standard on the market first, ultimately undermining competition.[209]

While an independent standard of care accommodates technological developments in which electronic agents may outperform humans, it will differentiate between algorithms and humans as to the standard against which they will be measured. Yet, the better algorithms become and the more tasks they can take over, such differentiation can again become problematic. From the users' perspective, a higher standard of care for algorithms could provide an incentive to go back by relying on humans for their actions, as this would leave them with a smaller risk of liability. The use of technology would be discouraged rather than encouraged. Therefore, some authors suggest that an autonomous standard for the 'reasonable algorithm' should even influence reasonable care standards for humans.[210] Hence, the more common it is to delegate specific tasks to electronic agents and rely on their capacities, the more humans acting in these areas of decision-making will need to be held to the same standard of care.

In line with the constant adaption of the standard of care to technological developments, the capacities of electronic agents will set the basis for a narrowly confined higher standard of care for comparable algorithms. Subsequently, this will gradually lead to new standards for particular decision-making contexts.

G. Who is Liable?

If vicarious liability in tort applies to algorithmic wrongful conduct, a final question remains: Who is the principal that is held liable? Our preceding discussion

[208] Lemley and Casey, 'Remedies for Robots' 1383 f.

[209] See: Wagner, 'Produkthaftung für autonome Systeme' 737; MA Geistfeld, 'A Roadmap for Autonomous Vehicles: State Tort Liability, Automobile Insurance, and Federal Safety Regulation', (2017) 105 *California Law Review* 1611, 1680.

[210] Abott, 'Reasonable Computer' 5 f; Tjong Tijn Lai, '(Semi)autonomous System' 72.

has summarised a wide-ranging debate in which authors consider liability for different actors involved, ie users, manufacturers, operators, programmers. Some argue for the user as principal, others for the operator or the manufacturer. In contrast, our proposal remains embedded within the rules on vicarious liability. As a consequence, we treat only the user as the principal. Ultimately, the user is putting the algorithm in operation. However, some authors see here a considerable weakness of vicarious liability, compared to product liability, making the producer responsible. They argue that the producer should be the target of liability in terms of policy since he is mainly in control of the digital risks.[211] The appropriate answer to the risks of algorithmic autonomy seems to be: Not the user but the producer should be exposed to digital liability. Moreover, the producer usually disposes of considerable financial resources and organisational capacities. He should organise insurance and bear insurance costs.

However, according to the principles of principal-agent relations, these are weak arguments. They do not take sufficient account of the different risks that vicarious liability and product liability are reacting to. Vicarious liability compensates for the division of labour between principal and agent, making the principal liable for delegation to the agent. In contrast, product liability compensates for risks on decentralised distribution markets that derive from production and product monitoring.[212] Concerning production risks, control of the electronic agent's behaviour is in the producer's hands; concerning the division of labour in principal-agent relations, control is in the user's hands.[213] It is the user who chooses the computer as an assistant for achieving his own ends. It is the user who has the information about the concrete circumstances of the use. It is the user who decides to put the computer in operation and choose the relevant context, thus exposing third parties to the considerable risks of digital autonomy. And it is the user who benefits from digital assistance. Although this decision in itself is not negligent behaviour, as we said above, these are sufficient reasons for qualifying the user as the responsible principal for the algorithmic agent. To put an algorithm into operation cannot be equalised with a breach of a duty of care; in contrast, liability is justified based on the tortious behaviour of a person who has been employed by the principal and who is under his control.[214] Therefore, vicarious liability law is correct in targeting only the user as the actual principal. Additional liability of the backend operator (through, for instance, providing software updates and backend support, as suggested by the Expert Group as

[211] See especially: Wagner, 'Digitale Techniken' 738.

[212] See: J Salminen, 'From Product Liability to Production Liability: Modelling a Response to the Liability Deficit of Global Value Chains on Historical Transformations of Production', (2019) 23 *Competition & Change* 420, 422 ff.

[213] This differential treatment of algorithmic risks in relation to production on the one side and use on the other is accentuated by Linardatos, *Aktanten* 199 ff.

[214] This clear distinction is emphasised by G Wagner, 'Grundstrukturen des Europäischen Deliktsrechts', in R Zimmermann (ed), *Grundstrukturen des Europäischen Deliktsrechts* (Baden-Baden, Nomos, 2003) 274.

an additional criterion for strict liability)[215] remains at odds with the principles of vicarious liability and the characteristics of digital assistance. Of course, this does not mean that programmers, producers and distributors are relieved from any liability. According to principles of tort law and product liability, they remain responsible for the production risks whenever they violated their own duties of care. But for the failures of an autonomous computer that has been assigned to fulfil individual tasks in concrete circumstances with a considerable amount of discretion, the user alone is subject to vicarious liability to the same degree as he would be assigning the task to a human assistant.

[215] European Expert Group, Report 2019, 39 ff.

4

Hybrids: Association Risk

In response to the autonomy risk, we have so far proposed to confer limited legal capacity to algorithms and treat them in law as autonomous decision-making actors. Based upon the socio-digital institution of digital assistance, the law treats them as contractual agents in principal-agent relations and as vicarious agents in contractual and tortious liability. These are still reasonably secure solutions for current law because contractual agency and vicarious liability serve as a well-developed body of rules. Moreover, such a solution does not require full legal personhood for machines. However, the solution risks giving in to the quasi-natural tendency in law to resort to individualist principles where they are not adequate anymore. There is indeed a tendency to ascribe individual action capacity for software agents in a variety of situations. And sometimes, this is stretched too far. In the words of an observer:

> The legal system is trying as much as possible to associate the actions of autonomous machines and their consequences to individuals or groups of human beings, and the doctrines used include individual liability for human individuals, products liability, agency, joint criminal enterprise, aiding and abetting, conspiracy, and command responsibility.[1]

However, such individualist concepts fail once one is forced to focus on the human-algorithm association itself as the unit of action. This occurs when the actions of humans and machines intertwine so closely that there is 'no linear connection between the emergent structures, cultures, or behaviour that comprise collectives and the complex interactions of the individuals from which they arise'.[2] Humans and algorithms seem to become a symbiotic entity – thus developing into something 'greater than just the sum of their parts'.[3]

Here, the socio-digital institution of digital assistance does not govern the interactions anymore. It is replaced by a different socio-digital institution – human-algorithm associations. Accordingly, contractual agency and vicarious liability are

[1] MA Chinen, 'The Co-Evolution of Autonomous Machines and Legal Responsibility', (2016) 20 *Vanderbilt Journal of Law & Technology* 338, 342, relying on insights of complexity theory.

[2] MA Chinen, *Law and Autonomous Machines* (Cheltenham, Elgar, 2019) 101; S Schuppli, 'Deadly Algorithms: Can Legal Codes Hold Software Accountable for Code That Kills?', (2014) 187 *Radical Philosophy* 2, 4 ff.

[3] J Turner, *Robot Rules: Regulating Artificial Intelligence* (London, Palgrave Macmillan, 2018) 167.

of no help because, in joint decision-making, the human's or the algorithm's individual contributions can no longer be identified. Human-machine interactions develop emergent collective properties when taking on a distinct cooperative, hybrid or organisational character. Will collective liability be appropriate here? In this chapter, we will indeed propose treating human-machine associations as quasi-organisational hybrids that, legally, are to be understood as composite networks with respective liability rules.

I. Socio-Digital Institution: Human-Machine Associations

A. Emergent Properties

On several occasions, dense human-machine interactions will turn into collectivities. 'Computational journalism' is a clear example of this; human actors and non-human actants are assembled in a newswork, and their workflows are iteratively re-engineered. In some constellations, the algorithms' and journalists' contributions to their common text intertwine so densely that it becomes virtually impossible to establish individual responsibility:[4]

> Algorithms are beginning to make headway in cognitive labor involving rule- and knowledge-based tasks, creating new possibilities to expand the scale and quality of investigation. Some of this technology … will be symbiotic with core human tasks and will, for instance, make finding entities and interpreting a web of relationships between banks, lawyers, shell companies, and certificate bearers easier. … The challenge is to figure out how to weave algorithms and automation with human capabilities. How should human and algorithm be blended together in order to expand the scale, scope and quality of journalistic news production?[5]

Other situations of dense human-algorithm interaction occur when algorithms are integrated into collective decision-making.[6] In corporate governance, algorithms have already been integrated into corporate boards.[7] There is an ongoing discussion of whether they can be serving as self-standing board members,[8] or as algorithmic

[4] See: N Diakopoulos, *Automating the News: How Algorithms are Rewriting the Media* (Cambridge/Mass., Harvard University Press, 2019) 13 ff, 204 ff. For a concrete case of liability in computational journalism, ch 6 IV.B.

[5] ibid, 15 f.

[6] See: H Shidaro and NA Christanikis, 'Locally Noisy Autonomous Agents Improve Global Human Coordination in Network Experiments', (2017) 545 *Nature* 370.

[7] For examples, see: GD Mosco, 'AI and the Board Within Italian Corporate Law: Preliminary Notes', (2020) 17 *European Company Law Journal* 87, 88 f.

[8] For a detailed analysis of robo-directors and the implications for corporate law, F Möslein, 'Robots in the Boardroom: Artificial Intelligence and Corporate Law', in W Barfield and U Pagallo (eds), *Research Handbook on the Law of Artificial Intelligence* (Cheltenham, Edward Elgar, 2017).

sub-organisations within a corporate group structure.[9] In these cases, algorithms do not simply assist in the decision-making process but become themselves decision-makers within a collective decision-making unit. This fundamentally alters the character of corporate decision-making. Finally, the classical case of a human-machine collective is the cyborg with both algorithmic and human contributions and a diminishing role of the human.[10] Sometimes machines dominate human decision-making, sometimes vice versa, sometimes there is a densely intertwined human-machine co-behaviour.[11]

The emergent properties of human-machine collectives appear in three constellations: First, a fusion of human and machine impulses results in joint actions, eg in cyborgs. Second, in institutionalised collective decision-making, algorithms become integrated as self-standing participants within an organisation, eg as board members in corporate governance. Third, human-machine interaction intensifies within a project so that human and algorithmic contributions become indistinguishable. Hybrid writing, composition and journalism are cases in point. One can also refer to newer legal advice or litigation services in which lawyers make use of machines that contribute to the file or translation services by which humans check machine-driven translations. Feedback loops in social media are another example when communications between bots and humans together cause a 'scandal' or 'shitstorm'. Combined algorithmic and human trading in financial markets or alteration of traffic patterns by both human-driven and driverless cars denote similar but more spontaneous phenomena.[12] An observer describes the emergent properties:

> Due to their technical/systemic foundation in system behaviour, successful interaction processes within hybrid actor constellations (eg depending on the frequency, the density, the duration and the quality of the use) can lead to non-predictable effects, which can be characterised as 'emergent'. … At the same time, they result from joint action within the hybrid action constellation.[13]

In these situations, human-computer interaction defies widespread ideas of algorithms acting in isolation because human operators do not understand the rationale of decision-making rules produced by algorithms.[14] The peculiar emergent effects exclude *a priori* the responsibility of the individual actors, humans or machines.

[9] J Armour and H Eidenmüller, 'Self-Driving Corporations?', (2019) 475/2020 *ECGI-Law Working Paper* 1, 26 f.

[10] See: P Haselager, 'Did I Do that? Brain-Computer Interfacing and the Sense of Agency', (2013) 23 *Minds & Machines* 405, 413 f.

[11] See: I Rahwan et al., 'Machine Behaviour', (2019) 568 *Nature* 477, 483.

[12] ibid.

[13] B Gransche et al., *Wandel von Autonomie und Kontrolle durch neue Mensch-Technik-Interaktionen: Grundsatzfragen autonomieorientierter Mensch-Technik-Verhältnisse* (Stuttgart, Fraunhofer, 2014) 62 (our translation). For a precise analysis of emergent properties in human-machine-relations, J Weyer and R Fink, 'Die Interaktion von Mensch und autonomer Technik in soziologischer Perspektive', (2011) 20 *TATuP – Journal for Technology Assessment in Theory and Practice* 39, 41ff.

[14] See: C Messner, 'Listening to Distant Voices', (2020) 33 *International Journal for the Semiotics of Law – Revue internationale de Sémiotique juridique* 1143. For a detailed account of how the introduction of

Moral philosophers discuss such emergent properties under the 'collective moral autonomy thesis': In some situations, a group is morally responsible for an outcome even though its individual members are not.[15] The group disposes – beyond the intentions and actions of the members – of its own intentions, acts voluntarily, and has knowledge of the possible results of its activities so that the group itself becomes morally responsible.[16] The human-machine interaction develops a phenomenal inner perspective. It acts with self-awareness in a 'living' process, creates its own hierarchy of preferences, social needs and political interests. None of this can be reduced to a singular actor.[17] Hanson, for example, applies the concept of 'extended agency' to the human-algorithm association, which explains causation and responsibility better than moral individualism does. Accordingly, moral responsibility 'lies with the extended agency as a whole and should not be limited to any part of it.' The result is a 'joint responsibility', where 'moral agency is distributed over both human and technological artefacts'.[18] Attribution theory arrives at similar conclusions using Dennett's concept of intentional stance to hybrids as 'a combination of human, electronic and organisational components'.[19]

B. Hybridity

These insights into emergent collective properties require taking seriously the ideas on collective responsibility for human-algorithm interaction. Two important theoretical strands are pertinent for a deeper understanding. Actor-Network-Theory describes the conditions under which dense human-machine interactions form hybrid associations. And systems theory elaborates on new forms of co-evolution between the societal and technological sphere.

Latour's Actor-Network Theory is relevant here again. In chapter two, we used his concept of 'actants' to personify free-standing algorithms and suggested vicarious liability of the operator. In the present context, Latour's concept of 'hybrids' becomes relevant.[20] Sometimes, the interaction of actants and humans turn into a

AI-based decision support systems in the clinic transform the modes of interaction between different agents, M Braun et al., 'Primer on an Ethics of AI-Based Decision Support Systems in the Clinic', (2020) 0 *Journal of medical ethics* 1.

[15] D Copp, 'The Collective Moral Autonomy Thesis', (2007) 38 *Journal of Social Philosophy* 369.

[16] See: P Pettit, 'Responsibility Incorporated', (2007) 117 *Ethics* 171; JA Corlett, 'Collective Moral Responsibility', (2002) 32 *Journal of Social Philosophy* 573, 575.

[17] See: Rahwan et al., 'Machine Behaviour' 482 f.

[18] FA Hanson, 'Beyond the Skin Bag: On the Moral Responsibility of Extended Agencies', (2009) 11 *Ethics and Information Technology* 91, 94 ff; on the appropriate distribution of responsibility between humans and machines in complex interactions, K Yeung, *Responsibility and AI: A Study of the Implications of Advanced Digital Technologies (Including AI Systems) for the Concept of Responsibility within a Human Rights Framework* Council of Europe study DGI(2019)05, 2019), 64 ff.

[19] G Sartor, 'Cognitive Automata and the Law: Electronic Contracting and the Intentionality of Software Agents', (2009) 17 *Artificial Intelligence and Law* 253, 264.

[20] B Latour, *Politics of Nature: How to Bring the Sciences into Democracy* (Cambridge/Mass., Harvard University Press, 2004) 70 ff.

'hybrid', as a collective actor. Latour liberates the concept of action from its intentionalist components and constructs a consequentialist concept of action which integrates operations of non-humans. Such action is distributed among many entities within one assemblage. For digital actants, the potential of forming associations is essential. There are many situations where action capacities are required on a higher level than algorithms dispose of. Regularly, this would leave actants in a position of paralysis, even if they have the capacity to choose among alternatives. Algorithms lack the communicative skills needed in a variety of contexts. Latour expresses this with a metaphor: 'Actants' need not only a language and a resistant body but also the capacity to form 'associations'. To give non-humans, nevertheless, the capacity for action in those circumstances, one needs to recognise the existence of hybrids, ie associations of human actors and non-human actants. In this situation, 'actants', become members in 'hybrids', ie in full-fledged associations. Now, as in any association, a pooling of resources takes place. The troubling recalcitrance of the actants is now pooled with the communicative skills of real people. 'The distributed intelligence of social systems compensates the psycho-systemic competence deficits of non-humans.'[21] Now, the combination of human and non-human communicative properties within hybrids allows the algorithms to participate fully in political negotiations, economic transactions and legal contracting.

Storms, Neyland and Möllers have explicitly used Actor-Network Theory for algorithmic hybrids, particularly Callon's concept of *agencement*. The hybrids' capacity to act is generated through the arrangement of heterogeneous elements in a network of socio-technical assemblages, where human and non-human actors intertwine.[22] Thus, in certain situations, the individualistic principal-agent relation between humans and algorithms is transformed into a hybrid collective actor in its own right. By the same token, organisational theory has provided insights into how the behaviour of algorithms is shaping and altering the behaviour of their users, planners, operators. Even the most passive digital environments, it is argued, shape social organisations and the participating individuals and lead to dense technological-organisational-human actor-networks.[23] All of this has consequences for making the hybrid as such responsible.[24]

[21] KF Lorentzen, 'Luhmann Goes Latour: Zur Soziologie hybrider Beziehungen', in W Rammert and I Schulz-Schaeffer (eds), *Können Maschinen handeln? Soziologische Beiträge zum Verhältnis von Mensch und Technik* (Frankfurt, Campus, 2002) 110. On the personification of hybrids, JC Gellers, *Rights for Robots: Artificial Intelligence, Animal and Environmental Law* (London, Routledge, 2021) 118 ff, 154 ff.

[22] E Storms, 'Exploring Actor-Network Theory in the Investigation of Algorithms', (2019) *Conference Paper, HCI workshop 'Standing on the Shoulders of Giants', May 4-9, 2019* 1; D Neyland and N Möllers, 'Algorithmic IF … THEN Rules and the Conditions and Consequences of Power', (2017) 20 *Information, Communication & Society* 45; see generally: M Callon, 'What Does It Mean to Say That Economics Is Performative?', in D Mackenzie et al. (eds), *Do Economists Make Markets? On Performativity in Economics* (Princeton, University Press, 2007).

[23] See: E Monteiro, 'Actor-Network Theory and Information Infrastructure', in CU Ciborra et al. (eds), *From Control to Drift: The Dynamics of Corporate Information Infrastructures* (Oxford, Oxford University Press, 2001); CU Ciborra and O Hanseth, 'From Tool to Gestell: Agendas for Managing the

Social systems theory provides additional insights.[25] Technological and social systems become a collective unit in its own right when autonomous actants connect to the social world via stable digitalised communication. Human-machine interaction then forms a space in which information signals from the technological world are understood and responded to in social communication, albeit in a reflexively integrated form in each of the systems involved.[26] In this space of digital communication, human-machine associations arise under certain conditions. Such associations integrate social communication, human consciousness, and technical information via dense structural coupling.

Similar concepts of collective responsibility appear in other disciplines, such as moral philosophy. Artificial intelligence systems, Heinrichs argues, 'will form mixed agents in close cooperation with their human users, systems whose actions are not easily ascribed to the human user or the AI's programming but rather emerge from their ongoing interaction'.[27] Similarly, in a discussion of digital ethics, Loh and Loh perceive human-algorithm cooperation as a hybrid system that will become itself responsible due to its common purpose.[28] And Neuhäuser advocates a collective moral responsibility of man-machine associations as 'responsibility networks'.[29]

C. The Organisational Analogy

In several aspects, human-machine hybrids are comparable to human associations and outright corporate actors. The humans and algorithms involved do not act on their own behalf but 'for' the hybrid as an emergent entity, as a genuine association. They act for the hybrid in the same way as managers in a company do not act

Information Infrastructure', (1998) 11 *Information Technology & People* 305, 316: 'they constitute the background condition for action, enforcing constraints, giving direction and meaning, and setting the range of opportunities for undertaking action. Infrastructure as a formative context can shape both the organisation of work and the set of social scripts which govern the invention of alternative forms of work, the future ways of problem-solving and conflict resolution, the revision of the existing institutional arrangements and the plans for their further transformation.'

[24] See especially: B Latour, 'On Technical Mediation', (1994) 3 *Common Knowledge* 29, 34.

[25] See extensively ch 2, I.C.

[26] A Nassehi, *Muster: Theorie der digitalen Gesellschaft* (Munich, C.H.Beck, 2019) 96 ff, 257, 262. *Cf* for a successful experiment relying on the value of 'cheap talk' as signals readable by both algorithms and humans in co-operation, JW Crandall et al., 'Cooperating With Machines', (2018) 9 *Nature Communications* Art 233, 1, 4 f.

[27] J-H Heinrichs, 'Artificial Intelligence in Extended Minds: Intrapersonal Diffusion of Responsibility and Legal Multiple Personality', in B Beck and M Kühler (eds), *Technology, Anthropology, and Dimensions of Responsibility* (Heidelberg/New York, Springer, 2020) 171.

[28] W Loh and J Loh, 'Autonomy and Responsibility in Hybrid Systems', in P Lin et al. (eds), *Robot Ethics 2.0: From Autonomous Cars to Artificial Intelligence* (Oxford, Oxford University Press, 2017).

[29] C Neuhäuser, 'Some Sceptical Remarks Regarding Robot Responsibility and a Way Forward', in C Misselhorn (ed), *Collective Agency and Cooperation in Natural and Artificial Systems* (Heidelberg, Springer, 2015) 143 f.

in their own name, but as 'agents' on behalf of their 'principal', ie for the company. And there are conflicts of interest between the members and the human-machine association, similar to the well-known agency problems faced by corporate actors, for which numerous legal norms have developed solutions. Analogous rules are needed for the conflicts in the human-algorithm associations. At first sight, this sounds counter-intuitive since algorithms are not supposed to have interests of their own. But when autonomous algorithms are capable of choosing different means under pre-programmed goals, this conflict potential is created.[30] And comparable institutional norms – eg duties and responsibilities of the managing director, the ultra-vires doctrine, the examination of representativeness in class action lawsuits – are needed to contain the agency problem.[31]

Viewing the hybrid as a self-standing actor opens a collectivist perspective that frees the law from the problematic individualist alternative of assigning the actions exclusively to the human or the algorithm.[32] In contrast to individual attribution, collective attribution is capable of doing justice to the emergent human-machine association in a twofold sense.[33] First, it accounts for the internal dynamics of the human-machine interactions, which, beyond the properties of several individual actors, is responsible for the particularities of their association. Second, it does justice to the new quality of external relations. Now, the human-algorithm association itself communicates with third parties. It is no longer either the human or the algorithm to whom external communication is attributed. In both respects, the risks of the inextricable interweaving of human and algorithmic actions can be better counteracted by identifying the human-algorithms association as a common point of attribution for actions, rights, and obligations. Moreover, under some circumstances, the human-algorithm association, as already mentioned, can be found to be responsible for an outcome even though its members are not.[34]

However, a nagging question remains. The move from actants to hybrids, is this not simply a return to ascribing agency to human actors? At first sight, yes, since it is often the humans within the hybrid who are acting more visibly. The more elaborate action capacities will often be identified in human actors in the hybrid. But this would neglect the critical difference between the actions of human

[30] Such conflicts of interests are discussed by GI Zekos, *Economics and Law of Artificial Intelligence: Finance, Economic Impacts, Risk Management and Governance* (Cham, Springer, 2021) 139 ff. See also: N Bostrom, *Superintelligence: Paths, Dangers, Strategies* (Oxford, Oxford University Press, 2017) 157 ff for a discussion on several methods of controlling the algorithm's capabilities.

[31] In ch 3, III.F and G, we discussed some of these problems which arise in the relation between digital agents and their human principals. See in general JL Daniel, 'Electronic Contracting under the 2003 Revisions to Article 2 of the Uniform Commercial Code: Clarification or Chaos?', (2004) 20 *Santa Clara Computer & High Technology Law Journal* 319, 344 ff.

[32] See: S Schuppli, 'Deadly Algorithms' 4 f.

[33] See: J Kersten, 'Menschen und Maschinen: Rechtliche Konturen instrumenteller, symbiotischer und autonomer Konstellationen', [2015] *Juristenzeitung* 1, 4 ff; A Ingold, 'Grundrechtsschutz sozialer Emergenz: Eine Neukonfiguration juristischer Personalität in Art. 19 Abs. 3 GG angesichts webbasierter Kollektivitätsformen', (2014) 53 *Der Staat* 193, 220 ff.

[34] So for human associations in general, Copp, 'The Collective Moral Autonomy Thesis'.

actors and hybrids. It is the strong influence that algorithms exert on humans within the association that makes the difference.[35] Frequently, due to its immense calculative capacities, the influence of the algorithm is even overwhelming. Both the massive permanent irritations that algorithms exert on humans and their substantial impact on the hybrid's decisions are so typical for the hybrid that they should not be ignored in ascribing responsibility. Otherwise, one would run again into the untenable fiction of identifying algorithmic calculations with actions of people, which we had critiqued harshly in our discussion of algorithmic contracts in chapter three.

II. The Association Risk

Thus, the difference between digital actants and hybrids is due to the varieties of socio-digital institutions in which they are embedded: principal-agent relation versus association. This has consequences for their different modes of personification, but also for the social risks that they pose. The autonomy risk differs from the association risk in relevant aspects. In hybrids, the Arrow theorem prescribes that collective decisions cannot be calculated as an aggregation of individual preferences.[36] The participation of algorithms intensifies this intransparency. Bostrom analyses this risk under the title 'collective intelligence' or even 'collective superintelligence'.[37] The human-machine interactions cannot be fully controlled, which leads to 'perverse instantiation': an algorithm efficiently satisfies the goal set by the human participant but chooses a means that violates the human's intentions.[38] And the subtle influence of algorithms on human behaviour is even riskier, as the invisibility of the calculating machines as an integral element of the decision-making may conceal where the actual decision has taken place.

When it comes to accountability, the association risk makes it difficult to determine the damage-causing event as well as individual responsibility. It may still be possible to identify the illegal action – errors in journalistic work as defamation, a corporate board decision as breach of fiduciary duties, social media interaction as collective defamation. But it is excluded to attribute responsibility to an individual contribution. Was it the human action or the algorithmic calculation that was at fault? The contrast to the autonomy risk we dealt with in chapter three is obvious. For autonomous agents' decisions, it remains possible to delineate individual action, violation of duty, damage, and causality between action and damage; here, the algorithm's decisional autonomy creates the liability gap. In digital hybrids, it

[35] R Werle, 'Technik als Akteurfiktion', in W Rammert and I Schulz-Schaeffer (eds), *Können Maschinen handeln? Soziologische Beiträge zum Verhältnis von Mensch und Technik* (Frankfurt, Campus, 2002) 126.

[36] K Arrow, 'A Difficulty in the Concept of Social Welfare', (1950) 58 *Journal of Political Economy* 328.

[37] Bostrom, *Superintelligence* 58 ff, 65 ff,155 ff.

[38] ibid 146 ff.

remains possible to identify damage and action, but the typical responsibility gap comes up here because it is impossible to identify the individual actor. The only way out is to consider the hybrid as a responsible collective actor.[39] And it is this collective decision-making of hybrids that the law needs to respond to.

III. Solution *de lege ferenda:* Hybrids as Legal Entities?

The crucial question is: Can liability law cope with a 'cyborg turn in law', ie 'a development where humans, non-humans, persons and things enmesh and combine to form an unprecedented legal mode of existence, one that runs perpendicular to the creeping hybridisation of humans and non-humans'?[40] A radical answer is: the law should attribute legal personality and impute responsibility to a human-machine association. Indeed, this would be a radical but still a serious option, even if it has not yet been tried out for algorithmic communication. Already today, several authors suggest granting legal capacity to hybrids. This would integrate human and non-human actors into one legal personality.[41] Just for clarification, legal personhood would, in this case, not be attributed to the algorithm, rather to the association between actants and humans.

In this vein, Taylor and De Leeuw propose

> to rethink personhood from a relational perspective – where we consider Robotic AI systems as a new form of experience, impacting our emotional, rational, and social relations with ourselves, machines and the world. This new form of algorithmic hybridisation of human and algorithmic sensing and 'acting' needs a novel legal account of attribution, action and accountability.[42]

One may refer to other human-non-human hybrids whose attribution of legal personhood is discussed today to support this argument. Personhood for animals, rivers, the natural environment are cases in point. According to Fischer-Lescano, close interactions between non-human and human actors form 'hybrid persons

[39] The difference between the types of responsibility gaps will become clearer when we later discuss (ch 5, II.) the interconnectivity risk. Human-machine associations can be understood as collective decision-making units where the risky action of a collective can be identified. The interconnectivity risk appears when it is not possible anymore to identify even the risky action at all. Interconnected machines exclude to identify any concrete collective decision as a damage-causing event.

[40] M Viljanen, 'A Cyborg Turn in Law?', (2017) 18 *German Law Journal* 1277, 1278.

[41] D Linardatos, *Autonome und vernetzte Aktanten im Zivilrecht: Grundlinien zivilrechtlicher Zurechnung und Strukturmerkmale einer elektronischen Person* (Tübingen, Mohr Siebeck, 2021) 100 f, 479 ff; J Kersten, 'Die Rechte der Natur und die Verfassungsfrage des Anthropozän', in J Soentgen et al. (eds), *Umwelt und Gesundheit* (Baden-Baden, Nomos, 2020) 113 f; MW Monterossi, 'Liability for the Fact of Autonomous Artificial Intelligence Agents. Things, Agencies and Legal Actors', (2020) 6 *Global Jurist* 1, 11; G Teubner, 'Rights of Non-Humans? Electronic Agents and Animals as New Actors in Politics and Law', (2006) 33 *Journal of Law and Society* 497.

[42] SM Taylor and M De Leeuw, 'Guidance Systems: From Autonomous Directives to Legal Sensor-Bilities', (2020) *AI & Society (Open Forum)* 1, 6.

(which) constitute legal persons sui generis'. In litigation, the non-human person, he submits, is complemented by a natural person (individual plaintiff) or juridical (collective plaintiff). Together, they form a juridical association and a new legal person.[43]

For our particular case of human-algorithm associations, Gruber defines the conditions under which hybrids should become legal persons:

> Once humans and information technology systems can count as connected parts of an expanded web of human-artificial legal subjects under conditions of increased unpredictability, we can consider the next step: provided that the artificial components reach a sufficient degree of independence and resistance to appear as 'intentional systems' and independently acting agents, they can also be reconstructed as independent legal subjects within the law.[44]

Allen and Widdison argue as well for the juridification of such a 'hybrid social person', consisting of a computer and natural person operating in tandem. This 'partnership could exhibit behaviour that is not entirely attributable to either constituent and yet is the product of their joint efforts'. It is easier to accept in law that a 'human-machine "partnership" has a will and a personality – compared to that of a machine alone – and yet distinct from that of the human alone'.[45] Dahiyat wants to strengthen sharing responsibility with intelligent computer systems, which will create a new type of 'hybrid' personality consisting of a human and software agent operating together.[46] Similarly, Asaro submits that the law needs theories of agency and responsibility that apply to complicated systems of humans and machines working together. Responsibility and agency should be shared so that large organisations of people and machines can produce desirable results and at the same time be held accountable and reformed when they fail to do so.[47] Perlingieri suggests that the operative reality necessitates treating hybrids as a juridical unit and imputing responsibility directly to this unit for the behaviour of the two inseparable actors.[48] Thus, individual acts of the humans and algorithms would transform into collective acts of the association and would create both binding legal ties and liability claims against the association.

In contract law, the human-machine association itself would become the actual party to the contract. This is in contrast to the law of agency, which clearly separates the individual actions of principals and agents and declares the principal to

[43] A Fischer-Lescano, 'Nature as a Legal Person: Proxy Constellations in Law', (2020) 32 *Law & Literature* 237, 246 f.

[44] M-C Gruber, 'Why Non-Human Rights?', (2020) 32 *Law & Literature* 263, 267.

[45] T Allen and R Widdison, 'Can Computers Make Contracts?', (1996) 9 *Harvard Journal of Law & Technology* 25, 40.

[46] E Dahiyat, 'Law and Software Agents: Are They "Agents" by the Way?', (2021) 29 *Artificial Intelligence and Law* 59, 78 ff.

[47] See: PM Asaro, 'Determinism, Machine Agency, and Responsibility', (2014) 2 *Politica Società* 265, 265.

[48] C Perlingieri, 'Responsabilità civile e robotica medica', (2020) 1 *Tecnologie e diritto* 161, 175 f.

be the contractual partner. Indeed, Linardatos develops plausible arguments to give hybrid associations full legal personality so that they can serve as attribution points for contracts; attribution to the multiplicity of actors involved can be avoided.[49] The human-machine association's legal personification would be desirable, and the emergent unit would serve as an endpoint of attribution. For liability in contract and tort, the precondition for making the hybrid liable would be their composite conduct, without needing to calculate their individual contributions apart, as it would be necessary in the case of vicarious liability for auxiliary persons.

However, constructing the hybrid itself as a legal entity implies that the law dramatically expands the traditional law of associations and creates an entirely new kind of corporate entity, the human-machine association.[50] This would indeed be a bold – if not daring – step, for which today's law of associations is hardly prepared. Algorithms as full members of a novel association? This would be a more radical move than granting software agents limited legal capacity as representatives of their human principal, as we proposed in chapter three. Although such a collectivist legal solution seems to be ultimately more appropriate to the reality of dense human-machine interaction, courts and legal doctrine are likely to prefer a solution that attributes behaviour to individuals rather than associations.[51] This is why our proposal for the legal treatment of hybrids develops two different perspectives: Legal personhood for hybrids, as presented in the preceding paragraphs, remains preferable since it captures the hybrids' collective action more accurately. The alternative of an individualist liability of actors in light of their collaborative enterprise, as will be developed in the coming sections, is probably less adequate. Yet, it respects existing constraints in the law.

IV. Our Solution *de lege lata*: Enterprise Liability for Human-Machine Networks

A. Human-Machine Interactions as Networks

The resistance in law to entirely re-imagine the law of associations suggests looking for alternatives with a firmer grounding in legal doctrine. What is needed is an individualist solution that, simultaneously, takes account of the quasi-collective properties of the human-algorithm association.

Legal network theories are of help. They make it possible to conceive hybrids as multiple bilateral relations between humans and algorithms but simultaneously

[49] Linardatos, *Aktanten* 177 ff.

[50] See: M-C Gruber, 'Zumutung und Zumutbarkeit von Verantwortung in Mensch-Maschine-Assoziationen', in J-P Günther and E Hilgendorf (eds), *Robotik und Gesetzgebung* (Baden-Baden, Nomos, 2013) 158. Courageous steps *de lege ferenda* in this direction, Linardatos, *Aktanten* 413 ff.

[51] See also: Chinen, *Law and Autonomous Machines* 141.

as overarching networks or quasi-associations. Thus, the unity of the hybrid would still become effective in law and open to limited legal personification: 'Networks produce hybrids, and here, non-humans attain aspects of personhood.'[52] An incipient network model is already offered by current contract law once the 'common purpose' is introduced as a legal concept, ie the shared purpose of the individual parties in the exchange relationship.[53] A common purpose will not transform the contractual relationship into a fully collective unit. Instead, the relation will continue to be a multilateral relationship between the contracting parties. The common purpose, oriented to a combination of exchange and cooperation, brings the overarching unity of the contractual relationship to bear but it remains different from full legal personhood. The common purpose creates legal consequences in many respects – for contract interpretation, for good faith and fiduciary duties, and for breach of contract.

Moreover, in relational contracts and contractual networks, eg in supplier and distribution networks, the common purpose is gaining more and more weight – now under the titles of 'association purpose', 'final nexus' or 'network purpose' – without having to be subsumed under the 'corporate purpose' or other corporate law constructs.[54] In a parallel fashion, the human-computer association would not need to have legal capacities itself. Instead, introducing 'common purpose' injects a dose of collectivity into a purely individualist relation, brings the unity of the human-machine association to bear in legal terms, and does justice to their hybrid character.[55]

'Common purpose' is the point where network theory starts to introduce a third attribution method, different from individual or collective attribution.[56] This theory conceives networks neither as markets nor as hierarchies but as social systems in their own right, which operate between multilateral contracts and fully-fledged associations. Such organisational contracts imply that network participants must adapt to a contradictory double orientation: following their own individual interests and realising the overarching network purpose in one and the same operation. While in corporate law, management functions are not

[52] G Sprenger, 'Production is Exchange: Gift Giving between Humans and Non-Humans', in L Prager et al. (eds), *Part and Wholes: Essays on Social Morphology, Cosmology, and Exchange* (Hamburg, Lit Verlag, 2018) 258.

[53] Chinen, 'Legal Responsibility' 369.

[54] On network purpose and its delineation from other types of common purpose in contract and association, G Teubner, *Networks as Connected Contracts* (Oxford, Hart, 2011) 184 ff; *cf* also R Brownsword, 'Contracts with Network Effects: Is the Time Now Right?', in S Grundmann and F Cafaggi (eds), *The Organizational Contract: From Exchange to Long-Term Network Cooperation in European Contract Law* (London, Routledge, 2013).

[55] For similar arguments on ethical responsibility, Loh and Loh, 'Autonomy and Responsibility in Hybrid Systems' 41 ff.

[56] *Locus classicus*, WW Powell, 'Neither Market nor Hierarchy: Network Forms of Organization', (1990) 12 *Research in Organizational Behavior* 295. For networks in law, F Cafaggi and P Iamiceli, 'Private Regulation and Industrial Organization: Contractual Governance and the Network Approach', in S Grundmann et al. (eds), *Contract Governance: Dimensions in Law and Interdisciplinary Research* (Oxford, Oxford University Press, 2015).

allowed to be oriented toward an individual interest but only toward the common purpose, in purely contractual relations, the exchange purpose invites the parties to follow their own personal interests. In contrast to both contract and corporate law, network law creates a never-ending oscillation between individual and collective orientation. Networks have an exchange contract character but still, react like formal organisations. They expect individual members to pursue their own individual goals but simultaneously to remain faithful to the contradicting demand for cooperation and the pursuit of the common purpose. This double orientation of network participants forces the law to recognise the coexistence of collective and individual goal setting in relation to the same sphere of action.

In a parallel fashion, the human-algorithm cooperation would be a network that imposes the individual and the collective orientation on its members simultaneously. Machines and humans each are treated as acting individually and according to their own logic, eg human action and algorithmic calculation, and these remain – at the very basic level – not compatible; yet, through co-production they accumulate to develop a common purpose that sets the collective human-machine action into being. Qualifying human-algorithm associations as networks will have repercussions, too, on responsibility. In this sense, Gunkel argues that networks include

> not only other human beings but institutions, organisations, and even technological components like the robots and algorithms that increasingly help organise and dispense with social activity. This combined approach, however, still requires that someone decide and answer for what aspects of responsibility belong to the machine and what should be retained for or attributed to the other elements in the network.[57]

Thus, the common purpose constitutes a network that comprises both algorithms and the human participants as a single group and renders them subject to new forms of joint liability – 'network liability'.[58]

B. Networks and Enterprise Liability

For such networks, the established doctrine of 'common enterprise liability' will be the appropriate legal base for liability rules in human-algorithm interaction.[59] Under common enterprise liability, when individual actors share a common

[57] DJ Gunkel, 'Mind the Gap: Responsible Robotics and the Problem of Responsibility', (2020) 22 *Ethics and Information Technology* 307, 318.

[58] For three aspects of a genuine network liability, see Teubner, *Networks as Connected Contracts* ch 4–6.

[59] See: Chinen, *Law and Autonomous Machines* 83; DC Vladeck, 'Machines without Principals: Liability Rules and Artificial Intelligence', (2014) 89 *Washington Law Review* 117, 129, fn 39; JS Allain, 'From Jeopardy! to Jaundice: The Medical Liability Implications of Dr. Watson and Other Artificial Intelligence Systems', (2013) 73 *Louisiana Law Review* 1049, 1073 ff; similarly for medical negligence, TR Mclean, 'Cybersurgery: An Argument for Enterprise Liability', (2002) 23 *Journal of Legal Medicine* 167, 181.

purpose and form a network, responsibility is imposed on the network itself, ie on the enterprise, rather than on the individuals. Enterprise liability oscillates between market-based and organisation-based concepts. Market share liability is a market-based enterprise liability holding all manufacturers in the industry liable for a tort when it is impossible to identify the actual harm-causing manufacturer.[60] It does not determine the extent of liability according to the substantial contribution to the damage. Instead, it refers to the share of a particular manufacturer in selling the product on the market. Economic benefit is the central aspect for determining the share. Organisation-based enterprise liability is on the other side of the spectrum. It is a kind of corporate group liability that treats the organisational parts of a common enterprise as one responsibility unit.[61] It then attributes responsibility to the dominating actor within the common enterprise.[62]

Control and economic benefit – these two criteria are thus commonly used for enterprise liability. While market competition results in pro-rata liability based on economic benefit, organisational cooperation results in the central hub's liability based on control capacities.

For the liability of human-algorithm hybrids, we depart from the alternative of either market-based or organisation-based liability and integrate both components in network liability. In contrast to competition-based enterprises, human-machine hybrids have a stronger cooperative character. And in contrast to tightly coupled corporate groups, hybrids have more loosely structured network relations. A controlling actor cannot be singled out. Therefore, a third type – network liability – is required: 'Network liability thus builds on enterprise liability to expand the concept to a broader group of actors connected through subtle modern modes of intermediation.'[63] Under such a theory, 'each entity within a set of interrelated companies may be held jointly and severally liable for the actions of other entities that are part of the group.'[64] The courts will be able to attribute collective responsibility to the team without disentangling the single but intertwined actions of algorithms or humans. Liability then will be distributed between the stakeholders. In contrast to organisation-based enterprise liability, not one controlling entity is singled out as the responsibility unit. And different from market-based enterprise liability, it is not the individual share within the enterprise that appears as the basis for liability on a pro-rata basis. Instead, the network itself is responsible.

[60] See generally: the famous DES lawsuits in which market share liability was introduced in the US, *Sindell v Abbott Labs.*, 607 P.2d 924, 928 (Cal. 1980).

[61] M Dearborn, 'Enterprise Liability: Reviewing and Revitalizing Liability for Corporate Groups', (2009) 97 *California Law Review* 195, 198 ff, 252 ff.

[62] The clearest move towards control-based enterprise liability has been made by the European Court of Justice for EU competition law, fundamentally C-97/08 P *Akzo Nobel and Others v Commission*, ECLI:EU:C:2009:536, para 58.

[63] RV Loo, 'The Revival of Respondeat Superior and Evolution of Gatekeeper Liability', (2020) 109 *Georgetown Law Journal* 141, 186, fn 314.

[64] *FTC v Tax Club Inc.*, F. Supp. 2d, 2014 WL 199514, 5 (S.D.N.Y. Jan. 17, 2014); see also *FTC v Network Servs. Depot, Inc.*, 617 F.3d 1127, 1142–43 (9th Cir. 2010); *SEC v R.G. Reynolds Enters., Inc.*, 952 F.2d 1125, 1130 (9th Cir. 1991).

However, externally, it is the participating individual units that appear as attribution points for liability. This doctrine of joint and several liability potentially applies to human-machine associations. Vladeck argues:

> A common enterprise theory permits the law to impose joint liability without having to lay bare and grapple with the details of assigning every aspect of wrongdoing to one party or another; it is enough that in pursuit of a common aim, the parties engaged in wrongdoing. That principle could be engrafted onto a new, strict liability regime to address the harms that may be visited on humans by intelligent autonomous machines when it is impossible or impracticable to assign fault to a specific person.[65]

This liability regime for human-algorithm associations would distinguish between the hybrid as the centre of the network and the bilateral contracts as its periphery. Such asymmetric networks, consisting of a central hub organisation and a multitude of connected contracts around the hub, have been frequently analysed in network studies.[66]

C. Action Attribution and Liability Attribution in Hybrids

At this point, we need to introduce the distinction between action attribution and liability attribution, a distinction that is indicative of enterprise liability.[67] Typically, in networks, financial resources and control capacities are distributed among the nodes, while action capacities are bundled in collective network actions. Consequently, attribution of action is collectivised, while the attribution of liability for these actions is re-individualised. Action attribution targets the hybrid as such, but this does not mean that the hybrid as the acting unit becomes financially liable. Instead, the action attribution to the hybrid serves as channelling the liability to a series of actors.

Distinguishing action and liability attribution allows the victim to direct compensation claims to the individual participants of the network, but – and this is the trick – simultaneously releasing the victim from the burden of proving individual fault. It is sufficient to prove that the defendant is a member of the actor-network and that a breach of a duty of care took place that is attributable to an action of the network.

D. Liable Actors

This inevitably leads to the question of who of the network participants will be liable for unlawful computer decisions. Who is to be sued? The answer is – as

[65] Vladeck, 'Machines without Principals' 149.

[66] For the combination of network and hierarchy see, eg: T Thomadsen, *Hierarchical Network Design* (Kongens Lyngby, Technical University of Denmark, 2005).

[67] See: Allain, 'From Jeopardy! to Jaundice' 1074.

the leading figure in information philosophy Floridi points out: Distributed responsibility! He argues:

> The effects of decisions or actions based on AI are often the result of countless interactions among many actors, including designers, developers, users, software, and hardware. … With distributed agency comes distributed responsibility.[68]

In human-machine hybrids, the association is surrounded by a satellite network of independent actors, ie users, operators, dealers, manufacturers, programmers. If these actors were forming a formal organisation, collective liability would apply since it is the organisational duty of management to coordinate intersections of various actions. In contrast, if these actors were interacting in pure market-based relationships, the liability risk would shift to the client, who becomes responsible for coordinating partial performances.[69] However, problems do arise in our case of a hybrid with a surrounding actor-network where neither attribution of causal responsibility to the manufacturer nor the network centre nor the human actor nor the algorithmic network nodes is convincing. Individual apportionment of responsibility is equally arbitrary, especially where it ignores the structural diffusion of responsibilities within cooperative networking or even seeks to reverse it.

The alternative is a collective attribution of responsibility to the network or the narrower cooperative relationship between those network participants within which incriminating operations arise. This is precisely parallel to imposing collective liability upon various actors, should causal attribution to individual actors be no longer possible.[70] Liability should then extend to the concrete 'responsibility focus' of the network. This will result in the joint and several liability of (concretely involved) network members without getting bogged down in the impossible task of a legal reconstruction of individual causal relationships. This procedure is an expression of 'double attribution' within external network liability.[71] Separate apportionment of responsibility to members of the network or to the network centre is no longer appropriate. Given the division of labour within networked operations, apportionment of causal responsibility to individual actors is empirically defeated. This suggests apportioning responsibility for the wrongful actions first to the network as a whole or the concrete project within the network,

[68] M Taddeo and L Floridi, 'How AI can be a Force for Good: An Ethical Framework Will Help to Harness the Potential of AI while Keeping Humans in Control', (2018) 361 *Science* 751, 751. For transforming this ethical responsibility into legal liability of many actors involved, I Martone, 'Algoritmi e diritto: appunti in tema di responsabilità civile', (2020) 1 *Teconologie e diritto* 128, 151.

[69] See: G Wagner, 'Robot, Inc.: Personhood for Autonomous Systems?', (2019) 88 *Fordham Law Review* 591, 607.

[70] On undermining traditional causal attribution of liability to collective actors under conditions of intense interdependency, G Teubner, 'The Invisible Cupola: From Causal to Collective Attribution in Ecological Liability', in G Teubner et al. (eds), *Environmental Law and Ecological Responsibility: The Concept and Practice of Ecological Self-Organization* (Chichester, Wiley, 1993).

[71] See generally: PM Baquero, *Networks of Collaborative Contracts for Innovation* (Oxford, Hart, 2020) 41; M Amstutz, 'The Constitution of Contractual Networks', in M Amstutz and G Teubner (eds), *Contractual Networks: Legal Issues of Multilateral Cooperation* 2009) 340.

then making it possible to extend liability to those individual actors who have actually participated.[72] The initial apportionment of action to the network takes on the role of channelling responsibility and attributing the wrongful action to the human-machine hybrid. Subsequently, liability for this action is transferred to the network's members and apportioned amongst them. In contrast to collective liability of formal organisations, this liability re-individualises collective network liability and attributes it amongst the individual units.

As a consequence, after the attribution of action to the hybrid, the attribution of liability would be distributed among the members of the surrounding contractual network who are benefitting from the hybrid's activities, ie operators, owners, manufacturers, and deliverers of the electronic technology. This solution finds some support in the literature. Chinen, for example, attributes the liability for the hybrid's damaging actions to a group of human operators behind the hybrid itself. When software developers, manufacturers, and engineers share the common purpose of producing an autonomous machine, he submits, they can be liable for harms caused by that machine.[73] Allain convincingly argues that future legislation should create a new digital liability regime. Restitution will be equally shared among actors to spread the risk of loss better and reduce the economic disincentives.[74] Navas proposes that a conception of (market) share liability could be suitable in case of liability for AI.[75] And Vladeck is correct in suggesting that such a common enterprise liability would be a form of court-compelled insurance.[76] Similarly, the European Expert Group discusses joint liability of all actors connected to a 'commercial and technological unit'.[77] Operators, manufacturers, dealers and programmers of the software agent are bundled in such a liability network. Network theory will be of help, identifying the boundaries of the liability unit as well as their relative involvement in the damage dynamics.[78] The boundaries will be defined by the purposive interwovenness of contracts around the production of the algorithmic machine. The network of contracts related to the activities of the hybrids establishes the group of liable actors.

[72] See generally: Teubner, *Networks as Connected Contracts* 258 ff.

[73] Chinen, *Law and Autonomous Machines* 83; similarly for medical negligence, Mclean, 'Cybersurgery: An Argument for Enterprise Liability' 181.

[74] See: Allain, 'From Jeopardy! to Jaundice' 1074.

[75] S Navas, 'Robot Machines and Civil Liability', in M Ebers and S Navas (eds), *Algorithms and Law* (Cambridge, Cambridge University Press, 2020) 169 f and the related blog entry 'Robotics and Civil Liability', Robotics & AI Law Society, 12 December 2019, https://ai-laws.org/2019/12/robotics-and-civil-liability-in-the-eu/; also discussed by G Spindler, 'User Liability and Strict Liability in the Internet of Things and for Robots', in R Schulze et al. (eds), *Liability for Robotics and in the Internet of Things* (Baden-Baden/Oxford, Nomos/Hart, 2019) 139.

[76] Vladeck, 'Machines without Principals' 129, fn 39.

[77] European Expert Group on Liability and New Technologies – New Technologies Formation, Report 'Liability for Artificial Intelligence and Other Emerging Technologies', 2019, 55f.

[78] For more details, A Lior, 'The AI Accident Network: Artificial Intelligence Liability Meets Network Theory', (2021) 95 *Tulane Law Review* forthcoming, sections C.3. and C.5.b.

E. Pro-Rata Network Share Liability

Up to now, we have suggested first attributing the wrongful action collectively to the network and subsequently distributing financial liability individually among its members. But how can one calculate the concrete share, the basis for any liability claim? What factors does one need to consider here?

Drawing an analogy to the well-known market share liability, we suggest 'network share liability'.[79] The network itself has no collective pool of resources that could be made liable. However, as we said above, the network serves as an initial attractor for the attribution of action (because the individual contributions of humans and algorithms cannot be disentangled). Then follows a re-individualisation of liability among the network nodes. Re-individualisation is suitable in cases like ours, where the imposition of joint liability would be an exaggerated solution. Individual nodes should be made liable on a pro-rata basis according to their substantial involvement. It mirrors networking structures that demand simultaneously individual and collective orientation but which do not pool resources. As a result, responsibility is re-individualised in line with the 'network share' of various actors, rather than by analysing their 'causal contributions', which may even be wholly impossible to effect.

Thus, responsibility for digital failure falls on the network participants. The criteria according to which the liability share is calculated should, we suggest, be their network share. Network share is specified by two aspects: network benefit and network control. Both aspects are essential for forming and sustaining a network. Normatively, they are an appropriate basis for attributing liability. The focus on benefit may weigh in the advantages that a party gains from the network structure. In particular, economic advantages come from integrating a component, software, or service into an overall network compared to their isolated selling on the market. Not all parties are assigned the same benefit, but a participant's higher network gain will result in a higher share.[80] Control serves as a balancing factor to ensure that the act of putting and keeping an algorithm in operation is co-determining liability. On the one side, the justification is the actor's proximity to the perceived wrongful act given the importance of controlling actions for the network. On the other side, responsibility is assigned to the party with the most robust problem-solving capacity in prevention and restitution. As a result, all those actors will be liable that are involved in putting the algorithm in operation and maintaining its function. As the European Expert Group argues convincingly, there are often central backend providers who continuously define the features of the technology and provide backend support services. The backend operator has a high degree of control over the operational risk. Moreover, the *ratio legis* of liability is to link

[79] Network share liability as a special form of collective liability has been proposed in general by Teubner, *Networks as Connected Contracts* 266 ff, 268.

[80] See: Chinen, 'Legal Responsibility' 86.

financial responsibility not only to effective risk control but equally to the financial benefits resulting from the agent's operations.[81]

The issue then is how to attribute liability when several participants control the hybrid's actions and benefit from them. This is a problem well-known in labour and tort law. To be sure, this is not to be confused with multi-causation when the proportion of different causal contributions to damage are unclear. Instead, the issue is the proportion of control exerted by various participants and their benefits. According to the labour and tort law principles, control and benefit are the relevant criteria. And the backside of control is the risk that people accept in the absence of effective control. Therefore, the amount of risk that different actors have taken is another good indicator of the proportion of liability they have to bear.[82] Here, we can take inspiration from the 'Robotic Liability Matrix', which distributes responsibility between the producer and the user.[83] Regularly, in the hybrid's actions, several actors are involved, and the control of the algorithm's actions is distributed between them. They include the programmer who writes the general instructions, the producer responsible for the whole production process and the user who puts the autonomous agent in operation. In addition, the central backend operators also benefit from the algorithm's operations.

As a result, it is not only the user who should pay the damage, but all the participants who are involved in control and benefit that should be liable, ideally, on a pro-rata basis. In case of doubt, the shares should be equally divided between them. Regularly, the producer will make contractual arrangements between the persons controlling the algorithms and, if the risk is considerable, will take out insurance. A related proposal has already been suggested for the specific case of car accidents. Concerning liability for hazardous vehicles, the courts have summarised drivers, owners and insurance companies.[84] Hanisch's proposal of a tiered liability between the operator and the manufacturer, according to which the operator is primarily liable and the manufacturer secondarily so, is also worth considering in this context.[85] A compulsory insurance policy for digital risks that affects manufacturers would cushion the burden of hardship for the operators, especially if they are not acting commercially.[86] The introduction of maximum sums would correspond to the insurance logic.

[81] See: European Expert Group, Report 2019, 41 f.

[82] See: M Bashayreh et al., 'Artificial Intelligence and Legal Liability: Towards an International Approach of Proportional Liability Based on Risk Sharing', (2021) 30 *Information & Communications Technology Law* 169.

[83] JA Pepito et al., 'Artificial Intelligence and Autonomous Machines: Influences, Consequences, and Dilemmas in Human Care', (2019) 11 *Health* 932, 940f.

[84] H Zech, 'Zivilrechtliche Haftung für den Einsatz von Robotern: Zuweisung von Automatisierungs- und Autonomierisiken', in S Gless and K Seelmann (eds), *Intelligente Agenten und das Recht* (Baden-Baden, Nomos, 2016) 204.

[85] J Hanisch, 'Zivilrechtliche Haftungskonzepte für Robotik', in E Hilgendorf (ed), *Robotik im Kontext von Recht und Moral* (Baden-Baden, Nomos, 2014) 55 ff.

[86] See: European Parliament, Resolution of 16 February 2017 with Recommendations to the Commission on Civil Law Rules on Robotics, 2015/2103(INL), para 29; S Horner and M Kaulartz,

F. External Liability Concentration: 'One-Stop-Shop' Approach

However, there is a weak point in this network liability – high transaction costs for the victim when trying to recuperate the damage. Although such proportional liability leads to an overall fairer outcome, the victim remains in a difficult position. He must collect compensation from each potential injurer and bear the risk of each injurer's insolvency.[87] In addition, the victim would be overburdened with providing evidence for each network node's share. The victim would remain in a very undesirable situation with all the uncertainties in identifying the actors involved and calculating their network share.

We suggest external liability concentration as a way out. According to a 'one-stop-shop approach', one needs to identify ex-ante a single, unmistakable and unquestionable entry point for all litigation. Ideally, the entry point would be the party who is in the best position to: (1) identify the risk; (2) control and minimise its decisions; and (3) manage it. Managing the risk means pooling and distributing it among the other parties, eventually through insurance and/or no-fault compensation funds.[88] Indeed, this suggestion resonates with the principles of enterprise liability. Once the enterprise's responsibility is established, a single actor, generally the head of the enterprise, must make financial restitution.[89] Here,

> the core doctrinal and policy question is what firm sits at the nexus of power such that it could cost-effectively monitor and punish wrongdoing in its web of business associations. This emerging worldview amounts to network keeper liability, in which actors are responsible in proportion to their influence over a sphere of activities.[90]

Network theory can be of considerable assistance to determine the most influential node in the network. Network theorists have designed a method that ranks the nodes to identify influential nodes. The proposed measure strikes a balance between the degree and strength of every node in a weighted network. Probability assignments represent the influences of both the degree and the strength of each node. The combination of these assignments determines the proposed result of centrality. In this vein, Condon recently suggests a liability regime for network gatekeepers that perform public and steering functions in a network.[91] Given governing and participating nodes in networks, liability would centre on the

'Haftung 4.0: Rechtliche Herausforderungen im Kontext der Industrie 4.0', [2016] *InTeR Zeitschrift zum Innovations- und Technikrecht* 22, 26.

[87] This problem is also recognised by the European Expert Group, Report 2019, 58.

[88] See: A Bertolini, *Artificial Intelligence and Civil Liability* (Brussels, European Parliament, Study Commissioned by the Juri Committee on Legal Affairs, 2020) 97 ff, 101 f.

[89] See: Vladeck, 'Machines without Principals' 129.

[90] Loo, 'Respondeat Superior' 189.

[91] R Condon, *Network Responsibility: European Tort Law and the Society of Networks* (Cambridge, Cambridge University Press 2021 forthcoming) ch 4, 4.

governing nodes. In an algorithmic responsibility network, the manufacturer network will usually exert gatekeeping. In a similar vein, Wagner provides a robust economic case for manufacturers as the governing network nodes:

> Manufacturers of robots and IoT devices will be able to exercise much more control over the performance and behaviour of their creatures than manufacturers of mechanical products. To the extent that manufacturers do or can exercise control, liability must follow. This is particularly obvious in the case of a closed software system that prevents third parties, including the user, from tampering with the algorithm that runs the device. Here, it is only the manufacturer who is in a position to determine and improve the safety features of the device; nobody else can. Phrased in economic terms, the manufacturer is clearly the cheapest cost avoider.[92]

Consequently, the victim would target the most influential node in the network, ie the manufacturer. For the victim, this would release the burden significantly. Essentially, the victim would only need to prove the damage and action attributable to the network.

G. Internal Liability Distribution: Pro Rata Network Share

Notwithstanding this external liability channelling, the internal principles of network share should remain intact. This means that our proposed external liability channelling needs to be complemented with internal liability distribution in the form of a redress action. The manufacturer who paid damages to the victim needs to be able to file redress action against the other participants. Authors who have suggested collective liability, particularly the Expert Group, come up with the same solution. Arguing for an external joint and several liability of actors connected to a technical and commercial unit, they propose introducing redress action that considers pro-rata liability according to individual share.[93]

Such redress action can take two forms: Usually, the participants will have made contractual arrangements to distribute risks. This implies redress action based on contractual clauses. According to the principles of judicial review of standard contracts, the courts will scrutinise the arrangements to ensure that the agreements do not unduly overburden one of the contracting parties. The network share, related to economic benefit and control, again plays a role in this context. The courts will consider it as an unfair arrangement if the party benefitting most from the network contractually arranges an exclusion or strong limitation of liability.

In the absence of contractual arrangements, courts will have to identify each participant's 'network share'. The participants will make financial restitution on a

[92] G Wagner, 'Robot Liability', in R Schulze et al. (eds), *Liability for Robotics and in the Internet of Things* (Baden-Baden/Oxford, Nomos/Hart, 2019) 40 f.

[93] European Expert Group, Report 2019, 57f.

pro-rata basis according to their share. According to the criteria of control and benefit, the share will be determined with the weight between the two depending on the network structure. In hierarchical networks, control will be the determining factor, whereas, in heterarchical networks, economic benefit will be more important. Courts will have to develop case law to specify these criteria continuously.

V. Conclusion

Altogether, enterprise liability of human-algorithm hybrids has a somewhat complex structure. It proceeds in three steps:

First step – Action attribution: Without needing to disentangle the intertwined actions of algorithms and humans and analyse each individual violation of duties or causal contribution to the damage, the damaging action will be collectively attributed to the human-algorithm hybrid. Since the hybrid does not dispose of financial resources, the action attribution only channels the liability transferring it to the other enterprise members.

Second step – Liability attribution: Once the wrongful action is attributed to the hybrid, liability for this action will be attributed to the actor who has the highest amount of economic benefit and operative control over the network. This is usually the manufacturer, as the head of the enterprise, but depending on the particular network in question, it could also be other actors. Thus, the victim can recuperate the damage from one single actor. As a basis for the claim, the victim only needs to prove the damage and the wrongful action of the hybrid.

Third step – Liability regress: The manufacturer will be in a position to charge reimbursement from the other members of the enterprise on a pro-rata basis according to their share of responsibility. In this process, responsibility follows both economic benefit and technical control.

5

Multi-Agent Crowds: Interconnectivity Risk

I. Socio-Digital Institution: Exposure to Interconnectivity

For autonomous electronic agents, we have shown that several legal scholars seem to ignore their specific risks when they argue that the existing rules on contract formation and liability can simply be applied to the new situation. For hybrid human-algorithm associations, we have shown that legal doctrine is not yet prepared to accept them as new collective actors. For the interconnectivity between multiple autonomous electronic agents, the situation seems to be even worse. Most scholars do not touch upon the problem at all or limit themselves to problematising the autonomous decision-making processes of machines. Others clearly identify the risks of interconnectivity but do not seem to offer a clear-cut solution.[1] So far, the only area where interconnectivity is discussed extensively is by experts on security law and critical (public) infrastructures.[2] There are very few voices that acknowledge the difficulty of capturing system interconnectivity in legal categories openly.[3]

In this chapter, we will argue that exposure to algorithmic interconnectivity is a self-standing socio-digital institution. It can neither be reduced to individual decision-making in digital assistance nor to collective decisions by human-machine associations.[4] Interconnectivity is a configuration in its own right, and its relation to society results in a specific socio-digital institution. Moreover, the idea of personification needs to be abandoned: In contrast to AI agents and

[1] eg: G Wagner, 'Verantwortlichkeit im Zeichen digitaler Techniken', [2020] *Versicherungsrecht* 717, 725, 739 f.

[2] H Zech, 'Liability for AI: Public Policy Considerations', [2021] *ERA Forum* 147, 148f.

[3] On the difficulties of understanding interconnectivity legally, M-C Gruber, 'Zumutung und Zumutbarkeit von Verantwortung in Mensch-Maschine-Assoziationen', in J-P Günther and E Hilgendorf (eds), *Robotik und Gesetzgebung* (Baden-Baden, Nomos, 2013) 126, 144 f.

[4] In this regard, our solution differs from M-C Gruber, 'On Flash Boys and Their Flashbacks: The Attribution of Legal Responsibility in Algorithmic Trading', in M Jankowska et al. (eds), *AI: Law, Philosophy & Geoinformatics* (Warsaw, Prawa Gospodarczego, 2015) (interconnectivity as extended hybrids) and those authors who seek to extend the liability rules for individual machine behaviour, such as vicarious or product liability, to interconnectivity (see below n 42 ff).

human-machine hybrids, interconnectivity cannot be personified. It represents a systemic 'un-person' without communicative capacities in the strict sense. Nevertheless, such machine interconnectivity influences society substantially but is different from communicative contacts. From the perspective of society, this interconnectivity risk is linked to the unpredictability, incomprehensibility, and invisibility of interconnected operations. In this regard, the interconnectivity risk differs from the autonomy risk of independent decision-making and from the association risk of collectivisation. Interconnectivity risks do not stem from the appearance of new actors in social communication that can cause damage. Instead, we encounter a latent technical configuration lying 'underneath' society that is inherently prone to failure. To sketch in advance our result: To the specific interconnectivity risk, we argue, liability law needs to respond by decreeing risk pools, which, through a fund solution, compensate damages and cover the costs of undoing consequences.

A. Non-Communicative Contacts

Early on, with the advent of the computer, the social sciences have begun to discuss the interconnectivity of machines. They became aware that the human-machine encounter takes place in two distinct spaces. Within a relatively limited area, communication between humans and computers is indeed possible. Earlier, we have shown that this communicative space is populated by algorithmic actants and by human-machine hybrids. Via narrow interfaces, humans and algorithms gain the capacity to communicate with each other. However, for the sizeable remaining space of internal algorithmic operations, their dynamics are not accessible, neither for social communication nor for human consciousness. Here we are no longer dealing with human-machine interactions but with non-communicative human-machine relations.[5] Characteristically, interconnected machines exert a highly indirect but enormous influence on society, which is difficult to grasp with the instruments of the social sciences:

> There are already computers in use whose operations are accessible to neither consciousness nor communication, neither simultaneously nor reconstructively. Although they are manufactured and programmed machines, such computers function non-transparently for consciousness and communication; their operations nevertheless affect consciousness and communication through structural couplings. Strictly speaking, they are invisible machines.[6]

[5] See: B Gransche et al., *Wandel von Autonomie und Kontrolle durch neue Mensch-Technik-Interaktionen: Grundsatzfragen autonomieorientierter Mensch-Technik-Verhältnisse* (Stuttgart, Fraunhofer, 2014) 51 ff.

[6] N Luhmann, *Theory of Society 1/2* (Stanford, Stanford University Press, 2012/2013) 66.

'Structural coupling with invisible machines' is a somewhat enigmatic concept for the non-communicative relation of society with the internal operations of interconnected algorithms. Technological systems do not operate in the medium of meaning but through electronic operations and their interconnections.[7] These formalised binary processes are not accessible via communication. Nonetheless, a substantial impact on communicative events, social structures, and their media is exercised through surface interfaces. Coming from a different theory tradition, Hildebrandt uses the metaphor of the 'digital unconscious' to describe this mysterious interrelation. She explains how society is exposed to algorithmic interconnectivity, without being able to communicate with it, neither to control it nor to make single algorithms responsible for failures:

> Big Data Space extends our minds with a digital unconscious that is largely beyond the reach of our conscious mind. This digital unconscious is not owned by any one person and cannot be controlled by any one organisation. It has been created by individuals, enterprises, governments and machines, and is rapidly becoming the backbone of our education, scientific research, economic ecosystem, government administration and our critical infrastructures. It enables data-driven agency in software, embedded systems and robotics, and will increasingly turn human agency itself into a new hybrid that is partly data-driven. The onlife world that we now inhabit is data-driven and feeds on a distributed, heterogeneous, digital unconscious.[8]

Other authors describe the same situation as 'structural shifts' in society caused by interconnected algorithms. They might unintentionally – and, at times 'invisibly' – shift actors' incentives in hazardous ways, for various reasons, and at both the global and local levels. Such sociotechnical change would be all the harder to anticipate and mitigate, because it might not be intended by any one actor.[9]

Thus, the personification of algorithms is limited to the comparably small number of contacts via the monitor's surface when the machine can re-organise itself in response to human use, and the user knows how to respond to the machine's messages. As described in chapter two, to a limited degree, communication of digital systems with humans is done via readable displays, while the deeper invisible structure remains a 'black box'. In a different constellation, as described in chapter four, the ongoing communication between computers and humans can be so dense so that they form together a new hybrid social system; this hybrid has the potential to be personified in diverse social practices. But apart from these two constellations, the algorithmic processes in their interconnectivity remain opaque. Their personification remains problematic. This core of the system is invisible, incomprehensible, and unpredictable for social interaction. In such a situation, human users 'see themselves as variables of the system who can influence

[7] See: A Nassehi, *Muster: Theorie der digitalen Gesellschaft* (Munich, C.H.Beck, 2019) 154 f.
[8] M Hildebrandt, *Smart Technologies and the End(s) of Law* (Cheltenham, Edward Elgar, 2015) 40.
[9] MM Maas, *Artificial Intelligence Governance under Change: Foundations, Facets, Frameworks* (Copenhagen, Dissertation University of Copenhagen, 2021),179 (describing several examples).

the processes only insofar, as they optimally subsume themselves under the requirements of the system in order to receive its gratifications'.[10]

Organisation theory describes such complex interconnected digital infrastructures as autonomous. Together with the human operators, they form actor-networks within a formal organisation.[11] In a first approximation, such infrastructures appear as organisational tools that should help the organisation to operate efficiently. Yet, in contrast to what corporate managers regularly suggest, they do not work as willing tools in the organisation's hands; instead, they are regularly 'out of control'.[12] Accordingly, as early organisational theorists suggest, successful strategies to govern even the most passive, only response-oriented interconnected technological infrastructures are never about straightforward control of technology-as-a-tool. Instead, surface improvisation, patching or hacking takes place until the technology is functioning satisfactorily without anyone having necessarily understood why the system was not working in the first place.[13] Hence, technological infrastructures are not understandable, and humans cannot control them; yet the dependency of social organisations on their functioning reveals how such technological systems resonate with society.

B. Distributed Cognitive Processes

The novelty with interconnected autonomous systems is the dramatic increase in unpredictability of processes and outcomes and the complex architecture of the underlying digital structure. Interconnectivity includes heterarchical machine-machine relations as well as hierarchical machine-machine meta-processes, which seek to control autonomous AI agents. Identifiable humans behind complex systems are replaced by controlling software that in itself acts autonomously. Such hierarchical forms of interconnectivity between autonomous systems do not lead to Bostrom's superintelligence.[14] Instead, we encounter a phenomenon that is neither purely hierarchical in the machine-machine interaction nor purely heterarchical as an aggregate of individual AI actants' decisions.[15] Network theory is of

[10] Gransche et al., *Mensch-Technik-Interaktionen* 53.

[11] See: E Monteiro, 'Actor-Network Theory and Information Infrastructure', in CU Ciborra et al. (eds), *From Control to Drift: The Dynamics of Corporate Information Infrastructures* (Oxford, Oxford University Press, 2001).

[12] See: CU Ciborra et al., *From Control to Drift: The Dynamics of Corporate Information Infrastructures* (Oxford, Oxford University Press, 2001); CU Ciborra and O Hanseth, 'From Tool to Gestell: Agendas for Managing the Information Infrastructure', (1998) 11 *Information Technology & People* 305.

[13] See: CU Ciborra, *The Labyrinths of Information: Challenging the Wisdom of Systems* (Oxford, Oxford University Press, 2004) 29 ff.

[14] N Bostrom, *Superintelligence: Paths, Dangers, Strategies* (Oxford, Oxford University Press, 2017).

[15] See: J Chen and P Burgess, 'The Boundaries of Legal Personhood: How Spontaneous Intelligence Can Problematize Differences Between Humans, Artificial Intelligence, Companies and Animals', (2019) 27 *Artificial Intelligence and Law* 73; Nassehi, *Muster* 236 ff.

no help either, as interconnectivity cannot be delineated as a relational network of identifiable actors and does not follow any delineated common purpose.

Such interconnected processes exhibit what cognitive sociologists describe as 'distributed cognition', ie cognitive processes without an identifiable subject distributed across a social group structure.[16] Distributed cognition means processes by which collective action occurs heterarchically and even without direct interaction between the group members but nonetheless produces a collective action due to mutual responsiveness.[17] This resembles what sociologists call a 'collectivity without collective', commonly associated with swarms or crowds. Crowds are uncoordinated collectives that appear as acting together without engaging in coordinated collective action. In contrast to genuine collectives with group identity, crowd behaviour is connectivity of individual actions, which is enabled through a (physical or technological) infrastructure. In contrast to networks, crowds develop neither a 'common purpose' nor an elaborate organisational structure. Also, they are much more dynamic than the network's image suggests, with its nodes connected by relatively stable relations.[18] The early sociological analysis by Blumer describes crowds as a form of 'circular reaction', defined as 'interstimulation wherein the response of one individual reproduces the stimulation that has come from another individual and in being reflected back to this individual reinforces the stimulation'.[19] This is 'restless collectivity'.[20] Sociologists argue that the concept of crowds can explain interconnected individual behaviour acting on social infrastructures, such as trading on financial markets.[21] Consequently, crowds are a collective phenomenon of interconnected and mutually responsive individual actions enabled by a social and material infrastructure that produces collective results spontaneously.

We submit that interconnected digital systems precisely exhibit this form of 'restless collectivity'. Now, autonomous electronic agents rather than humans responsively interact on digital infrastructures. In interconnected AI systems,

[16] See generally: G Salomon, 'No Distribution Without Individuals' Cognition: A Dynamic Interactional View', in G Salomon (eds), *Distributed Cognitions: Psychological and Educational Considerations* (Cambridge, Cambridge University Press, 1993) 111ff, 128ff; extending that conception M Viljanen, 'A Cyborg Turn in Law?', (2017) 18 *German Law Journal* 1277, 1286.

[17] See for digital relations: V Rauer, 'Distribuierte Handlungsträgerschaft. Verantwortungsdiffusion als Problem der Digitalisierung sozialen Handelns', in C Daase et al. (eds), *Politik und Verantwortung: Analysen zum Wandel politischer Entscheidungs- und Rechtfertigungspraktiken* (Baden-Baden, Nomos, 2017) 440 ff, relying predominantly on the work of E Hutchins, *Cognition in the Wild* (Boston, MIT Press, 1995).

[18] See generally: E Thacker, 'Networks, Swarms, Multitudes', (2004) *CTheory – Journal of Theory, Technology, and Culture* https://journals.uvic.ca/index.php/ctheory/article/view/14542.

[19] See generally: H Blumer, 'Collective Behaviour', in A Mcclung Lee (ed), *New Outline of the Principles of Sociology* (New York, Barnes & Noble, 1946) 170f.

[20] See generally: C Wiedemann, 'Between Swarm, Network, and Multitude: Anonymous and the Infrastructures of the Common', (2014) 15 *Distinktion: Scandinavian Journal of Social Theory* 309, 313.

[21] See generally: C Borch, 'Crowds and Economic Life: Bringing an old figure back in', (2007) 36 *Economy and Society* 549; U Stäheli, 'Market Crowds', in J Schnapp and M Tiews (eds), *Crowds* (Stanford, Stanford University Press, 2006).

the relations between autonomous decisions do not follow a coherent collective purpose. Rather, it is a spontaneously produced reciprocity between algorithms that, in its indirect but strong influence on society, leads to new types of sense-making. The single algorithms may work autonomously, but their operations develop into routines within the broader network context.[22] Accordingly, Chen and Burgess have argued convincingly that a difference exists between what is commonly defined and personified as 'artificial' intelligence and a strange type of 'social' intelligence that is enabled by a passive human-created infrastructure but operates in an uncoordinated fashion that is 'not owned or controlled by anything'.[23]

Such distributed action creates a massive problem for personification, for social actorship and legal subjectivity. While isolated decision-making agents can possess action capacity and human-machine hybrids can be personified as collective actors, interconnectivity lacks the qualities of collective decision-making units. The same is true for the relation of structural coupling of human communication and algorithmic interconnectivity. Thus, the techniques of personifying actants or hybrids reach their absolute limits in situations when a multi-agent system connects several autonomous algorithms.[24] Personification needs a determinable socio-technical substrate, which is not present in computer interconnections. The best approximation to this phenomenon is the notion of the 'unperson', someone or something located outside communication and inaccessible to personification. Unperson refers to humans (or technological processes for our purpose) that are as such not included in social communication.[25]

II. The Interconnectivity Risk

The specific social risk caused by interconnectivity lies in the inaccessibility of the interconnected calculations and the impossibility of predicting and explaining the results. The authors of the interdisciplinary study on machine behaviour summarise these unexpected properties under the term 'collective machine behaviour':

> In contrast to the study of the behaviour of individual machines, the study of collective machine behaviour focuses on the interactive and systemwide behaviours of collections

[22] See: C Messner, 'Listening to Distant Voices', (2020) 33 *International Journal for the Semiotics of Law – Revue internationale de Sémiotique juridique* 1143.

[23] Chen and Burgess, 'Legal Personhood' 78.

[24] See: Messner, 'Distant Voices'; W Rammert, 'Distributed Agency and Advanced Technology: Or: How to Analyze Constellations of Collective Inter-agency', in J-H Passoth et al. (eds), *Agency Without Actors: New Approaches to Collective Action* (London, Routledge, 2012) 101, 103; Wagner, 'Digitale Techniken' 725; I Spiecker, 'Zur Zukunft systemischer Digitalisierung: Erste Gedanken zur Haftungs- und Verantwortungszuschreibung bei informationstechnischen Systemen – Warum für die systemische Haftung ein neues Modell erforderlich ist', [2016] *Computer und Recht* 698, 701.

[25] See: AC Braun, *Latours Existenzweisen und Luhmanns Funktionssysteme: Ein soziologischer Theorienvergleich* (Heidelberg, Springer, 2017) 102 f.

> of machine agents. In some cases, the implications of individual machine behaviour may make little sense until the collective level is considered. … Collective assemblages of machines provide new capabilities, such as instant global communication, that can lead to entirely new collective behavioural patterns. Studies in collective machine behaviour examine the properties of assemblages of machines as well as the unexpected properties that can emerge from these complex systems of interactions.[26]

The study group refers to studies on microrobotic swarms found in systems of biological agents, on the collective behaviour of algorithms in the laboratory and in the wild, on the emergence of novel algorithmic languages between intelligent machines, and on dynamic properties of fully autonomous transportation systems. In particular, they discuss huge damages in algorithmic trading in financial markets. The infamous flash crashes are probably due not to the behaviour of one single algorithm but to the collective behaviour of machine trading as a whole, which turned out to be totally different from that of human traders resulting in the probability of a larger market crisis.[27]

The interconnectivity risk destroys fundamental assumptions constitutive for action and liability attribution. Interconnectivity rules out the identification of actors as liable subjects.[28] And it does neither allow for foreseeability of the damage nor causation between action and damage.[29] Dafoe speaks of 'structural dynamics', in which

> it is hard to fault any one individual or group for negligence or malign intent. It is harder to see a single agent whose behaviour we could change to avert the harm, or a causally proximate opportunity to intervene. Rather, we see that technology can produce social harms, or fail to have its benefits realised, because of a host of structural dynamics. The impacts from technology may be diffuse, uncertain, delayed, and hard to contract over.[30]

Accordingly, legal scholars refer to complexity theory and philosophers of the tragic when attempting to understand interconnectivity and its potential damages.[31] According to complexity theory, linearity of action and causation

[26] I Rahwan et al., 'Machine Behaviour', (2019) 568 *Nature* 477, 482.

[27] ibid.

[28] See: Zech, 'Liability for AI' 148 f; Spiecker, 'Digitalisierung' 701 ff; T Schulz, *Verantwortlichkeit bei autonom agierenden Systemen: Fortentwicklung des Rechts und Gestaltung der Technik* (Baden-Baden, Nomos, 2015) 76 f; S Beck, 'Dealing with the Diffusion of Legal Responsibility: The Case of Robotics', in F Battaglia et al. (eds), *Rethinking Responsibility in Science and Technology* (Pisa, Pisa University Press, 2014); L Floridi and JW Sanders, 'On the Morality of Artificial Agents', in M Anderson and SL Anderson (eds), *Machine Ethics* (Cambridge, Cambridge University Press, 2011) 205 ff.

[29] See: CEA Karnow, 'The Application of Traditional Tort Theory to Embodied Machine Intelligence', in R Calo et al. (eds), *Robot Law* (Cheltenham, Edward Elgar, 2016) 73: 'With autonomous robots that are complex machines, ever more complex as they interact seamless, porously, with the larger environment, linear causation gives way to complex, nonlinear interactions.'

[30] A Dafoe, 'AI Governance: A Research Agenda', (2018) *Centre for the Governance of AI Future of Humanity Institute University of Oxford* 1, 7.

[31] C Wendehorst, 'Strict Liability for AI and other Emerging Technologies', (2020) 11 *Journal of European Tort Law* 150, 152 f; MA Chinen, *Law and Autonomous Machines* (Cheltenham, Elgar, 2019) 94 ff; Karnow, 'Traditional Tort Theory' 74.

cannot be assumed, and surprises are to be expected. Unpredictability and uncontrollability result neither from insufficient information nor from a poorly designed system, for which someone can be made responsible; they are inherent in the nature of complex systems. Latent failures characterise complex systems that are always run as 'broken systems'.[32] Coeckelbergh compares the catastrophes resulting from interconnectivity to experiences of the tragic. Conventional understandings of blame, responsibility and even causation fall short.[33] Any retrospective identification of a disaster's cause cannot be but 'fundamentally wrong', and responsibility attributions are 'predicated on naïve notions of system performance'.[34]

Many scholars agree that for interconnectivity, neither ex-ante nor ex-post analyses can identify the actors as attribution endpoints and their causal contribution to the damage.[35] And European legislative initiatives are well aware of the difficulties for liability law:

> AI applications are often integrated in complex IoT environments where many different connected devices and services interact. Combining different digital components in a complex ecosystem and the plurality of actors involved can make it difficult to assess where a potential damage originates and which person is liable for it. Due to the complexity of these technologies, it can be very difficult for victims to identify the liable person and prove all necessary conditions for a successful claim, as required under national law. The costs for this expertise may be economically prohibitive and discourage victims from claiming compensation.[36]

Yet, why, if attribution of action, causation and responsibility is impossible, should the law respond to the risks of interconnectivity at all? Once we accept that interconnectivity is inevitably prone to failure, then we might just conclude that nothing needs to be 'fixed' by law. Interconnectivity risks may just be a price to pay for the use of technology. However, there is a plausible counterargument. Despite being invisible, unpredictable in their operations and incomprehensible in their underlying structure, interconnected systems do produce results that may represent a productive surplus of meaning.[37] They generally result in intended results.

[32] See generally: RI Cook, 'How Complex Systems Fail', (2002) *Unpublished Research Paper* www.researchgate.net/publication/228797158_How_complex_systems_fail, point 4 ff.

[33] M Coeckelbergh, 'Moral Responsibility, Technology, and Experiences of the Tragic: From Kierkgeaard to Offshore Engineering', (2012) 18 *Science and Engineering Ethics* 35, 37. For an application in relation to interconnected autonomous machines, Chinen, *Law and Autonomous Machines* 98f.

[34] Cook, 'How Complex Systems Fail', points 5 and 7.

[35] K Yeung, *Responsibility and AI: A Study of the Implications of Advanced Digital Technologies (Including AI Systems) for the Concept of Responsibility within a Human Rights Framework* Council of Europe study DGI(2019)05, 2019) 62 ff; K Heine and S Li, 'What Shall we Do with the Drunken Sailor? Product Safety in the Aftermath of 3D Printing', (2019) 10 *European Journal of Risk Regulation* 23, 26 ff; H Zech, 'Zivilrechtliche Haftung für den Einsatz von Robotern: Zuweisung von Automatisierungs- und Autonomierisiken', in S Gless and K Seelmann (eds), *Intelligente Agenten und das Recht* (Baden-Baden, Nomos, 2016) 170.

[36] European Commission, 'Report on the Safety and Liability Implications of Artificial Intelligence', The Internet of Things and Robotics, COM(2020) 64 final, 14.

[37] See: Nassehi, *Muster* 197 ff.

Automatic and even more so autonomous infrastructure may be regularly out of control but still fulfils a distinct purpose, which allows for automation of processes, alignment of procedures and reasonable calculations. This has two consequences: First, digital technology does not require consensual practices of actual people; acceptance originates in its problem-solving capacity. Second, human actors tend to be paralysed when the risks materialise, when complex technological systems do not function, when they go astray and cause damage. This means, once society has accepted complex technological systems, it cannot tolerate their malfunctions. Technological risks must be mitigated, and their damages compensated, even if no culprit can be identified. Therefore, de-personalised compensatory rules need to counteract the risks of new evolving technologies.

In addition, relying on liability law to cope with the risks of uncoordinated complex processes is not entirely new for the law. To mention just two examples: Nuclear plants as promising sources of energy production had been accompanied by international negotiations on a liability system. This ended up in international agreements that specify direct and strict liability for power plants' operators.[38] Another example is the immense risks associated with complex commodity production chains. In particular, the tragedy of Rana Plaza in 2013, where a building collapsed in Bangladesh, has revealed the immense dangers that commodity production chains may cause. And recent litigation revealed the apparent difficulties of fault-based liability for global 'distributed irresponsibility'.[39] Despite many attempts to bring action against 'lead firms', the result for affected parties seems nothing more than the insight that the aggregated decisions of buying companies, suppliers, auditors, and government inspectors have caused the disaster. Still, none of the participants involved has made a clear and identifiable decision that could lead to a clear and delineated liability.[40] As a response, one may increasingly see suggestions on new liability models that accommodate shared contributions and irresponsibility.[41] The failure of addressing interconnected networks through individual responsibility and related liability regimes underlines the necessity for a change in the system of liability. Digital interconnectivity requires a similarly drastic change.

[38] Arts II and IV of the Convention on Civil Liability for Nuclear Damage, (Vienna, 21 May 1963); Art 3 of the Convention on Third Party Liability in the Field of Nuclear Energy (Paris 29, July 1960) as amended by the Additional Protocols (Paris, 28 January 1964 and Paris, 12 February 2004).

[39] For a similar argument KH Eller, 'Das Recht der Verantwortungsgesellschaft: Verantwortungskonzeptionen zwischen Recht, Moral- und Gesellschaftstheorie', (2019) 10 *Rechtswissenschaft* 13, 36 ff.

[40] eg: *Rahaman v JC Penny Corp., The Children's Place* und *Wal-Mart Stores*, Superior Court of Delaware, C.A. No. N15C-07-174 MMJ; *Arati Rani Das v Weston Ltd., Loblaws Comp.*, 2017 ONSC 4129; *ECCHR et al v TÜV Rheinland* AG, OECD Specific Instance Procedure, concluded 2 May 2016.

[41] J Salminen, 'Contract-Boundary-Spanning Governance Mechanisms: Conceptualizing Fragmented and Globalized Production as Collectively Governed Entities', (2016) 23 *Indiana Journal of Global Legal Studies* 709; M Anner et al., 'Towards Joint Liability in Global Supply-Chains: Addressing the Root Causes of Labor Violations in International Subcontracting Networks', (2013) 35 *Comparative Labor Law and Policy Journal* 1.

III. Mismatch of New Risks and Existing Solutions

But what does the existing law and the reform debate have to offer? Confronted with the difficulties in attributing action, responsibility and causation, the current legal debate remains rather silent. And the few solutions that are on offer seem to shy away from grasping the problem in its entirety. Instead, they recur to familiar legal categories that may be comparably easy to integrate into the existing legal structure but do not solve the problem. In the following, we explain why all current ideas, namely applying existing legal rules, vicarious liability or collective liability, inevitably fail. A new legal category is required.

A. Applying Existing Categories

Very few voices suggest that the existing liability rules are adequate for the interconnectivity risk. It is a well-known strategy in legal doctrine to argue that existing liability rules are well-equipped to deal with the dangers of new technologies. The classic example is self-driving cars, for which the current liability regimes for ordinary vehicles still apply. The result would be a co-existence of different types of liability, product liability for the hardware and software manufacturer, strict liability for the operator, and fault-based liability of the actor causing the damage.[42] But the counterarguments are overwhelming. First, simply applying existing rules without causing a liability gap is only possible in very few sectors where strict liability rules exist. This works for self-driving cars since strict liability combined with compulsory insurance is well established. Yet, it does not exist in numerous other sectors where interconnected systems are used, such as financial trading, industrial robotics and algorithmic search engines. Relying on strict liability for self-driving cars has the potential of concealing the problem. Second, even where strict liability rules exist, liability gaps do emerge. An identifiable operator is needed who can be held strictly liable. This may be possible for ordinary cars in which the owner of the vehicle is simultaneously the operator. Yet, individualising the responsible system component becomes immensely difficult when overlapping decisions of autonomous components operated by different actors cause the damage. Even for self-driving cars that heterarchically interact with the sensor-based environment, it is unclear how to identify the owner who could be strictly liable. Breaking down the various components is often impossible when several components contribute to causing the damage. Third, simply applying and combining existing strict and fault-based liability to interconnected systems effectively creates an

[42] See: B Koch, 'Product Liability 2.0 – Mere Update or New Version?', in S Lohsse et al. (eds), *Liability for Robotics and in the Internet of Things* (Baden-Baden/Oxford, Nomos/Hart, 2019) 116.

intransparent liability system. No justification can be given why some contributions should be subject to strict liability and others not. If a consistent liability system is developed for interconnectivity, it cannot simply rely on the existing fragmented conceptions.

B. Vicarious or Product Liability of the Whole Interconnected AI-System?

A serious alternative is to concentrate liability on the whole system – vicarious or product liability.[43] Such suggestions are similar to the liability for autonomous actants as we have suggested in chapter three. Here it re-appears as liability for interconnected AI systems as a whole. Vicarious liability would apply to all distributed decisions in the network, not only to an isolated electronic agent. In addition, liability would need to be linked to the operators behind the network as the principals. Or one principal is singled out as having to bear the entire liability risk.[44]

However, this suggestion would create difficulty for singling out the overarching system operator as principal that can be held strictly liable. As Wagner puts it: 'The system operator of a complex interconnected system as equivalent to the product manufacturer [in product liability rules] still needs to be identified.'[45] The criteria that we have been developing for networks in the previous chapter, ie control and economic benefit of actors in the system, are of no help here. Given the interwoven decision-making processes in complex systems where the interaction of several systems causes damage, any identification of one responsible actor seems nothing but arbitrary. No doubt, concentrating liability risks on one actor, such as the immediate operator, cannot be justified based on the individual responsibility for the damage. There are simply too many agents in their interconnected decision-making and too many principals for justifying a coherent form of vicarious or product liability. Complex interconnected systems disrupt the concept of individual responsibility.[46]

Are there persuasive policy considerations assigning the interconnectivity risk to a particular actor? Such justifications would need other criteria than responsibility for fault, causation of damage, or the potential of control. They could be either economic considerations, such as an actor's financial capacity, the rule of the cheapest cost avoider, or the risk-affinity of certain activities.[47]

[43] See: G Wagner, 'Digitale Techniken' 739 f ('Produkt-Gefährdungshaftung'). See also: Zech, 'Liability for AI' 154.

[44] For the argument that liability should fall on the party who puts the final product onto the market, eg: Koch, 'Product Liability 2.0' 106, 111.

[45] See: Wagner, 'Digitale Techniken' 725 (our translation).

[46] See: Chinen, *Law and Autonomous Machines* 96.

[47] For these ideas, Wendehorst, 'Strict Liability for AI' 172 ff; J Hanisch, 'Zivilrechtliche Haftungskonzepte für Robotik', in E Hilgendorf (ed), *Robotik im Kontext von Recht und Moral* 2014) 55 ff.

Platform liability seems to be a case in point. For damages caused by interconnected agents, the platform would be responsible for the system. This would be justified by their surveillance power, their capacity to operate as a central actor and the economic benefits they generate. Yet, interwoven complex systems have such a multitude of operators so that it is nothing but arbitrary to single out one operator.[48] Moreover, given the severe damage that interconnected systems can cause, it seems unlikely that a single system operator will be able to secure against the risk through insurance.

C. Collective Liability of Actors Connected to the 'Technical Unit'?

As a way out, some scholars suggest collective liability for all the parties who operate the system. If not one principal can be identified for the system, then, so the reasoning goes, all actors involved are responsible. Technically, different solutions are currently proposed. The preferred solution in the literature would be joint and several liability,[49] while some others suggest pro rata liability.[50] It would cover all actors involved in the operations.[51] The victim would be able to sue one of the operators for the entire damage, irrespective of whose system component caused the damage. The party being sued would then need to take redress with the other involved parties. Such a solution resembles the category of network liability as we have proposed for closing the liability gap for hybrids.[52] Essentially, it suggests viewing interconnected algorithmic operations as a system for which a joint responsibility of the involved actors within the actor-network be established, possibly combined with policy considerations on how liability is to be channelled and distributed.

[48] See: Spiecker, 'Digitalisierung' 702.

[49] In German law, the main rule discussed is § 830(1) 2 BGB; in the common law, the doctrine of joint and several liability.

[50] M Bashayreh et al., 'Artificial Intelligence and Legal Liability: Towards an International Approach of Proportional Liability Based on Risk Sharing', (2021) 30 *Information & Communications Technology Law* 169, 180 ff; H Zech, 'Künstliche Intelligenz und Haftungsfragen', [2019] *Zeitschrift für die gesamte Privatrechtswissenschaft* 198, 208 f; Spiecker, 'Digitalisierung' 703 f. See also: C Cauffman, 'Robo-Liability: The European Union in Search of the Best Way to Deal with Liability for Damage Caused by Artificial Intelligence', (2018) 25 *Maastricht Journal of European and Comparative Law* 527, 531.

[51] See: G Spindler, 'User Liability and Strict Liability in the Internet of Things and for Robots', in R Schulze et al. (eds), *Liability for Robotics and in the Internet of Things* (Baden-Baden/Oxford, Nomos/Hart, 2019) 139; Spiecker, 'Digitalisierung' 703; DC Vladeck, 'Machines without Principals: Liability Rules and Artificial Intelligence', (2014) 89 *Washington Law Review* 117, 148 ff; in a similar direction A Lior, 'AI Entities as AI Agents: Artificial Intelligence Liability and the AI Respondeat Superior Analogy', (2020) 46 *Mitchell Hamline Law Review* 1043, 1094; European Expert Group on Liability and New Technologies – New Technologies Formation, Report 'Liability for Artificial Intelligence and Other Emerging Technologies', 2019, 55 ff.

[52] ch 4, IV.E and G.

Yet, the interconnectivity risk is different from the association risk of hybrids. The literature concentrates on the difficulty of proof: For the victim, it is impossible to prove the chain of causation, to identify what digital action has caused the damage, and to disentangle the contributions.[53] Therefore, so the argument goes, the solution is to be found in shifting the burden of proof.[54] However, the proposed solution of reversing the burden of proof so far extends only to the problem of causality between the action and the damage leaving the victim still in the position of having to substantiate that an action potentially having caused the damage occurred.[55] To recall, for hybrids, the situation was somewhat similar in the sense that not an individual action but only a collective action was identifiable. Our way out was to distinguish between action and liability attribution. This relaxes the burden of proof for the victim. He needs to prove only the hybrid's collective action as a precondition for the liability of one of the members.[56] Yet, this solution does not hold for interconnectivity given that there is regularly a problem identifying the responsibility action.[57] Here, the difference between hybrids and interconnectivity comes in. Hybrids allow for action attribution to a networked collective. In contrast, in interconnected systems, neither individual nor collective action can be identified.

Hence, the reversal of the burden of proof would need to reach further. Essentially, it would require the victim only to prove the damage.[58] The result is a prima facie assumption for a damaging action, which qualifies as a breach of the duty of care. But this would create excessive disadvantages for the operators. How can operators or manufacturers rebut such prima facie assumption? They would need to provide evidence that no action responsible for the damage has occurred in the whole interconnected system. This is impossible!

A seemingly elegant way out is the requirement for operators to 'open the black box' and reveal all types of actions that have happened. Or, more broadly, in order to be able to prove 'what happened', exclusively 'explainable' and 'traceable AI' could be placed on the market.[59] Still, this gives a false sense of security. The interconnectivity risk is due to emerging properties of interacting algorithmic decisions which are inaccessible to society.[60] They are still not visible when the black box of one of its components is opened. Opening the black box may perhaps provide transparency on the underlying data and programs but does not

[53] Zech, 'Liability for AI' 149; Wagner, 'Digitale Techniken' 739: 'Vernetzung als Beweisproblem'; J Oster, 'Haftung für Persönlichkeitsverletzungen durch Künstliche Intelligenz', [2018] *UFITA – Archiv für Medienrecht und Medienwissenschaft* 14, 50.

[54] Oster, 'Persönlichkeitsverletzungen' 50 f; Spindler, 'User Liability' 139.

[55] See: European Expert Group, Report 2019, 56.

[56] ch 4, IV.C and F.

[57] See: Bashayreh et al., 'Artificial Intelligence and Legal Liability' 173, 176; Zech, 'Künstliche Intelligenz' 208, 218.

[58] For such a suggestion, Wendehorst, 'Strict Liability for AI' 178.

[59] Oster, 'Persönlichkeitsverletzungen' 50.

[60] See: Rahwan et al., 'Machine Behaviour' 482.

give access to the black box's actual actions. Data as such are meaningless; only their interrelation with society creates meaning. This problem relates to the more profound logic of emergent properties of interconnected systems. They operate outside society and process programs and raw data in the form of information. But for action attribution, reconstruction in social communication is required. And for liability attribution, a normative assessment needs to come in. Opening the black box will neither reveal who was the actor nor who should be responsible. It will provide mere information that requires additional reconstruction through interpretative practices.[61] In law, a normative decision is needed that re-frames codes and operations in terms of liability. For interconnected algorithmic systems, the difficulty is immense: From the perspective of society, interconnectivity is only understandable at either the surface of an interface or at the most basic level of the binary code structure. The operations in-between are, to recall, unpredictable and unforeseeable. Any 'reading' of the binary operations through an opening of the black box is thus already a normative decision in the law regarding who is acting on behalf of an unpredictable system.

But the impossibility of proof in interconnected systems is not the only problematic aspect. Joint and several liability has an inherent tendency to shift the risk unduly to only one of the parties involved. If the victim can successfully sue one of them, it is pivotal that this party can take recourse with the other parties. After all, this is the idea behind collective responsibility. Yet, this merely transforms the problem of identifying individual decisions rather than solving it. The party who had to pay the damage would need to engage in the impossible endeavour to prove how the damage was caused and define the own share against all other parties involved. Thus, the full risk eventually falls upon the party that the victim has chosen. This is likely either the most financially viable party or the party that is most easy to 'access'. For hybrids, this consequence is acceptable due to the small number of participants. Yet, it seems considerably more difficult in interconnected systems without clearly defined boundaries. Pro-rata liability is of no help since it faces a similar problem: How to delineate the share of responsibility of different actors in the system?

Is it promising to impose joint and several liability on those participants that are contractually linked to a 'commercial or technical unit'?[62] No, in the case of interconnectivity, neither an individual contribution nor a collective 'unit' can be identified. Perhaps one could develop a variation of a network share liability that does not use the technical unit as a reference point but the interconnected system. Such a 'system share liability' might indeed lead to better risk distribution since

[61] Explicitly, M Ananny and K Crawford, 'Seeing without Knowing: Limitations of the Transparency Ideal and its Application to Algorithmic Accountability', (2016) 20 *New Media & Society* 973 who discuss this using the relational concept of transparency.

[62] European Expert Group, Report 2019, 56.

it targets those operators that economically profit the most.[63] Perhaps one might consider the risk share of each actor.[64] But the main problem remains. Calculation of the share is impossible due to uncertainties to determine the interconnected system's boundaries. Interconnected systems are not identifiable action 'units' where a set of 'connected actors' can be defined. Therefore, even the duty of all operators involved to disclose their share does not provide a solution. Determining the parties involved, not to speak of weighing each risk, is plainly impossible.

IV. Our Solution: Socialising the Interconnectivity Risk

A. Entire or Partial Socialisation?

Given these difficulties of individualising responsibility, socialising the interconnectivity risk remains the only viable option. Here, 'structural coupling' of social communication to algorithmic operations, as theorised by Luhmann, is pertinent. It precludes any direct access to the 'invisible machines' despite their enormous impact on society. Similarly, Hildebrandt's 'digital unconscious' metaphor suggests that we have no access to something which nevertheless influences our daily lives strongly. What follows for responsibility? According to the concept of 'mutual irritation', the two systems involved, social communication and digital operations, do not influence each other via identifiable causal chains but reconfigure themselves internally after external events of perturbation, such as damage events.[65] Damages stemming from digital interconnectivity are comparable to 'force majeure', external events that cannot be controlled and exclude individual or collective liability. These damages concern the whole society. The remote and indirect connection created by mutual irritation suggests socialising the risk. Therefore, the most recent debate increasingly prefers mandatory insurance and fund solutions.[66] However, the question is: What form of risk socialisation is appropriate for interconnectivity damages? Complete socialisation through mandatory insurance (potentially with state participation) or partial socialisation by choosing the industrial sector that economically benefits from interconnectivity?

Indeed, if interconnectivity is widespread in the digital society,[67] it is tempting to make society as a whole responsible for adverse consequences. Some authors

[63] For this argument, Spiecker, 'Digitalisierung' 702f. (linking liability share to who profits economically).

[64] See: Bashayreh et al., 'Artificial Intelligence and Legal Liability' 180.

[65] See: M Mölders, 'Irritation Expertise: Recipient Design as Instrument for Strategic Reasoning', (2014) 2 *European Journal of Futures Research* 32.

[66] Zech, 'Liability for AI'; G Borges, 'New Liability Concepts: The Potential of Insurance and Compensation Funds', in S Lohsse et al. (eds), *Liability for Artificial Intelligence and the Internet of Things* (Baden-Baden, Nomos/Hart, 2019) 153 ff, 159 ff; Wagner, 'Digitale Techniken' 741 f.

[67] This is the core thesis of Nassehi, *Muster* 145ff.

suggest that comprehensive social insurance systems with or without state participation take care of interconnectivity externalities.[68] However, complete socialisation through social insurance comes with many problems. It provides wrong incentives for the developers of interconnected systems, encourages careless behaviour, and considerably limits the steering function of tort law.[69] Moreover, the long-term sustainability of insurance solutions will be jeopardised when interconnected systems cause high, diffuse and unpredictable damages, which overburden private insurance regimes. Reversely, the risk mitigation of the insurance market induces strategies to socialise the risks through high premiums and limited coverage.[70] In short, insurance solutions are not suitable for securing unpredictable and incalculable damages, for which no experience exists.[71] Public-funded insurance will likely overburden public finance. Mandatory private insurance is of no help either since it will have to identify concrete actors who need insurance. Moreover, mandatory private insurance is based on a disputable prediction. Will a private insurance market evolve in response to related demands following obligations to carry out insurance if there is an immense uncertainty of the risks involved?

B. Risk Pools Decreed by Law

Rather than overburdening either public finance or relying on the private insurance market, a more appropriate strategy will link legal responsibility to the substantial involvement in interconnectivity. We have in mind here to attribute responsibility to the series of identifiable operations, ie to the social and digital processes themselves, rather than to individual operators or collective units of affiliated parties. The actual attribution points for responsibility are 'crowds' of algorithmic operations and no longer the decision-makers. Ultimately, it would not be people, organisations, networks, software agents, hybrids, but rather the operations themselves in their interconnectivity that would have to be made responsible.[72] These operations will be aggregated as risks pools that serve as a basis for liability.

[68] For coverage by social security schemes, R Janal, 'Extra-Contractual Liability for Wrongs Committed by Autonomous Systems', in M Ebers and S Navas (eds), *Algorithms and Law* (Cambridge, Cambridge University Press, 2020) 205; H Zech, 'Entscheidungen digitaler autonomer Systeme: Empfehlen sich Regelungen zu Verantwortung und Haftung?', (2020) I/A *73. Deutscher Juristentag* 11, 105 ff; A Bertolini and E Palmerini, *Regulating Robotics: A Challenge for Europe* (Brussels, European Parliament, Study Commissioned by the Juri Committee on Legal Affairs, 2014) 188 f.

[69] See: OJ Erdélyi and G Erdélyi, 'The AI Liability Puzzle and a Fund-Based Work-Around', (2020) *AIES '20: Proceedings of the AAAI/ACM Conference on AI, Ethics, and Society* 50, 53; Wagner, 'Digitale Techniken' 741.

[70] This problem is mentioned by the European Parliament, Civil Liability Regime for Artificial Intelligence, Resolution of 20 October 2020, 2020/2012(INL), para 25.

[71] See: Chinen, *Law and Autonomous Machines* 118 f.

[72] See: CEA Karnow, 'Liability for Distributed Artificial Intelligences', (1996) 11 *Berkeley Technology Law Journal* 147, 201 (translating the responsibilisation of actions instead of actors into the technical requirement of 'tagging' the electronic messages). For risk pooling, see also: H Smith and K Fotheringham, 'Artificial Intelligence in Clinical Decision-Making: Rethinking Liability', (2020) 20 *Medical Law International* 131.

However, how can the boundaries of interconnected operations be delineated? This is the haunting question that has already been present in our discussion on joint liability above. The Gordian knot needs to be cut. It is the law itself that has to take hard decisions. On its own authority, it needs to interrupt interdependencies, delineate interrelations, and define risk pools. Here, the law finally has to leave the actor perspective because it no longer looks for individual actors or collectives but instead focuses on the risky operations as such.[73] It makes single chains of operations responsible for their consequences without caring for organised decision centres. There is a decisive difference between such a risk liability and known forms of organisational liability. Liability law can neither refer to existing organisations nor cooperative relationships but instead has to define on its own – not to say, it has to decree – the contours of new risk pools. And as soon as the actions of individual, collective actors, or the calculations of algorithms move into such a space, they all become 'compulsory members' of such a risk pool – by the authoritative order of state law. Admittedly, there is still voluntary action involved but limited to the decision to enter the risk pool.[74]

The risk pool can no longer be defined by the boundaries of existing cooperative, organisational or technical structures. Instead, it would be constituted as a 'digital problem area'. The suitability for algorithmic risk management should determine the limits. Ultimately, neither causal connections nor pre-defined cooperative structures are decisive, but the ability to manage risk. Admittedly, this would amount to 'opportunistic' risk attribution.[75] The law identifies concrete digital risk contexts in the offline and online world by its own authority with the ulterior motive of creating a social institution that can control these risks to a certain extent to prevent and settle damages.

Risk management deals first with the settlement of losses already incurred. In a situation of multiple causation, the law balances the losses so that it creates an adequate financial pool that covers the losses and distributes the risk ('deep pocket', 'risk spreading'). Second – and perhaps more importantly – risk management means collective action focussing on future behaviour. The law designates

[73] Hildebrandt, *Smart Technologies* 26, as well defines actions and not actors as points of attribution, although she formulates perhaps more cautiously and returns at the end on the concept of agency: 'Because the agents may be distributed on and possibly mobile between different hardware applications and because as a multi-agent system it is capable of changing shape (polymorphous), it is not always easy to identify where the emerging agent is located and what is and is not a part of it at any point in time. However, in so far as the emergent behaviours of the system allow its identification as a unity of action, it can be qualified as an agent, whatever the underlying embodiment.'

[74] On concurrent considerations in environmental liability law, G Teubner, 'The Invisible Cupola: From Causal to Collective Attribution in Ecological Liability', in G Teubner et al. (eds), *Environmental Law and Ecological Responsibility: The Concept and Practice of Ecological Self-Organization* (Chichester, Wiley, 1993). In the same direction D Linardatos, 'Künstliche Intelligenz und Verantwortung', [2019] *Zeitschrift für Wirtschaftsrecht* 504, 509; European Parliament, Resolution of 16 February 2017 with Recommendations to the Commission on Civil Law Rules on Robotics, 2015/2103(INL), para 59 b) and c).

[75] See: N Luhmann, *Risk: A Sociological Theory* (Berlin, de Gruyter, 1993) ch 5.

the limits of the risk pool to create a realistic basis for active and joint damage prevention in sensitive areas. From both points of view, the law shapes the risk pool so that a functioning digital technology can cope with the risks of digital interconnectivity.

C. Public Administration of the Risk Pool: The Fund Solution

Therefore, in line with a few authors, we suggest a no-fault, fund-based system for dealing with the interconnectivity risk.[76] A fund solution provides several advantages, most importantly, it allows the law to play an intermediate role between the parties to an interconnected system. On the one side, the law determines ex-ante the risk pool of potentially responsible parties. It needs to rely on criteria other than the actual risk contribution; instead, it will take into account the economic benefits of actors and their ability to manage the risk and compensate for the damage. On the other side, the law sets up ex-post rules for distributing fund capital among the victims. More specifically, the law may prioritise the accessibility of certain victims to the fund capital. A law-mediated fund solution helps to foster social trust in the system by providing an ex-ante guarantee that damages will be compensated.[77]

Such a fund-based solution is inspired by other issue areas where risk funds have equally been developed to respond to large-scale damages caused by complex systems – environmental disasters,[78] financial system crises,[79] medical injuries[80] and damages caused in complex corporate groups and supply chain structures.[81] However, in most cases, funds have been set up only ex-post and have been actively lobbied for by those involved that also face a threat of liability. Against this background, several authors have criticised fund solutions for their deficiencies: lack

[76] For similar approaches see especially: Erdélyi and Erdélyi, 'AI Liability Puzzle'; see also: TH Pearl, 'Compensation at the Crossroads: Autonomous Vehicles & Alternative Victim Compensation Schemes', (2019) 60 *William & Mary Law Review* 1827; W Barfield, 'Liability for Autonomous and Artificially Intelligent Robots', (2018) 9 *Paladyn. Journal of Behavioral Robotics* 193, 202. See further on discussion of funds as a solution for AI damage, A Panezi, 'Liability Rules for AI-Facilitated Wrongs: An Ecosystem Approach to Manage Risk and Uncertainty', in P García Mexía and F Pérez Bes (eds), *AI and the Law* (Alphen aan den Rijn, Wolters Kluwer, 2021), section 3; Borges, 'New Liability Concepts'; J Turner, *Robot Rules: Regulating Artificial Intelligence* (London, Palgrave Macmillan, 2018) 102 ff.

[77] See: Erdélyi and Erdélyi, 'AI Liability Puzzle' 54.

[78] A prominent example is the Gulf Coast Claims Facility (created individually by BP in the aftermath of the Deepwater Horizon Catastrophe).

[79] S Schich and B-H Kim, 'Guarantee Arrangements for Financial Promises: How Widely Should the Safety Net be Cast?', (2011) 2011 *OECD Journal: Financial Market Trends* 201.

[80] Examples are the foundation established after the Contergan scandal in Germany (ContStiftG) or the National Vaccine Injury Compensation Program (NVICP) in the US.

[81] On compensation funds after the Bhopal disaster, J Cassels, 'The Uncertain Promise of Law: Lessons from Bhopal', (1991) 29 *Osgoode Hall Law Journal* 1, 48 f., and the Rana Plaza building collapse, Rana Plaza Donors Trust Fund, established by the ILO, www.ranaplaza-arrangement.org/trustfund/.

of sufficient financing, intransparency of fund allocation, waivers of victims' right to sue, delegation of decisions on fund contributions to potentially liable actors.[82] Therefore, a trustworthy fund solution requires public authorities to administer the fund. 'Quasi-judicial funds' need to be financed by private parties but administered by public regulatory authorities, which, if possible, already have been set up within that sector. Pearl suggests a publicly administered crash fund for victims in the context of self-driving cars set up by the transport authorities.[83] Erdélyi and Erdélyi propose an AI guarantee scheme analogous to existing financial system guarantees.[84] Indeed, given the specificity of sectors and their different degree of relying on digital interconnectivity, it makes sense to establish sector-specific funds instead of a society-wide fund. This would also allow linking to existing schemes that have been proven successful in the particular sector.

D. Financing: Ex-Ante and Ex-Post Components

In setting up a fund, one may distinguish between ex-ante and ex-post funding. Pre-funding entails a mandatory or tax-financed initial funding base. Post-funding requires payment into the fund once a guarantee-triggering event has occurred. It is usually based on a pre-issued compulsory guarantee. Both options have their advantages and disadvantages, but in reality, most of the existing sector-specific fund solutions combine ex-ante and ex-post financing. This also seems the royal road for a secure financial basis, which would not run the risks of either under- or overcapitalisation. In addition, requiring small-scale, ex-ante financing combined with additional ex-post liability by potentially responsible parties seems to provide the right incentives. A small-scale ex-ante contribution does not overburden those developing products. At the same time, ex-post liability in case of interconnectivity damages will effectively help maintain the liability system's steering function.[85]

The most promising combined pre- and post-financed funds are those where initial funding is conducted through tax or mandatory contributions backed up by ex-post mechanisms. Fund solutions have been backed up by existing mandatory insurances in the transport sector, which lowered the fund capital. However, this construction is only possible when insurance solutions are established and thus still leaves victims with uncompensated damages where this does not exist.[86]

[82] Pearl, 'Compensation at the Crossroads' 1872 f.

[83] ibid.

[84] Erdélyi and Erdélyi, 'AI Liability Puzzle' 54.

[85] The argument against a fund solution is made by Zech, 'Liability for AI' 157; Wagner, 'Digitale Techniken' 741; Cauffman, 'Robo-Liability' 531. Yet this critique applies only if the fund solution is proposed instead of liability schemes whereas we propose to combine fund solution with priority for a system of liability.

[86] See: EU Parliament, Resolution 2020, Preamble para 22: 'Special compensation funds could also be set up to cover those exceptional cases in which an AI-system, which is not yet classified as high-risk AI-system and thus, is not yet insured, causes harm or damage.'

In the financial system, guarantees are partially industry-funded, but due to difficulties in assessing the extent of damages, they are government-backed up; thus, the systemic risk is fully socialised ex-post if the private guarantees do not suffice.[87] In the environmental sector, the 'Superfund' for environmental damages has been developed in the US as a particularly interesting combination of an ex-ante fund and an ex-post strict liability. It provides sufficient fund capital and fulfils the goal of recovery action. Initially financed by a tax for companies in the sector to provide a stable financial basis, the fund now relies on ex-post financing through a hard background liability regime. The public agency that administers the fund is entitled to sue those actors considered potentially responsible. This results either in a far-reaching strict joint and several liability or in an agreement on equitable remedies.[88] The advantages of a fund that facilitates damage compensation are combined with the advantages of a background liability on a share basis. Hence, the Superfund initially taxed ex-ante risk-prone companies to pay into the fund. Later on, it determined ex-post potentially responsible parties in the light of their connection to the problem area. Liability was made dependent on their problem-solving capacity.

For algorithmic interconnectivity, such a model seems appropriate. It will rely on initial small-scale financing through taxes on specific products. Alternatively, an industry-centred mandatory contribution will be required. This can be backed up with a liability regime in which the regulatory agency makes strictly liable those parties with close connections to the system. Such liability should be based on problem-solving capacity. This would allow for small scale, ex-ante financing. Simultaneously, large scale, ex-post financing in areas with large scale damage would come from those closely connected to the system. Such a system may also be suitable because it would allow calculating ex-post financing through strict liability claims in light of the scale of the damage. Since the interconnectivity risk may range from small-scale risks to systemic threats, it makes sense to secure a financial basis for small-scale damages. Systemic damages should be left with those actors closely connected to the network.

E. Participation and Administration

This leaves the question of how to delineate the risk pool, both ex-ante and ex-post. Who are those 'connected to a technical system', the 'potentially responsible parties', those economically benefitting from interconnectivity, and those with problem-solving capacity? How should the law determine the boundaries of algorithmic interconnectivity, which in itself does not have clearly defined limits?

[87] See: Schich and Kim, 'Guarantee Arrangements'.

[88] 42 US Code § 9607 (strict joint and several liability) and § 9613 (agreement on equitable remedies).

This is a general problem well-known to network analysis.[89] There, the only way out seems to be that the observer determines the network's boundaries. Hence, the law's decision cannot rely on existing social boundaries. Instead, the law's own authority makes the determination. As Lior puts it: 'the observer would be the judicial or administrative authority observing an AI accident'.[90]

Notwithstanding law's autonomy in this decision, delineating the risk pool still needs justifiable criteria. First, it needs to identify the industry sector that should be responsible for financing the fund. Generally, it can be said:

> In order to form 'AI risk pools' for legal purposes, legislators and later judges, should take into account industry clusters, horizontal, upstream, and downstream interconnections between AI products and services. They should also take into account how industries self-identify within the market at large, including vis-à-vis their customers. Industry members in well-defined risk pools should then be in the best position to cooperate to mitigate the risk of causing damage.[91]

For sectors where the interconnectivity risk is centred around a particular product, such as autonomous vehicles, a levy for that product or the component to be paid by involved manufacturers and users may be the most cost-efficient to realise. This would also allow the consideration of the degree of autonomy and interconnectedness in calculating the levy or tax,[92] as well as hierarchising the coverage among the actors that typically produce the most risk-affinitive components.

For professional use in financial markets, an entry charge for accessing the market through the stock exchange may probably be most suitable. Such an entry charge may be imposed on traders seeking to act on the market and those operating in financial markets. This applies to stock exchange operators who will have to contribute if they actively pursue the use of interconnected systems within their own regulatory reach.

In general, such a sector-specific approach to delineating the risk pool may also include actors who serve as central 'responsibility nodes' in the interconnected systems, such as organisations that have certified interconnected systems or components in advance, hereby instituting trust in the system.[93]

Such ex-ante funding may provide an initial basis for capitalising the fund. However, given the difficulty of estimating the total amount of capital needed and

[89] See generally: S Heath et al., 'Chasing Shadows: Defining Network Boundaries in Qualitative Social Network Analysis', (2009) 9 *Qualitative Research* 645; EO Laumann et al., 'The Boundary Specification Problem in Network Analysis', in RS Burt and M Minor (eds), *Applied Network Analysis* (Beverly Hills/Cal., SAGE Publications, 1983).

[90] A Lior, 'The AI Accident Network: Artificial Intelligence Liability Meets Network Theory', (2021) 95 *Tulane Law Review* forthcoming, section C.1.

[91] Panezi, 'AI-Facilitated Wrongs' 17.

[92] See: Pearl, 'Compensation at the Crossroads' 1879.

[93] On the essential role of certification in limiting liability, MU Scherer, 'Of Wild Beasts and Digital Analogues: The Legal Status of Autonomous Systems', (2019) 19 *Nevada Law Journal* 259, 394 ff. See generally for the possibility and limits of certifier liability, P Rott (ed), *Certification – Trust, Accountability, Liability* (Heidelberg/New York, Springer, 2019).

in order to minimise the risk of 'dead capital', one should combine initial funding with rules for ex-post funding, which apply once a damaging event occurs. Ex-post funding will be relevant, especially when interconnectivity risks are realised only rarely but may cause large-scale damages. Ex-post funding elements allow a more precise risk allocation retrospectively in the light of the particular damage and the problem-solving capacity of involved actors.

When setting up the rules for ex-post funding, one may take inspiration from other backup funds. There are three choices: (1) Guarantee schemes require participants to commit ex-ante to an ex-post contribution when large-scale damage has occurred; (2) government will back up funding, as is the case for financial guarantee schemes; (3) a public agency administrates a background liability system, which holds involved parties liable to contribute to the fund or directly finance the restitutory action. This has successfully been implemented in environmental superfund liability. Government-back-up should be least preferable since this would again fully socialise the risk and provide the wrong incentives for the private actors involved.[94] Here, the classical 'too big to fail' dilemma comes up. Private guarantee-based funding faces the difficulty of predicting the financial size of the risk pool and estimating the contributions so that parties can insure against the risk. Moreover, guarantee-based funding does not address the insolvency risk of actors. Hence, fund solutions combined with background liability systems seem to be the royal road. Such a combination has the additional advantage of introducing liability considerations that would maintain liability law's steering function. Altogether, this would amount to 'a multilayered approach to AI liability that combines individual and collective liability: identifying different risk pools and applying rules of collective liability together with regulations that enforce or incentivise the (re)allocation of liability within the separate risk pools'.[95]

Therefore, it seems preferable to combine a broad but small-scale ex-ante funding with precisely tailored ex-post determination as a general strategy. This will establish a background liability system that the administrative agency manages. The Superfund could provide the model: The regulatory agency pays out fund capital after damage occurs. Subsequently, the agency sues the potentially responsible parties according to their connection to the specific problem area. Strict joint and several liability of those involved in the problem area will apply.[96] As part of a fund-based system, it is not a classical fault-based liability regime; instead, it is a regulatory regime where an administrative agency has broad discretion to make decisions based on various considerations. In contrast to our suggestions for hybrids, such liability cannot be oriented on share or control of the risk but rather require the agency to single out actors for compensation according to the

[94] This is the reason why policy actors are sceptical about fund-based solutions for high-risk AI systems, see EU Parliament, Resolution 2020, para 25.

[95] Panezi, 'AI-Facilitated Wrongs' 16.

[96] Such a system of strict joint and several liability is proposed by the EU Parliament, Resolution 2020, Proposed Regulation, Art 4, 11.

overarching criterion of problem-solving capacity. Network theory and its statistical methods of measuring power and influence within a network can be of great assistance here, which would make the abstract legal categories workable.[97] In this way, it would be possible to delineate the concrete responsibility network within the broader risk pool of interconnectivity.

A variety of aspects can be weighed. (1) Higher responsibility should be borne by those actors that take over central risk controlling functions. Here, antitrust regulations measuring market power via micro-level indicators such as price, activity-level profits, and market share could identify the relative weight of control.[98] (2) The economic benefits that parties gain from the system may serve as a component.[99] (3) Finally, considerations on deep pocket and insurability of the risk should come in.

F. Compensation and Recovery Action

The fund's primary function will be to compensate victims.[100] To close the liability gap arising caused by interconnectivity, compensation is necessary not only for physical damage but also for non-economic losses.[101] To avoid 'opening the floodgates', compensation for damages resulting from interconnectivity needs to be limited to those outputs of interconnectivity that involve a breach of the law, similar to what we have already suggested for actants and hybrids.[102]

In addition, access to the fund will depend on other existing regimes of individual liability within a sector. Fund-based regimes will have to remain a subsidiary solution. Hence, for self-driving cars, access to the fund will be open only under the condition that the existing private insurance system does not cover the losses.[103] For high-frequency trading, the fund coverage would be subsidiary to any individual liability and would probably also need to specify conditions as to the threshold to be covered.[104] Several funds are administered by sector-specific agencies, such as road traffic authorities for autonomous vehicles, financial

[97] D Wei et al., 'Identifying Influential Nodes in Weighted Networks Based on Evidence Theory', (2013) 392 *PHYSICA A: Statistical Mechanics and its Applications* 2564.

[98] See: RV Loo, 'The Revival of Respondeat Superior and Evolution of Gatekeeper Liability', (2020) 109 *Georgetown Law Journal* 141, 183.

[99] See: Chinen, *Law and Autonomous Machines* 85 f.

[100] This is also emphasised by Pearl, 'Compensation at the Crossroads' 1876 ('victim compensation fund'); Erdélyi and Erdélyi, 'AI Liability Puzzle' 54 ('redistribution of losses').

[101] See extensively on the problem of non-economic losses as part of the liability gap, ch 3, V.D.

[102] For actants ch 3, V.D, for hybrids ch 4, IV.C.

[103] In this case, the sector-specific fund could be linked to a subsidiary fund solution wherever they already exist in national law, *cf* the German fund system that is subsidiary to private insurance, § 12 PflVG or the prominent New Zealand No-Fault Accident Compensation Scheme, explained in general and as applied to the context of AI liability by Turner, *Robot Rules* 102 ff.

[104] In ch 6, III, we will explain more specifically how the fund solution relates to individual and collective responsibility.

market authorities for interconnected trading, or digital network agencies for infringement of rights on social networks. For each of such funds, the administration needs to develop specific rules on the threshold for coverage, conditions for pay-out to victims, and required proof.

Thus, a delineation of the sector-specific interconnectivity risks covered by the fund is required. In autonomous vehicles, the victims will only claim individual damages in car accidents and need to apply existing coverage limitations.[105] In financial trading, an extension to economic and systemic losses will be necessary. It needs to prioritise groups that will have access to the capital. Caps on the extent of protection (similar to financial guarantee schemes) need to be defined.

Yet, a fund-based solution involving a regulatory agency needs to go beyond mere compensation. Complexity and unpredictability do not only pose problems for individual compensation but also have systemic consequences. Since technological systems have become part of the public infrastructure, the responsibility gap is no longer only problematic for individual losses. Interconnectivity damages impact the system as a whole. In this respect, algorithmic interconnectivity resembles the natural environment, public infrastructures, or public health. Interconnectivity risks cannot be reduced to the sum of individual damages. Public trust in the functioning of a complex technological system is the prevailing concern. This requires future-oriented action in terms of restoring the system. For this purpose, collective liability is better suited than individual liability since it promotes self-organisation within markets and motivates collaborative solutions.[106]

Consequently, the fund solution concentrates on undoing the negative consequences and engaging in recovery action. Again, environmental damages are a suitable analogy for this type of remedy. Regulations and case law on environmental pollution begin to move beyond individual compensation and focus increasingly on future-oriented recovery action of private actors. In particular, Superfund liability provides for detailed and sophisticated rules on remedies. They range from clean-up to payments for the agency's clean-up action and injunctive relief.[107] Similar remedies have been developed in environmental tort law. In the EU, courts establish concrete action plans aimed at ensuring clean air.[108] Recently, similar remedies have been developed in 'climate change litigation' against private actors.[109] In a recent case, a Dutch court made a company liable for contributing to climate change involving environmental and public health damage. Most interesting for our discussion, courts link such ecological damages to the private parties'

[105] See: Pearl, 'Compensation at the Crossroads' 1878.
[106] See: Panezi, 'AI-Facilitated Wrongs' 15.
[107] 42 U.S.C. § 9607 (liability) § 9622 (settlements).
[108] C-237/07 *Dieter Janecek v Freistaat Bayern*, ECLI:EU:C:2008:447.
[109] For the US: *City of New York v BP et al*, United States Court of Appeals for the 2nd Circuit, 1 April 2021, No 18-2188; for the Netherlands: *Milieudefensie v Royal Dutch Shell plc*, District Court of The Hague, 26 May 2021, ECLI:NL:RBDHA:2021:5339; for Germany *Lliuya v RWE AG*, Case number 2 O 285/15 (pending).

ability to control. The decisions focus on environmental recovery rather than on individual financial compensation.[110]

This provides a valuable model for digital interconnectivity. Here, as well, damages with potentially society-wide impact occur in a complex system where individual actors are difficult to identify. Appropriate remedies for systemic damages need to aim at restoring system integrity and mitigating future risks. Therefore, a digital fund solution will concentrate on preventing and undoing adverse consequences.[111] The regulatory agency will then organise a 'digital clean up' and aim at 'future mitigation' as equitable relief. The agency will either order those involved to conduct recovery action or ask for compensation when engaging itself in the recovery. In the digital world, this means infusing the concept of reversibility into technology.[112] Alternatively, firewalls will be built into interconnected systems, as some industry actors already develop today as a precautionary measure. An analogy to the famous 'right to be forgotten' in the context of interconnectivity will result in a claim for digital limitation of interconnectivity or even the claim for being disconnected. As a last resort, the 'robot death penalty' will undo the negative consequences of interconnectivity.[113]

G. Global Interconnectivity and National Administration

Interconnectivity is not a national but a global phenomenon. It encompasses manufacturers, operators, designers and programmers from different parts of the world. The infrastructural network on which interconnected technology operates is spread worldwide and detached from national territory and jurisdiction. At the same time, it is not spaceless. The damages caused by interconnectivity are located territorially, and compensation mechanisms need to be accessed via national regulatory systems.[114] In addition, the interconnectivity damages can result from household items running astray to catastrophes with a global reach, such as the shaking of financial markets by trading algorithms.

[110] Most prominently, *Milieudefensie v Royal Dutch Shell plc*, at 4.4.45, specifies this as a future-oriented 'reduction obligation'.

[111] Generally on the idea of relying on injunction orders and claims for undoing the consequences, MA Lemley and B Casey, 'Remedies for Robots', (2019) 86 *University of Chicago Law Review* 1311, 1386 ff. For a detailed model of restitution which involves co-regulation by governance by algorithms and a regulatory agency on the European level, M Sommer, *Haftung für autonome Systeme: Verteilung der Risiken selbstlernender und vernetzter Algorithmen im Vertrags- und Deliktsrecht* (Baden-Baden, Nomos, 2020) 452 ff.

[112] See: EU Parliament, Resolution 2017, Annex have suggested reversibility as an integral part of ethics guidelines in the field of robotics.

[113] See: Lemley and Casey, 'Remedies for Robots' 1390.

[114] This ambiguity of a global digital infrastructure with spatial characteristics has been analysed already by H Lindahl, 'We and Cyberlaw: The Spatial Unity of Constitutional Orders', (2013) 20 *Indiana Journal of Global Legal Studies* 697, 703 ff.

This twofold connection of AI interconnectivity to the global and the national sphere requires simultaneous alignment with national and international regulatory frameworks.[115] For a fund-based solution, the royal road seems to develop international rules on the specifics of the fund in terms of financing and compensation, while the particulars of administration and compensation procedures will be produced separately by the existing national administrative system.[116] Some authors suggest a new specialised international organisation for Artificial Intelligence.[117] Yet, one may equally think of existing international organisations, such as the International Organisation for Standardisation, that already develop specific AI-related standards.[118] Such international institutions need to be composed of technical experts, social scientists and lawyers. In its recent proposal for AI regulation, the European Commission proposes specific oversight bodies to be designated by Member States that oversee the conformity of AI in the internal market and compliance by operators with the specified obligations.[119] To be clear, these proposals are still different from the public oversight body as we propose should also administer compensation funds, but installing oversight bodies for AI systems in general could be a first step in the direction.

While such an international cooperative solution is needed, it will face significant obstacles. As the interconnectivity's benefits are distributed unequally over the globe, a robust international framework will probably not be established in the near future. At least for the time being, a uniform European solution will be satisfactory. Since there is an intense policy debate on liability and interconnectivity already ongoing, it may be easier to connect the fund-based solution to those existing debates. Such a European solution effectively may become an access requirement to the internal market. Maybe, it will be part of the 'Brussels effect'.[120] An EU standard subsequently spreads over the world and sets a de facto global standard. It is not unlikely that the EU will set the standard for regulating AI.

[115] See: R Brownsword, *Law 3.0* (London, Routledge, 2021) 96 ff, 99 ff.

[116] For a detailed analysis of this interaction between international (private technical) standard-setting and national public regulatory initiatives, E Fosch-Villaronga and AJ Golia, 'Robots, Standards and the Law: Rivalries between Private Standards and Public Policymaking for Robot Governance', (2019) 35 *Computer Law & Security Review* 129, 140 f.

[117] Bashayreh et al., 'Artificial Intelligence and Legal Liability', 186 f; OJ Erdélyi and J Goldsmith, 'Regulating Artificial Intelligence: Proposal for a Global Solution', (2018) *AIES '18: Proceedings of the AAAI/ACM Conference on AI, Ethics, and Society* 95, 99f.

[118] Specifically, ISO 26262 on driverless cars, see also the ISO-IEC joint committee 1, subcommittee 42 on Artificial Intelligence www.iso.org/committee/6794475.html.

[119] European Commission, Proposal for a Regulation of the European Parliament and the Council Laying Down Harmonised Rules on Artificial Intelligence (Proposal Artificial Intelligence Act) and Amending Certain Union Legislative Acts, COM(2021) 206, Art 30 I.

[120] See: A Bradford, *The Brussels Effect: How the European Union Rules the World* (Oxford, Oxford University Press, 2020) ch 5 (on data protection and online hate speech regulation).

To conclude, this chapter has outlined a fund solution combined with a background strict liability system for handling the interconnectivity risk. Such a fund solution will entail a significant regulatory process. As a subsidiary solution, it needs to be integrated with existing liability and insurance rules. The following last chapter will outline more in detail how the fund solution for interconnectivity interacts with vicarious and collective liability.

6

Conclusion: Three Liability Regimes and Their Interrelations

I. Synopsis and Rules

At the outset of this chapter, we present a condensed synopsis of our findings, which we discussed separately in the preceding chapters. Table 1 shows the differences between three liability regimes, their digital and social premises and their legal consequences. Subsequently, we will discuss in more detail the differences between the three liability regimes and the effects the differences have on the relations between digital technology, social institutions and legal regimes.

Table 1 Interrelations between machine behaviour, socio-digital institutions and liability regimes

Machine Behaviour	Socio-Digital Institution	New Actors: Emergent Risks	Liability Regime	Liable Subjects	Algorithms' Legal Status
Individual	Digital Assistance	Digital Actants: Autonomy Risk	Vicarious Liability	Users/ Operators	Limited Legal Personhood
Hybrid	Human-Machine Association	Digital Hybrids: Collective Action Risk	Enterprise Liability	Network Members	Membership in Hybrid
Collective	Exposure to Digital Interconnectivity	Crowds: Risks of Invisible Machines	Collective Funds	Industry Sector	Part of Risk Pool

We suggest the following rules for three liability regimes.

A. Digital Assistance: Vicarious Liability

Vicarious liability for wrongful decisions of an algorithm applies when: (1) a human principal (or an organisation) delegates a task to an algorithm; (2) the delegation requires the agent's freedom of decision; (3) the agent's action is neither foreseeable nor explainable by a programmer; (4) the action violates a contractual/tortious duty of care; and (5) causation between action and damage can be established.

(6) As a consequence, the algorithm's user as the principal is the liable person. (7) Compensation of damage is not limited to the narrow compensation principles of strict liability for industrial hazards but follows established principles of contract and tort law, particularly regarding the question of whether or not merely monetary damages will be compensated.

B. Human-Machine Associations: Enterprise Liability

If vicarious liability cannot be established, enterprise liability applies when: (1) in the cooperation between humans and machines; (2) a wrongful decision has been made; and (3) their activities are so densely intertwined; so that (4) the wrongful decision can be attributed neither to the human nor to the algorithm; and (5) causal links between individual actions and damage cannot be established; while (6) it can be proven that the collective decision has caused the damage.

(7) As a consequence, liable are those participants of the actor-network who constitute the enterprise initiating the hybrid, ie producers, programmers, dealers, and the human participants within the hybrid. (8) The primary target of enterprise liability is the producer as the hub of the networked enterprise. (9) The producer can seek redress on the other participants according to their network share. (10) Network share is defined by the combined criteria of economic benefit and control within the network.

C. Interconnectivity: Fund Liability

If neither vicarious liability nor enterprise liability can be established, compensation is possible only: (1) through a fund or insurance that will be set up to provide for compensation. Conditions for compensation by fund or insurance capital are (2) a violation of a contractual/tortious duty that can be attributed only to a series of interconnected algorithmic decisions; which (3) caused damage.

(4) As a consequence, a regulatory agency in the relevant branch of industry will be authorised to administer the fund. The agency determines (5) the actors in the industry sector who finance the fund ex-ante according to their market share,

and (6), in addition, determines actors for ex-post liability according to their problem-solving capacity.

II. Socio-Digital Institutions and Liability Law

A. One-Size-Fits-All or Sector-Specific Piecemeal Approach?

By distinguishing three liability regimes, we aimed to avoid the emptiness of an overgeneralising approach as well as the fallacy of misplaced concreteness of a sectoral approach.

Several authors favour a uniform treatment of algorithms under liability law. They argue for a one-size-fits-all solution. They treat algorithms in all situations indiscriminately, either as mere tools, as vicarious agents, or as autonomous self-interested e-persons. Against these positions, we distinguish typical responsibility situations according to the different risks they produce.[1] As an observer has it:

> A general rule for objective liability … may prove especially difficult to describe the particiuliarities or the necessary degree of a special, extraordinary risk in a sufficiently precise way (in order to prevent, for example, that every use of AI in a smartphone could be covered by strict liability).[2]

The general tool-solution, which is still the dominant opinion, would overburden the individual user. He would be liable in situations when other actors should bear the risks, sometimes the actor-network behind the algorithm, sometimes the branch of the computer industry involved. The fiction that the 'true' actor is always the human behind the computer is not only untenable but plainly unjust. Similarly, generally treating algorithms as autonomous e-persons makes sense only when they no longer play the role of digital assistants but when they become self-interested actors. Such a full personification will not provide for liability in the case of a human-machine association because, in its dense interactions, a responsible actor is not identifiable at all. Similarly, in situations of interconnectivity, it does not make sense at all to grant each algorithm involved the status of an autonomous e-person. How should one find the liable e-person in the multitude of e-persons and their interdependent action? The legal problems of actor-identification and multiple causation are not resolvable, which would open a considerable responsibility gap.

In contrast to this uniform approach, the sectoral approach suggests different liability rules for various algorithms, which are context-dependent on the industries in which they are used. In principle, this solution has some advantages. It

[1] Against a uniform approach: B Koch, 'Product Liability 2.0 – Mere Update or New Version?', in S Lohsse et al. (eds), *Liability for Robotics and in the Internet of Things* (Baden-Baden/Oxford, Nomos/Hart, 2019) 113 f; S Lohsse et al., 'Liability for Artificial Intelligence', in S Lohsse et al. (eds), *Liability for Robotics and in the Internet of Things* (Baden-Baden/Oxford, Nomos/Hart, 2019) 21 ff.

[2] Lohsse et al., 'Liability for Artificial Intelligence' 21.

can count on experiences with existing law and adapts well to technological and social particularities.[3] It works well in the public regulation of fund solutions as we suggested in chapter 5 but a situational approach is inappropriate for private liability law solutions. Bertolini has attempted to work out such a situational approach in detail. As it comes out, this requires numerous 'ad-hoc regulations' of algorithms based on a bewildering multitude of criteria, according to which

> a class of applications needs to be identified that is sufficiently uniform, presenting similar technological traits, as well as corresponding legal – and in some cases ethical – concerns. In such a perspective, a drone differs from a driverless car. They both are intended to operate in public spaces, and display some degree of autonomy. Yet the technologies they are based upon differ, the environment they will be used in as well, the dynamic of the possible accidents too. Moreover, their use, their social role, and potential diffusion also varies, and so do the parties that might be involved in their operation, and the structure of the business through which services might be offered.[4]

However, such ad-hoc regulation is a radically situationist approach, which has only a superficial plausibility. It will predictably be lost in numerous particularities. It suffers from excessive contextualism, which tries to master the infinite number of concrete circumstances by legislative fiat instead of building on emerging socio-digital institutions and their legal counterparts within existing liability law. Successful rules of liability law need to be embedded in social institutions, stabilising them over time. One of the ad-hoc regulations' concomitant disadvantages is that liability law would always be 'lagging behind' the technological, economic, social and ethical developments that the regulation hopes to take into account. What would be encountered by such an approach is the well-known problem that all regulatory law is facing: Situated in-between the eigen-dynamics of technological advancement and political and legal processes, regulatory intervention is unable to anticipate ex-ante the scale of the technological problem it ought to regulate and cannot intervene ex-post.[5]

The most significant problem, however, is that legislation will develop liability rules only for those digital actants whose damage producing actions have become a 'hot' political issue. This violates the principle of equal treatment blatantly. Why should strict liability regimes govern the car industry while patients in hospitals remain unprotected against algorithmic medical malpractice? Does it really make

[3] eg: G Borges, 'New Liability Concepts: The Potential of Insurance and Compensation Funds', in S Lohsse et al. (eds), *Liability for Artificial Intelligence and the Internet of Things* (Baden-Baden, Nomos/Hart, 2019) 145, 152; H Zech, 'Liability for Autonomous Systems: Tackling Specific Risks of Modern IT', in R Schulze et al. (eds), *Liability for Robotics and in the Internet of Things* (Baden-Baden/Oxford, Nomos/Hart, 2019).

[4] A Bertolini, *Artificial Intelligence and Civil Liability* (Brussels, European Parliament, Study Commissioned by the Juri Committee on Legal Affairs, 2020), 102.

[5] This problem has been commonly associated with the 'Collingridge Trilemma' (D Collingridge, *The Social Control of Technology* (New York, St. Martin's Press, 1980), or recently re-framed as the 'pacing problem' (eg: GE Marchant, 'The Growing Gap Between Emerging Technologies and the Law', in GE Marchant et al. (eds), *The Growing Gap Between Emerging Technologies and Legal-Ethical Oversight: The Pacing Problem* (Dordrecht/Heidelberg/London/New York, Springer, 2011)).

sense to develop a special liability regime for, say, lawnmowers, industry robots, smart kitchen devices, surgical robots, or military and emergency response robots, as some authors suggest?[6] One would leave liability law to the vagaries of local politics and the varying lobby power in different industry branches. Treating like cases alike and unequal cases unequally requires distinctions that develop sustainable normative criteria. In our opinion, the three different digital risks – autonomy, association, opaque interconnections – do provide a normatively robust base to distinguish liability regimes.

In the preceding chapters, we have treated each liability regime separately and in detail without, however, full regard for their interaction. This final chapter is devoted to how these regimes differ from each other and how they interrelate. Their differences appear in several dimensions. Differences in algorithmic behaviour correlate with different socio-digital institutions and their specific risks, which in their turn correspond to variations in liability rules. Yet, we also outline some overlaps and grey areas in which different socio-digital institutions play a role.

B. Socio-Digital Institutions

As discussed in chapter one, many authors in the current debate make an interdisciplinary short-circuit. They ignore the crucial interactions between technology and social behaviour. Instead, they connect technological characteristics of computers directly to liability rules. Thus, they remain locked in inadequate models of linear causation and simplified normative implications: technology -> legal liability.[7] In contrast, we are working with what we think is a more appropriate model. The starting point is a typology of machine behaviour developed in technology studies: individual, collective, and hybrid.[8] Similarly, others have framed this as the different modes of assisted, augmented and autonomous artificial intelligence.[9] To avoid the short-circuit, we have introduced the concept of 'socio-digital institutions'. These are stabilised complexes of social expectations, particularly expectations about social behaviour and related risks, which come up regularly when social systems use the new digital technologies. Socio-digital institutions emerge from three fundamental types of human-algorithm contacts. Individual machine behaviour denotes individually delineated algorithmic operations that humans can

[6] eg: the critical arguments by Koch, 'Product Liability 2.0' 114.

[7] As an example for the short-circuit, R Konertz and R Schönhof, *Das technische Phänomen 'Künstliche Intelligenz' im allgemeinen Zivilrecht: Eine kritische Betrachtung im Lichte von Autonomie, Determinismus und Vorhersehbarkeit* (Baden-Baden, Nomos, 2020).

[8] Our primary reference for this claim is I Rahwan et al., 'Machine Behaviour', (2019) 568 *Nature* 477.

[9] F Möslein, 'Robots in the Boardroom: Artificial Intelligence and Corporate Law', in W Barfield and U Pagallo (eds), *Research Handbook on the Law of Artificial Intelligence* (Cheltenham, Edward Elgar, 2017) 657. Similarly, the distinction between learning ability, robotics, connectivity by H Zech, 'Liability for AI: Public Policy Considerations', [2021] *ERA Forum* 147, 148 f.

understand through communication in the strict sense. Hybrid machine behaviour occurs in densely intertwined and stable interactions between humans and machines; here, a human-machine association emerges as a new collective actor. Collective machine behaviour, in contrast, is an indirect linkage of humans to the interconnectivity of invisible machines. Each of these contacts creates a different socio-digital institution.

Liability law should develop abstract legal rules based on these institutions and not solely on technological characteristics. This is what legal philosophy calls the embeddedness of law in concrete social institutions:

> Far from being reduced to an abstract set of rules, the law is materially embedded in the social structure from which it emanates. Rather than constituting order, regulating human relations or sanctioning deviant behaviour, the law gives expression to a web of relations already present in the social body. In this way, it does not merely unify subjective wills through a given system of norms but reveals their originally collective dimension. Just as law always has a social character, so society always has a juridical connotation of every type of organisation. This means that any relationship – even between two private parties – has an institutional profile, regardless of the public order in which it is embedded. Assumed at its point of emergence, it constitutes, indeed, the original cell of all law.[10]

In our case, socio-digital institutions are not *creationes ex nihilo*; instead, they are already rooted in existing social institutions of the offline world, which are now fundamentally transformed by the 'invasion' of algorithms. The first type of a socio-digital institution builds on traditional human principal-agent relations when humans delegate tasks no longer to humans but computers. The second type has its origin in inter-human associations and becomes a new hybrid collective actor. The third type builds on the traditional human exposure to machines that connects to society indirectly, now through new types of autonomous 'invisible machines'. Each of these socio-digital institutions develops its own risks, which are co-produced by computer technology and social relations: 'digital assistance' when tasks are delegated to algorithms, 'human-machine associations' when humans and algorithms together form a collective actor, and linkage to 'digital interconnectivity' when social communication is only indirectly coupled to a crowd of interacting algorithms.

Furthermore, we assume that the relations between digital technology, socio-digital institutions, and liability regimes are not linear but circular and recursive. While in the one direction digital technology anticipates the social use of algorithms and tries to avoid in advance potential liability risks, equally important are the feedback loops, which work in the opposite direction. Here, experiences of social use heavily influence further technological developments. And liability rules have a considerable impact on future programs of algorithms and their social use. These rules could work as incentives for precautionary measures and

[10] R Esposito, *Istituzione* (Bologna, Il Mulino, 2021) 62 (our translation).

activity levels[11] and have a particular deterrent/encouraging effect on technological developments.[12] These – *de facto et de jure* – mutual influences produce not only simple feedback loops but outright co-evolutionary dynamics between technology, sociality, and law. Liability law cannot orient itself only to legal consistency, political goals or economic efficiency but must be aware that it is an integral part of this co-evolutionary dynamics.

At this crucial point, we have introduced insights from the social sciences.[13] As intermediary disciplines between IT studies and legal doctrine, the social sciences are able to analyse the co-evolutionary dynamics between technological advancements and socio-digital institutions.[14] In these relations between digital technology and society, we have aimed to identify different risks, to which law needs to calibrate a variety of liability concepts and rules. When choosing between the relevant social sciences, liability law cannot rely exclusively on economic analyses, as many authors indeed do. While they focus on incentivising precaution standards and activity levels, they are relatively indifferent to broader social issues, particularly victims' interests for compensation of their damages. Analyses of monetary costs and benefits surely help determine an optimal level of liability, but they neglect liability law's contribution to the integrity of socio-digital institutions. According to the principle of 'transversality', developed in philosophy and sociology,[15] we have attempted to gain relevant insights from other social sciences, particularly from their contributions to personification of algorithms, to emergent properties of human-algorithm associations, and to distributed cognition of interconnected algorithms. To determine the concomitant risks of these institutions is the task not only of economic but equally of sociological risk theories. They are sensitive to risk perception in different social contexts.[16] In the end, it is the combination of economic and sociological risk theories that will give orientation to legal arguments about risk liability in socio-digital institutions.[17] Economics inform about balancing the precautionary and activity levels of risk avoidance, while other sociological disciplines and philosophy talk about the specific risk expectations and normative requirements of different socio-digital institutions.

[11] eg: G Wagner, 'Robot Liability', in R Schulze et al. (eds), *Liability for Robotics and in the Internet of Things* (Baden-Baden/Oxford, Nomos/Hart, 2019) 30 f.

[12] eg: P Hacker et al., 'Explainable AI under Contract and Tort Law: Legal Incentives and Technical Challenges', (2020) 28 *Artificial Intelligence and Law* 415.

[13] ch 1 IV. A and C, ch 2 I-II, ch 3, I-II, ch 4, I-II, ch 5 I-II.

[14] The co-evolution of digital and social 'patterns' is theorised by A Nassehi, *Muster: Theorie der digitalen Gesellschaft* (Munich, C.H.Beck, 2019) 15 ff.

[15] W Welsch, *Vernunft: Die zeitgenössische Vernunftkritik und das Konzept der transversalen Vernunft* (Frankfurt, Suhrkamp, 1996); G Wagner, 'Transversale Vernunft und der soziologische Blick: Zur Erinnerung an Montesqieu', (1996) 25 *Zeitschrift für Soziologie* 315.

[16] Prominently, N Luhmann, *Risk: A Sociological Theory* (Berlin, de Gruyter, 1993).

[17] For a risk-oriented legal analysis of algorithmic liability, D Linardatos, *Autonome und vernetzte Aktanten im Zivilrecht: Grundlinien zivilrechtlicher Zurechnung und Strukturmerkmale einer elektronischen Person* (Tübingen, Mohr Siebeck, 2021) *passim*.

C. Institution-Generating Liability Law

In their analyses of the new socio-digital institutions, the social sciences theorise not only their history and their present state but also consider their potential future development. These incipient institutions are still indeterminate in their role in different social sectors. Assisted by the social sciences, liability law needs to 'understand' this incipient status and respond accordingly. In this regard, Wielsch introduced a helpful distinction between two roles of liability law: developing either 'institution-preserving' or 'institution-generating' rules.[18] While in the past, law-in-context approaches have focused on preserving the law's embeddedness in customs and social norms, rapid developments in the digital world draw attention to new economic and social contexts where established social norms do not yet exist. Careful consideration is required on how to deal with future risks. It then becomes the task of legislators, judges, arbiters, and private ordering rule-makers to support incipient socio-digital institutions by designing rules that are open to future IT developments and their potential social trajectories.[19]

In more detail, Wielsch develops several methodological building blocks for a 'social hermeneutics in law'.[20] The legal process will 'understand' socio-digital institutions when it re-constructs the self-reference of both digital and social systems within the self-reference of law. For our purposes, three of these building blocks are particularly relevant:

(1) '[E]nabling and stabilising new forms of social cooperation via independent legal forms that cannot be traced back to other legal forms'. Accordingly, we replace vague ideas about the social use of algorithms with an elaborate typology of socio-digital institutions with concomitant liability regimes.
(2) '[T]he recourse to a special institution-generating interpretation in cases where an institutional context for interactions has not yet been established'. Indeed, all three socio-digital institutions proposed here – digital assistance, digital hybridity and digital interconnectivity – are not yet fully developed; thus, law's sensitivity for their social normativity as well as openness for their future developments will be required.
(3) '[T]he creation of new attribution points, especially for the legal constitution' of communication processes. In our context, the new attribution points

[18] For an institutionalist approach to private law, with a view on digital developments, D Wielsch, 'Contract Interpretation Regimes', (2018) 81 *Modern Law Review* 958, 961 ff, 976 ff; D Wielsch, 'Private Law Regulation of Digital Intermediaries', (2019) 27 *European Review of Private Law* 197.

[19] D Wielsch, 'Die Ordnungen der Netzwerke. AGB – Code – Community Standards', in M Eifert and T Gostomzyk (eds), *Netzwerkrecht. Die Zukunft des NetzDG und seine Folgen für die Netzwerkkommunikation* (Baden-Baden, Nomos, 2018); K-H Ladeur (ed), *Innovationsoffene Regulierung des Internet: Neues Recht für Kommunikationsnetzwerke* (Baden-Baden, Nomos, 2003).

[20] D Wielsch, 'Die Ermächtigung von Eigen-Sinn im Recht', in I Augsberg et al. (eds), *Recht auf Nicht-Recht: Rechtliche Reaktionen auf die Juridifizierung der Gesellschaft* (Weilerswist, Velbrück, 2020) 201 (our translation).

are digital 'actants' in principal-agent relations, digital 'hybrids' where a double attribution to collective and individual actors takes place, and 'funds' as artificially attribution points for non-individualisable responsibility.

Using these methodological building blocks implies refraining from designing abstract and universal rules of liability. Instead, legal doctrine needs to develop institution-specific standards and create several liability regimes that are responsive to the technological as well as to the social properties of algorithmic behaviour. Most important in our context are the three socio-digital institutions, to whose different risks liability law needs to respond: (1) 'digital assistance' which creates the hitherto unknown risk of a task delegation from humans to autonomous algorithms; (2) 'digital hybridity', which creates risks of a hitherto unknown dense cooperation between humans and algorithms; and (3) 'digital interconnectivity', which creates the hitherto unknown risk of humans' exposure to opaque algorithms' interactions. While each of these institutions has been analysed in the preceding chapters, here we describe how they differ from each other and how the social sciences will deepen our understanding of these differences:

'*Digital Assistance*': Individual machine behaviour, as analysed in IT studies, refers to intrinsic properties of a single algorithm, whose dynamics are driven by their single source code or design in its interaction with the environment.[21] These technical properties alone cannot determine whether or not algorithms can be qualified as autonomous actors. Instead, socio-digital institutions determine whether algorithms will have the social status of mere instruments, or whether they will be agents in principal-agent relations, or whether they will become – as a potential future development – independent self-interested socio-economic actors.

As discussed in chapter three, for potential principal-agent relations, several social science theories clarify under which conditions the incipient institution of 'digital assistance' will emerge. If the delegation of tasks from a human actor to an algorithm creates two independent streams of social action, a principal-agent relation appears between them. Such principal-agent relations presuppose necessarily personhood for both the principal and the agent. Thus, a selective attribution of personhood to specific digital processes is needed. Personification of algorithms – for this complex social process, several social theories deliver the relevant analytics.

Economics are relatively silent on this topic. More or less implicitly, they presuppose two rational actors as given. In contrast to narrow rational choice assumptions, sociological theory conceives personification as a performative act that institutes the social reality of an actor. In a complementary way, Actor-Network Theory defines the interactive qualities that transform an algorithm into an 'actant' different from a human actor.[22] Information philosophy defines the

[21] Rahwan et al., 'Machine Behaviour' 481.

[22] B Latour, *Politics of Nature: How to Bring the Sciences into Democracy* (Cambridge/Mass., Harvard University Press, 2004) 62 ff.

conditions under which algorithmic actions are determined as autonomous or non-autonomous.[23] Systems theory analyses in detail, how in a situation of double contingency, the emergent communication of human principals with algorithmic agents defines the algorithm's social identity and its action capacity.[24] This does not happen everywhere; instead, each social context creates for algorithms its own criteria of personhood, the economy being no different from politics, science, moral philosophy, or law. Different social systems attribute actions, rights and obligations in various ways to algorithms as their 'persons' and equip them with specific resources, interests, intentions, goals, or preferences. And political philosophy describes in detail how in a 'representing agency' relation, the transfer of the '*potestas vicaria*' constitutes the vicarious personhood of algorithms, 'implying distinct risks and dangers haunting modernity'.[25]

As a crucial result of social personification, technological risks are transformed into social risks. Causal risks stemming from the movement of objects are now conceived as action risks arising from the disappointment of Ego's expectations about Alter's actions. Thus, in 'digital assistance' situations, a principal-agent relation with its typical communicative risks will appear instead of an instrumental subject-object relation. Once this socio-digital institution comes into existence, the law will be required to decide according to its own criteria what degrees of legal personhood it attributes to the digital actants. Liability rules coping with action risks of digital actants differ substantially from rules reacting to causal risks of mere objects. As a consequence, strict liability rules for industrial hazards are inadequate. Instead, in the principal-agent relation of digital assistance, rules of vicarious liability for the actant's decisions are needed.

'Digital Hybridity': Quite different are the social sciences' contributions for hybrid human-machine behaviour, which is the outcome of closely intertwined interactions between algorithms and humans. If one attempted to use the individualistic approach of principal-agent relations and to separate single human and algorithmic actions, one would fail to notice that collective actors have been established. They develop properties whose risks differ qualitatively from the risks of individual action within digital assistance. While digital assistance has to cope with the risks of algorithmic autonomy, digital hybridity has to deal with the transformation of single human-algorithm interactions into collective actorship. As we discussed in chapter four, the social sciences play their intermediary role between IT studies and legal doctrine differently when they show how social practices constitute human-machine associations.

[23] L Floridi and JW Sanders, 'On the Morality of Artificial Agents', in M Anderson and SL Anderson (eds), *Machine Ethics* (Cambridge, Cambridge University Press, 2011) 192 ff.

[24] E Esposito, 'Artificial Communication? The Production of Contingency by Algorithms', (2017) 46 *Zeitschrift für Soziologie* 249

[25] K Trüstedt, 'Representing Agency', (2020) 32 *Law & Literature* 195, 196 f; K Trüstedt, *Stellvertretung: Zur Szene der Person* (Konstanz, Konstanz University Press, 2021 forthcoming).

Due to their adherence to methodological individualism, economic analyses are sceptical towards the reality status of collective actors. They conceive them as mere 'nexus of contracts', and they judge their personification as an abbreviation at best and as dangerous 'errors', 'traps' or 'fictions' at worst.[26] In contrast, sociology focuses closely on the differences in human-algorithm interactions.[27] They range from short-term, loose contacts to fully-fledged human-algorithm 'organisations' with an internal division of labour and distribution of competencies. Each of these hybrids creates its own risks. In loose contacts, the acts of humans and algorithms can be easily identified and can be qualified as principal-agent relations discussed above as our first socio-digital institution. Most conspicuous, however, are constellations of dense interaction, in which responsibility for actions can only be established for the whole hybrid entity, while it cannot be established for the individual algorithm or human involved.[28] Law then would have to react to the risks stemming from collective actorship. For these risks, vicarious liability is of no help. Instead, the law needs to develop collective liability rules, which, however, are below the threshold of liability of a fully-fledged legal person.

'Digital Interconnectivity': In contrast to the other two constellations, collective machine behaviour refers to the systemwide behaviour resulting from the interconnectivity of machine agents. As discussed in chapter five, looking at individual machine behaviour in principal-agent relations makes little sense when higher-order interconnectivity structures are responsible for the emerging risks. It is their specific risk that no single principal and no single agent can be identified. Neither are the risks of algorithmic interconnectivity identical with the risks of human-machine associations. What we encounter here are heterarchical interconnected processes between algorithms and not communication between humans and algorithms. Those interconnected processes are interdependent and spontaneous and can be qualified as what observers understand as a restless collective composed of distributive cognition.[29] Such a 'collectivity without collective' cannot be described as a deliberately designed network but simply as a crowd of algorithms. If it comes to how society relates to such algorithmic crowds, social theory informs us that we would qualify them as 'invisible machines'.[30] Their impact on society is difficult to describe. There is neither direct communication between an isolated algorithm and humans nor a collectivity combining humans and algorithms. Instead, an interconnected crowd of algorithms exerts an – only indirect but massive – influence

[26] M Jensen and WH Meckling, 'Theory of the Firm: Managerial Behavior, Agency Costs and Ownership Structure', (1976) 3 *Journal of Financial Economics* 306; FH Easterbrook and D Fischel, 'The Corporate Contract', (1989) 89 *Columbia Law Review* 1416, 1426.

[27] eg: Nassehi, *Muster* 224; A Hepp, *Deep Mediatization: Key Ideas in Media & Cultural Studies* (London, Routledge, 2020).

[28] eg: P Pettit, 'Responsibility Incorporated', (2007) 117 *Ethics* 171.

[29] ch 5, I.B.

[30] N Luhmann *Theory of Society 1/2* (Stanford, Stanford University Press, 2012/2013) 66; M Hildebrandt, *Smart Technologies and the End(s) of Law* (Cheltenham, Edward Elgar, 2015) 40.

on social relations. Interconnectivity between different algorithms influences social systems so that not one-to-one connections are at work, but a more diffuse structural coupling between algorithmic interconnectivity and human communication. As a result, this situation excludes legal liability for one among the various algorithms. Fund solutions are needed that require 'political' decisions of regulatory agencies to define the responsible industry sector.

D. Differential Treatment of Liable Actors

These variations of socio-digital institutions have consequences for the critical question: which human actors and which organisations will, in the end, be financially liable for wrongful algorithmic decisions? Again, we suggest a differential treatment according to institutional context and its typical risks. In a nutshell, for autonomous actions of isolated digital actants, vicarious liability falls exclusively on the user. For the activities of digital hybrids, enterprise liability applies. This results in the network of the actors involved being liable, ie producers, programmers, dealers, and users. For failures of interconnectivity, compensation funds need to be financed by the whole industry concerned. Negative consequences in cases of large-scale damages need to be borne by those actors with a strong problem-solving capacity and their needs to be recovery action available to limit or even undo interconnectivity.

This differential treatment of liable actors navigates again between overgeneralising and undergeneralising solutions. Many authors prefer to set up universal criteria for selecting the responsible actors and do not distinguish between special configurations. Managerial control and financial benefits – with these criteria, they want to establish joint liability of the main actors involved, ie producers, programmers, dealers and users.[31] Other scholars target the producer as the dominant player, cheapest cost avoider, and most efficient coordinator.[32] Both proposals end up in an overgeneralised digital liability, which is supposed to apply to all kinds of algorithmic externalities. However, paradoxically, using the same criteria, a third group of scholars ends up with undergeneralisation within a particularistic casuistry.[33] On a case-by-case basis, they attempt to identify the concrete actor with maximum control and benefit. Indeed, control and benefit are plausible criteria, but they need to be combined with the normative requirement to respond specifically to the typical risks of socio-digital institutions. While control refers to managerial capacities and benefit to economic incentives and rewards, institution refers to the inherent normative principles governing the social use of algorithms.

[31] eg: P Sanz Bayón, 'A Legal Framework for Robo-Advisors', in E Schweighofer et al. (eds), *Datenschutz / LegalTech* (Bern, Weblaw, 2019) section 7.
[32] eg: Zech, 'Liability for AI' 154.
[33] eg: Bertolini, *Artificial Intelligence* 102.

As a consequence, the institutional argument leads to the following differential treatment of liable actors.

'Digital assistance', as an institution in its own right, is governed by special responsibilities within the bilateral relation between algorithm and user/operator. As shown in chapter three, a principal-agent relation requires that the agent realises the principal's intentions and that the principal stands in for the algorithmic agents' actions. Out of a variety of potentially liable actors – programmers, producers, dealers, operators – the rules of vicarious liability target exclusively the actor who has delegated a task and has thus set the risks of the algorithm's autonomous decisions. For the particular risks of delegation, it is therefore only the *user/operator* who is responsible when things go wrong.

Some authors argue that the risks are shifted unfairly toward the user/operator; they wish to make other actors simultaneously liable, particularly the producer, including the backend operator.[34] However, they ignore the particular dangers of task delegation and violate principles of fair risk distribution between producers and users. Specific risks need to be precisely circumscribed and apportioned exclusively to those actors who actually took them. Vicarious liability reacts to the risk of a division of labour between user and algorithm. In contrast, product liability responds to the risk of producing the algorithm and product monitoring and the programmer's liability to the risk of defining the parameters. It is true, programmers/producers have set the risk of algorithmic unpredictability, and, of course, they remain liable under the condition that they have violated their specific duties under tort law or product liability. In particular, they are under the strict obligation of informing users about the autonomy risk which they have produced:

> The developer must disclose all risks, potential deficiencies, including the degree of the explainability of the AI system's decision making, and all 'built-in values or criteria' that the AI system uses in taking decisions (eg when facing the options of hitting children pedestrians crossing the road or another car with adult passengers). The developer should also disclose, to the extent possible, the factors that may make the AI system's behaviour unpredictable.[35]

But here, their responsibility ends. Against those voices who want to extend vicarious liability to producers or programmers, we maintain the position that the additional risk of setting an autonomous algorithm in action under concrete

[34] eg: Sanz Bayón, 'Robo-Advisors' section 7; For the consideration of backend operators as producers European Parliament, Civil Liability Regime for Artificial Intelligence, Resolution of 20 October 2020, 2020/2012(INL), para 8.

[35] M Bashayreh et al., 'Artificial Intelligence and Legal Liability: Towards an International Approach of Proportional Liability Based on Risk Sharing', (2021) 30 *Information & Communications Technology Law* 169, 181. *Cf* for a proposal of information duties to users for at least high-risk information systems, European Commission, Proposal for a Regulation of the European Parliament and the Council Laying Down Harmonised Rules on Artificial Intelligence (Proposal Artificial Intelligence Act) and Amending Certain Union Legislative Acts, COM(2021) 206, Art 13.

circumstances is solely the user's responsibility.[36] The user makes the crucial decision of whether or not he will delegate a specific task to an autonomous algorithm, and he decides under which concrete circumstances the algorithm is used. And he gains the benefits of the delegation, which are different from the benefits of producer/programmer under their contractual regimes. In economic parlance, when the algorithm's user is the cost-bearer, he has the optimum incentive to weigh up the benefits and costs of greater machine safety in a minimising manner.[37] This justifies applying the strict rules of vicarious liability and targeting the user/operator exclusively. *Potestas vicaria*, in its circumscribed potential, is the very reason why programmers, producers, dealers and owners, including so-called back-end controllers, cannot conceivably be declared as principals on whose behalf the algorithm is acting as an auxiliary. This is obvious in contract law. But also in tort law, the algorithm is qualified as auxiliary exclusively for the user/operator. Not the mechanics of digital technology but the hermeneutics of 'digital assistance' as the new socio-digital institution determines the scope of vicarious liability and excludes the extension to other actors than the user/operator. This argument is even stronger when it comes to professional users. They are able to make an informed risk assessment and influence the risk via permanently updating hardware and software.[38] As for corporate actors who are using algorithms,

> responsibility for algorithmic failure should ... lie with the entity using it, ie the corporation itself, and not with any third party vendors or an AI platform. This is obvious if the AI is a proprietary model developed by the corporation. But even with external input, it is ultimately the corporation itself that is responsible for its own data governance. The corporation decides on the design/specification of algorithms, their deployment, their interaction etc, and it benefits from them.[39]

This exclusive liability of the user/operator applies in particular to investors in the financial market whenever they take the adventurous risk of delegating their portfolio management to non-predictable algorithms.[40] Of course, all this does not exclude that the user/operator takes recourse to producers or programmers provided that they violated the rules of product or tort liability.

As opposed to this exclusive liability of users/operators, in the case of '*digital hybridity*', another socio-digital institution in its own right, the wrongful action

[36] See: Lohsse et al., 'Liability for Artificial Intelligence' 20; C Armbrüster, 'Verantwortungsverlagerungen und Versicherungsschutz: Das Beispiel des automatisierten Fahrens', in S Gless and K Seelmann (eds), *Intelligente Agenten und das Recht* (Baden-Baden, Nomos, 2016) 217 ff.

[37] See: P Hacker, 'Verhaltens- und Wissenszurechnung beim Einsatz von Künstlicher Intelligenz', (2018) 9 *Rechtswissenschaft* 243, 255.

[38] See: H Zech, 'Entscheidungen digitaler autonomer Systeme: Empfehlen sich Regelungen zu Verantwortung und Haftung?', (2020) I/A *73. Deutscher Juristentag* 11, 64.

[39] J Armour and H Eidenmüller, 'Self-Driving Corporations?', (2019) 475/2020 *ECGI-Law Working Paper* 1, 31. Their argument can be generalised for any vicarious liability for algorithmic failure.

[40] A graphic illustration is offered by the case *Li Kin-kan* v *Costa* pending before a London court, which will be discussed in IV.A below.

is attributed to the emerging human-algorithm association and liability is channelled to a multitude of actors, who are 'behind' the digital hybrid. As discussed in chapter four, a whole network of different actors is involved in initiating a dense human-algorithm interaction and profiting from its results. Since control is dispersed among the network nodes, responsibility follows this specific risk structure. For human-machine associations, a fully developed corporate liability of the association as such cannot be established, at least for the time being. Instead, the principles of enterprise liability are well suited to shape the responsibility of digital hybrids.[41] Enterprise liability works in two steps. In the first step, the wrongful action is attributed to the hybrid as a collective, without disentangling the contributions of humans and algorithms. In the second step, liability for the collective action is channelled to all the network nodes. These nodes have set up the hybrid and benefit from its activities. The hybrid is the source of their benefits. As a result, *all the nodes of the network* are liable according to benefit and control. If a hub enterprise contractually coordinates the network, primary liability should fall on this hub, usually the producer, who can take recourse on the network nodes.

'*Digital interconnectivity*' is again different. Responsibility shifts, as discussed in chapter five, toward the broader social collectivity. While in digital assistance, the human principal and the algorithmic agent are identifiable as individual actors, and while in digital hybrids, the network nodes and the hybrid are the relevant actors, in this third constellation, the liability situation is different. The 'invisible machine' excludes identifying any actor. Here, human communication depends on opaque algorithmic interconnectivity in only indirect 'structural coupling' so that no one-to-one responsibility relation can be established. Neither beneficiary nor contributor of the gain is identifiable. Setting up liability funds financed by the *industry sector* involved is the adequate solution.[42] The contributions of the relevant actors should be calculated according to their market share and their specific problem-solving capacity. The rules need to be oriented not only to compensation and precaution but also the broader social implications of interconnectivity damages. Recovery action as an additional principle of liability laws is required.

E. Calibrating Legal Personhood for AI

The specific risks of the new socio-digital institutions – autonomy, hybridity, interconnectivity – require treating the ascriptions of the algorithms' legal status differentially. A full legal personification of software agents, human-computer associations or multi-agent systems is excluded. Instead, in response to each of

[41] Similarly, DC Vladeck, 'Machines without Principals: Liability Rules and Artificial Intelligence', (2014) 89 *Washington Law Review* 117, 149; JS Allain, 'From Jeopardy! to Jaundice: The Medical Liability Implications of Dr. Watson and Other Artificial Intelligence Systems', (2013) 73 *Louisiana Law Review* 1049, 1074.

[42] See: OJ Erdélyi and G Erdélyi, 'The AI Liability Puzzle and a Fund-Based Work-Around', (2020) *AIES '20: Proceedings of the AAAI/ACM Conference on AI, Ethics, and Society* 50.

the three risks, we suggest carefully calibrating the legal status of algorithms to the substantial role they play within their socio-digital institution.

For the autonomy risk of digital assistance (chapter three), the correct answer is to grant software agents the status of limited legal personhood. For their principals, the algorithms' decisions are legally binding and give rise to liability consequences. The algorithms' limited legal subjectivity enables them to conclude binding contracts for others as a proxy. For contractual and tortious liability, they are recognised as vicarious agents so that the agent's misconduct itself (and not merely the conduct of the principals behind it) constitutes a breach of duty for which the principals must be held responsible.

The appropriate response to the association risk of digital hybridity (chapter four) is to give software agents the legal status as a member of a human-machine association. A maximum solution *de lege ferenda* would attribute actions, rights, and obligations as well as financial liability to the hybrid association itself – a solution that would break entirely new ground in private law. A minimal solution *de lege lata* is to introduce the legal concept of 'association purpose', which guides the interpretation of computer declarations and the determination of the participants' rights and obligations. A middle-ground solution, which we favour, uses an analogy to the established principles of enterprise liability. It treats the hybrid as an enterprise and channels liability toward the actors behind it. Here, the algorithm acquires the legal status of a member within the human-algorithm association.

Finally, the answer to the interconnectivity risks (chapter five) is a 'risk pool'. Liability law has to define its limits authoritatively. The unlawful behaviour of the pool itself would be the basis of liability. The algorithms' legal status would neither be personhood nor membership in a hybrid, but just a part of a digital problem area. The boundaries of this area would determine those actors who should finance the fund.

Algorithms thus acquire a differential legal status: either they become actors with limited legal subjectivity, or they are members of a human-machine association, or they serve as reference units for risk pools. We have attempted to define their status mainly with the question in mind of how to overcome the responsibility gaps of digitality and how to respond best to the status of algorithms within an evolving socio-digital institution. Finally, any definition of the algorithms' status must develop further the doctrines of contract and liability law and strive for conceptual and normative consistency. Doctrine's consistency is needed in the digital space as well, not as an end in itself, but as law's primary obligation to treat equal what is equal and to treat unequal what is unequal.

III. Interactions between Three Liability Regimes

A. Criteria for Delineating the Applicable Liability Regime

We are well aware that there are certain difficulties in delineating the three liability regimes' scope of application with sufficient precision. Which regime will govern when there are grey areas between them, when they appear overlapping, or when it is difficult to decide whether the rules of the one or the other regime apply? Such problems, we submit, are lawyers' bread and butter business, well-known from the offline world. Criteria related to action attribution will guide their solution.

To distinguish between digital assistance and digital hybridity, the relation between the human and the algorithm needs to be analysed closely. A first rather sharp criterion is whether or not the wrongful act can be attributed with certainty to one individualised decision. A second criterion is the density of the cooperation between the human and the algorithm. This can be concretised by asking whether the human-algorithm interaction occurs under the umbrella of a cooperative endeavour. A third criterion is whether there is an equality of cooperation or an asymmetry of unilateral instruction. For example, when humans and algorithms cooperate in digital journalism, distinguishing between vicarious liability and enterprise liability would require answering the following questions: Can the damage-causing action be attributed to the algorithmic operation or the human behaviour? In what context was the algorithm used, ie as an assisting tool for human investigative journalism or as a participant in the journalistic choices? And what was the relationship between human and algorithm in terms of human oversight? Admittedly, due to the graduality involved, there remains a grey area. As always with graduality, it needs a binary decision at one point on the sliding scale. But all these criteria are equally required in the offline world when the law draws the fine line between a principal-agent relation and a partnership.

When distinguishing between digital assistance and interconnectivity, different questions arise. Here, it is not so much the relation between humans and algorithms that is at stake but the identification of the wrongful act within a whole series of algorithmic operations. Does vicarious liability apply when an algorithm connected to an algorithmic network commits a wrongful act, or is this a case of interconnectivity? If the unlawful act can be clearly attributed to the algorithm to whom the task has been delegated, vicarious liability applies. If not, then only fund solutions will resolve the liability issue. If no fund regime is in force, then, regrettably, there is no compensation for the victims. Since fund regimes do not exist frequently, the search for identifiable algorithmic failures will become even more urgent.

On some occasions, social and legal attribution of action will tend to ignore existing technological interconnectivity. Attribution creates the fiction that one single algorithmic unit has committed the wrongful act, overrules the principle of collective liability, and makes vicarious liability applicable. The law of robots may serve as an illustration. Although some robots do not act in digital isolation but remain connected to an algorithmic network, the law treats them as single agents, and vicarious liability applies. In this case, the dangers of interconnective action cannot be externalised to third parties; they will remain with the user as the party to the contract.[43] When a hospital uses a multi-agent system for cancer

[43] See: Linardatos, *Aktanten* 262 f.

diagnosis and no funds are existing, interconnectivity rules cannot be used as a means to socialise the risk. Thus, legal liability rules will have to account for this difference between technological interconnectivity (excluding identification of one digital agent) on the one hand and social practices (working with the fiction of an isolated actor) on the other. Here, the strong influence of socio-digital institutions becomes visible. Social and legal attribution interrupt technological interdependencies and overrule the principles of interconnectivity. The socio-digital institution of digital assistance and the principles of agency law dictate to attribute manifold interconnections as individual action to the algorithm, and liability rules follow suit.

Finally, distinguishing between digital hybridity and interconnectivity requires a different perspective again. Here, both the human-algorithm relation and the wrongful algorithmic act need to be scrutinised. The guiding criterion is the role of humans in the unlawful behaviour. To the extent that humans participate in the broader algorithmic networks and shape the interdependent machine operations, it is more likely a case of digital hybridity. In contrast, a focus on autonomous and interdependent algorithmic operations suggests a case of interconnectivity. In addition, one needs to consider whether identifying an action is possible. If it is possible to delineate the damage-causing event in the interdependent operations between humans and machines, one may consider this a case of digital hybridity, whereas the lack to do so would instead suggest a constellation of interconnectivity.

B. No Priority for a Liability Regime

We do not agree with those authors who give priority to one liability regime over another, such as those arguing for a general priority for fund solutions when handling algorithmic externalities. Pointing to the non-predictability of computer behaviour, some authors propose insurance and fund solutions whenever autonomous algorithms are involved.[44] Alternatively, those who recommend a full personification of algorithms as e-persons face the problem of how to realise their financial capacity to pay for damages. Thus, they are under pressure to introduce mandatory insurance or compensation funds.[45] Finally, all those who want to apply strict liability for industrial hazards in all cases of algorithmic failures tend to recommend simultaneously mandatory insurance or fund solutions.[46]

All these authors show a more than generous attitude toward compulsory collective liability without good reasons. They ignore well-known negative side-effects of collective solutions. Mandatory collective liability regimes offer no

[44] eg: Erdélyi and Erdélyi, 'AI Liability Puzzle'.

[45] eg: Allain, 'From Jeopardy! to Jaundice' 1078 f.

[46] eg: European Commission, 'Report on the Safety and Liability Implications of Artificial Intelligence, The Internet of Things and Robotics', COM(2020) 64 final, 16.

incentives for damage-avoiding precautions. And, in contrast to fundamental principles of law and justice, they make individual actors liable for actions that other actors have committed. To combat these negative side-effects, particularly legal economists recommend preferring individual over collective liability. With good reason, they point to a set of abilities, which individual liability rules activate: the ability of an actor to prevent harm, to lower transaction costs, to insure against damages, and to reduce administrative costs.[47] Therefore, precisely calibrated rules of individual liability are to be preferred whenever the damaging action, the responsible actor and the causal nexus can be identified. In our threefold typology, this is indeed the case for vicarious liability as well as for enterprise liability, while only for interconnectivity such identification is impossible. When algorithms make autonomous decisions and vicarious liability steps in, there is no need for an additional compulsory insurance/fund solution. These are the reasons why we suggest using fund solutions only selectively in limited constellations.

Vicarious liability has the advantage of creating incentives for the user for diligent use of the computer as well as for voluntary insurance. And it locates responsibility precisely at the point where the decision is made to use the machine. We should hasten to make sure again, this does not mean that the user violates his duties when using the machine. He is entitled to do so. Only when the algorithm makes wrongful decisions, then the user becomes liable as a principal. Similarly satisfactory is the situation of hybridity when enterprise liability applies to a human-machine association. Here again, compulsory insurance/fund-solutions are not needed; it is sufficient to impose joint liability on a clearly defined range of actors. Thus, only in the third situation, in exposure to interconnectivity, mandatory insurance or fund solutions make sense when no responsible actor can be identified. Here they are indeed needed as compensation for the lack of personification.

Consequently, vicarious liability for isolated agents, enterprise liability for hybrid human-machine associations, and fund solutions for interconnectivity co-exist, side by side as independent legal regimes, with no priority for any of them. As Monterossi comments, each of these solutions 'could find its own slot of operability in the future, depending on the more or less equivocal contours of the entities involved and considering the heterogeneity of the mechanical devices associated with artificial autonomous agents'.[48]

In addition, we suggest an iterative procedure when applying the three liability regimes. The starting point would always be to look for the individual action

[47] See generally: S Shavell, 'Liability for Accidents', in MA Polinsky and S Shavell (eds), *Handbook of Law and Economics, vol I* (North-Holland, Elsevier, 2007) 149f.

[48] MW Monterossi, 'Liability for the Fact of Autonomous Artificial Intelligence Agents. Things, Agencies and Legal Actors', (2020) 6 *Global Jurist* 1, 11; similarly, I Spiecker, 'Zur Zukunft systemischer Digitalisierung: Erste Gedanken zur Haftungs- und Verantwortungszuschreibung bei informationstechnischen Systemen – Warum für die systemische Haftung ein neues Modell erforderlich ist', [2016] *Computer und Recht* 698, 703.

attribution of vicarious liability. When a human actor/organisation has delegated a task to an algorithm and the algorithm has violated a contractual/tortious duty, vicarious liability falls on the principal. Once these conditions are not fulfilled, in a second step, enterprise liability comes in. It is applicable when human actions and algorithmic calculations intertwine so densely that it is impossible to clearly identify an individual algorithm's wrongful act. Then the action is attributed to the hybrid association, and liability is channelled to the network of actors involved in setting up the human-machine association. Finally, when the interconnection of several algorithms has caused damage so that neither an isolated algorithm nor a hybrid can be identified, then, in a third step, the fund solution comes in.

Each liability regime is oriented toward a specific uncontrollable and opaque constellation: either the autonomy of an algorithmic decision, or the peculiarities of communication between human actors and digital agents, or the contingencies of algorithmic interconnectivity. Thus, a relation of subsidiarity exists between the liability regimes. Only when vicarious liability fails, hybrid liability comes in, and when both fail, collective funds are the solution of last resort.

This also means that the three liability regimes may be applied side-by-side in a particular sector. There is no sector-specificity of a particular regime. In financial markets, as we discuss later, there is a possibility of relying on algorithms for digital assistance through so-called robo-advisers. Still, there is also an exposure to interconnectivity when algorithms are interacting and produce flash crashes. In a similar vein, in corporate governance, different types of discussions on the use of artificial intelligence are ongoing. These discussions range from the use of algorithms in assisting the board in taking management decisions as digital assistants to the few cases of an appointment of algorithms as board members that we have qualified in chapter four as a case of hybrid decision-making. Fully autonomous corporate organisations that operate on technical infrastructure, most famously in the case of the DAO, could be qualified as interconnectivity, for which a fund solution is needed.

Finally, we conclude with a somewhat futuristic perspective. A likely trend towards ever-more interconnected systems is discernible. While at this stage, the real and most pressing liability gaps are related to the human-machine interaction, both in digital assistance and hybridity, the future may entail more significant risks of interconnectivity. Thus, the interconnectivity regime may gain broader prominence in the future. Risk pools will become the starting point, and the iterative analysis will 'work backwards' to individual contributions. Therefore, even for the interconnectivity constellation, it will be necessary to identify, as much as possible, individual actions within interconnected machines. Whenever an algorithm's decision is identifiable, that contribution needs to be subjected to liability. This may be necessary even when a fund is available.[49]

[49] This will be shown later in the exemplary case of flash crashes in algorithmic trading, see IV.C below.

IV. Exemplary Cases

We are well aware that our analysis so far has remained abstract and only occasionally provided examples to support our argument. Yet, it is ultimately the cases that make the law, and any new legal rules need to be tested in their practical application to cases. This is why we want to end this book with cases, real and fictitious ones, for each of the liability regimes and their interrelations.

A. Vicarious Liability: Robo-Advice

Samathur Li Ki-kan, a Hong Kong tycoon, is suing Raffaela Costa, an investment broker, for a loss of US$23 million due to wrongful algorithmic operations of a Robo Advice Computer. The supercomputer named K1 was supposed to comb through online sources to gauge 'investor sentiment' and make predictions on US stock futures. While simulations had been very promising, the computer, after starting trading, was regularly losing money. On 14 February 2018, due to a stop-loss order, Li lost over US$20 million.[50] This is the first known instance of humans going to court over investment losses triggered by autonomous machines. The case had to deal with the black box problem: If people cannot judge the algorithm's decisions, who is liable when things go wrong? Although the financial actors and the sums of money involved in this case are excessive, robo-advice is widespread today, including in small scale investment.

The individual liability of Costa for misrepresenting the algorithm's capacities for predictions of stock futures is, of course, the first issue to examine. However, if Li cannot demonstrate that Costa violated an investment broker's duties, the success of Li will depend on the question of whether the decisions of the algorithm can be the basis for liability.

According to the subsidiarity relation in our three liability regimes, a fund solution for such financial risks, which does not exist so far, could only come in when an illegal decision of an individual or collective actor cannot be identified. Clearly, here the supercomputer's stop-loss order was the algorithm's wrongful decision. Furthermore, since Costa's individual decisions on investment and K1's calculations are not wholly intertwined, enterprise liability for actions of a hybrid human-machine association does not come in. Thus, the relevant socio-digital institution is 'digital assistance', where an algorithm operates as agent in a principal-agent relationship. Unfortunately, in this context, product liability, if it

[50] For this case, eg: T Beardsworth and N Kumar, 'Going to Court Over Losses When Robot Is to Blame', [2019] *Insurance Journal* www.insurancejournal.com/news/national/2019/05/07/525762.htm. For liability in general, G Wagner and L Luyken, 'Haftung für Robo Advice', in G Bachmann et al. (eds), *Festschrift für Christine Windbichler* (Berlin, de Gruyter, 2020); B Hughes and R Williamson, 'When AI Systems Cause Harm: The Application of Civil and Criminal Liability', (2019) *Digital Business Law – Blog* 08 November 2019; Sanz Bayón, 'Robo-Advisors'.

is applicable for this kind of algorithmic decision at all, is of no help since Costa did not violate any duty of a producer. As a way out, many authors have therefore proposed strict liability *de lege ferenda*. However, strict liability would go much too far. It would 'open the floodgates' in financial liability. As a pure causation liability, it would make the principal liable for any action, legal or illegal, of the algorithmic agent which causes financial loss. Thus, only vicarious liability remains as a potential cause of action.[51] If Costa, the principal, had made a financial broker agreement with Li and delegated his contractual duties of portfolio management to K1 as his agent, he would be liable for any violations of contractual obligations that K1, the vicarious agent, had committed. However, according to current law, the algorithm has no legal capacity to act, which is necessary for a vicarious agent. The courts can attribute legal subjectivity to autonomous algorithms, as they had done in the past with associations of human actors. For vicarious liability, it is sufficient to endow them with partial legal capacity, namely the capacity to fulfil a principal's contractual duties. Still, vicarious liability requires intention or negligence of the agent's actions. However, the well-known objectivisation tendencies in private law alleviate this requirement. Altogether vicarious liability will be successful as a cause of action for Costa's liability.

B. Enterprise Liability: Hybrid Journalism

For constellations of hybrids, there are various examples in which algorithms and humans interact so densely that they form a self-standing human-machine association. The use of medical robots is a good case in point in which an unclear division of labour exists between algorithmic and human action. This is true particularly for sensor-driven robots that respond to and reinforce human impulses, but also occurs in human-algorithmic diagnosis decisions in the medical sector. The use of translation software is another example when algorithms are translating documents that are then reworked and revised by humans to an end product. Similarly, AI-powered research algorithms are introduced in professional contexts, eg Westlaw Edge used by lawyers. Such cases would qualify as an instance of hybrid liability once the human-algorithmic cooperation becomes so dense that it is impossible to distinguish between humans and algorithmic components.[52]

[51] In the US, breach of a fiduciary duty is the relevant cause of action on the basis of the Investment Advisers Act 1940. It is highly controversial whether an autonomous algorithm can be qualified as a registered investment adviser who satisfies the fiduciary standard elements laid out in the Act. At the end, the legal issue will be the same as under vicarious liability: Has the algorithm breached a contractual duty of a reasonable investment adviser. For details see BE Strzelczyk, 'Rise of the Machines: The Legal Implications for Investor Protection with the Rise of Robo-Advisors', (2018) 16 *DePaul Business & Commercial Law Journal* 54.

[52] See, for instance, Westlaw Edge: This service offers the possibility to upload litigation briefs into the system, which is then completed by the algorithm in the form of citing additional authorities and checked as to the overruling of referenced case law, see https://legal.thomsonreuters.com/en/products/westlaw.

If damage occurs – a libel, bad legal advice – it is often impossible to determine where precisely the wrongful act has occurred.

Panama papers: Investigative journalism frequently makes use of algorithms. In a complex investigation, an international consortium of journalists has been working collaboratively with technological help to identify the illegal tax practices of companies and individuals. The difficulty of the investigative work was the vast number of documents that needed to be analysed. Algorithms undertook the work of tagging, categorising, and selecting the relevant texts. The humans then reviewed their work.[53] In addition, the later publication of the work in the news and its distribution as news becomes influenced as well by algorithms on prioritising and filtering decisions.[54] *Panama papers* demonstrate how well algorithms and journalists can work together to reveal a scandal that otherwise would have never become public. Yet, such a practice has vast damage potential. What if such an investigation was blaming and shaming a person or a company that had not been involved? If an algorithmic error had occurred, digital assistance applies. However, what if an algorithmic mistake is not clearly delineable, but the cooperation between human investigation and algorithmic calculation led to the wrongful accusation? To make things more complicated, given the algorithms involved in news distribution, such false accusations could easily be spread and become a major topic of the news.[55]

Yet, liability for such false accusations by a collaborative human-machine interaction is difficult to establish. If the algorithm conducted the analysis precisely as programmed and the human journalists fulfilled their duties to check but had not been aware of the false statement, nobody will be liable.[56] The problem is a lack of knowledge. In such a case of 'collective moral responsibility', a group commits a wrongful act while the individuals involved have behaved correctly.[57] The algorithm worked as programmed and took decisions on labelling, classifying, selecting and preparing information for use by humans as intended, and the human journalists were reviewing that information with the required standard of care based on their knowledge. It is difficult to identify an individual wrongful act, although the collective endeavour between algorithms and journalists has produced illegal accusations. For these cases, network responsibility in the form of enterprise liability is appropriate. The human-machine association can be identified as the collective of journalists and algorithms. The cooperative character of the project, together with the difficulty of identifying an individual algorithmic

[53] See: N Diakopoulos, *Automating the News: How Algorithms are Rewriting the Media* (Cambridge/Mass., Harvard University Press, 2019) 13 ff.

[54] ibid 21.

[55] For an example, the US case against Facebook's 'rending topic algorithm', SC Lewis et al., 'Libel by Algorithm? Automated Journalism and the Threat of Legal Liability', (2019) 98 *Journalism & Mass Communication Quarterly* 60, 61.

[56] ibid 69. With a view to German law, J Oster, 'Haftung für Persönlichkeitsverletzungen durch Künstliche Intelligenz', [2018] *UFITA – Archiv für Medienrecht und Medienwissenschaft* 14, 29 ff.

[57] D Copp, 'The Collective Moral Autonomy Thesis', (2007) 38 *Journal of Social Philosophy* 369.

or human error, suggests on the one side that vicarious liability does not apply. On the other side, this cannot be qualified as a case of interconnectivity since a collective wrongful act in the form of false accusation through a newswork can be identified, and humans are involved.

For hybrid liability, there remains one problem in identifying the hybrid's wrongful act: attribution of knowledge to the hybrid. In order to qualify as a wrong assertion of facts, it is necessary that the tortfeasor knew the facts. This is of course difficult to construct for human-algorithmic networks, which is essentially a black box and, to complicate this problem, a two-fold black box, one the algorithm, the other the hybrid. If it is impossible to understand how exactly decisions were taken in the collective, how then can we prove knowledge about the wrong assertion of facts? When does a social system, in our case a human-digital hybrid, 'know'? When does a hybrid violate a duty of correct factual information? A promising criterion is: 'activate/passive information' or 'explicit/implicit knowledge'.[58] One needs to distinguish between passive information, somewhere lurking in the corners of the digital world and the active knowledge which is internally processed and used for internal communication. Passive information would not lead to liability. But whenever information is activated and transformed into explicit knowledge, regardless of its use by humans or by algorithms, then the wrongful act can be attributed to the hybrid.

Once the wrongful act is attributed to the human-machine hybrid, enterprise liability will hold the network liable. The victim can sue the central node of the network. In the case of hybrid journalism, this can be either the controlling news organisation of the hybrid or the manufacturer of the algorithm. In the context of the algorithmic news distribution, it could fall on the manufacturing company of the distributing algorithm, ie a news or social media company. Such liability would apply regardless of whether there are specific statutory strict liability rules for news providers and the decision of whether to apply them to platforms. Within the network, the internal pro rata distribution of liability would take place according to the economic benefit in the collaborative network and its control.

C. Collective Funds: Flash Crash

Algorithmic high frequency trading is the most prominent case of interconnectivity damages. Famous among them is the flash crash on the US market in 2010.[59] In the aftermath, the US Department of Justice charged one single trader, Navinder Saro, as the person responsible for the crash. Saro was accused of

[58] See: Hacker, 'Künstliche Intelligenz' 271 ff.

[59] US Commodity Futures Trading Commission and US Securities & Exchange Commission, Findings Regarding the Market Events of 6 May 2010, available at: www.sec.gov/news/studies/2010/marketevents-report.pdf.

so-called spoofing. His algorithm was supposed to have placed false orders on the market to trigger other trading algorithms to follow path, just to change his own strategy in the opposite direction. Investigations established that this spoofing had been a lateral cause of the algorithmic trading behaviour that ultimately had led to the crash. Yet, it was not possible to identify clearly where exactly within the algorithmic operations the wrongful action had taken place that led to the disastrous consequence. In other words, the individual fraudulent behaviour could be identified, but why this behaviour had caused a widespread crash could not be fully clarified. The algorithms had acted according to their programs and thus had faithfully executed the transactions; but it seemed that the immense size of the damage was correlated to the mere fact that the other high-frequency traders had used similar programs and algorithms.[60] This suggests that the risk of herd behaviour had materialised whereby individually pre-programmed decisions in their interdependency had been mutually reinforcing with catastrophic consequences. This is a classical case of machine interconnectivity.

Sentencing a single fraudulent trader for the crash of the entire stock market was received with scepticism.[61] While one may argue that the trader was responsible for fraudulently causing the algorithms to act in a particular manner, intuition seems to have it that one cannot extend such fraudulent action to cover the crash of an entire stock market. This was neither predictable nor foreseeable for the individual. The most plausible explanation is that the interconnected algorithmic operations had all acted in a similar manner. The conviction of a single trader for this collective behaviour cannot be anything but a helpless act in the face of viewing interconnected algorithms going astray.

In our terms, a flash crash caused by algorithmic trading would be a case of the interconnectivity risk. The hazardous operations of the crowd of algorithms might have been triggered from the outside, by a single human trader engaging in fraudulent behaviour, or from the inside, the infrastructure of the financial market itself. Yet, the direct cause of the crash is attributable to the series of interdependent algorithmic operations that engaged in spontaneous collective action. Similar trading patterns had been realised at a speed that widely outperforms any human capacities. Any human intervention had been impossible. Foreseeability and individual culpability, as would be required for negligence, becomes an empty concept in such a context.

For these cases we suggest a subsidiary fund solution instead of an obsessive search for a responsible individual trader. The fund will be established under the regulatory oversight of the financial market authorities.[62] It will be financed

[60] See: Y Yadav, 'The Failure of Liability in Modern Markets', (2016) 102 *Virginia Law Review* 1031, 1080.

[61] eg: M-C Gruber, 'On Flash Boys and Their Flashbacks: The Attribution of Legal Responsibility in Algorithmic Trading', in M Jankowska et al. (eds), *AI: Law, Philosophy & Geoinformatics* (Warsaw, Prawa Gospodarczego, 2015) 88f.

[62] For the similar suggestion of a 'market disruption fund' for algorithmic trading, Yadav, 'The Failure of Liability in Modern Markets', 1095.

through a small-market entry fee paid by users and manufacturers of algorithmic trading devices according to market share considerations. Rules on the accessibility will determine the threshold for accessing market capital. Here our criterion of a breach of the law comes into play. Not every flash crash should open access to the fund capital. Damage caused by the volatility of financial markets is not per se a damage for which liability rules are needed. Victims' access to fund capital following a flash crash need to be limited to those cases in which a breach of the law can be identified committed by algorithms collectively acting. There needs to be signs of illegal market manipulation as an ultimate cause of the flash crash that was initiated either by human traders and perpetuated by algorithms (as was the case in the 2010 flash crash) or caused by the construction of the algorithms as such. This criterion of a breach of law allows distinguishing damages caused by the normal volatility of financial markets and crashes that are the result of a breach of financial market laws.

The financial market authority should be empowered to order actors involved in algorithmic trading to engage in recovery action. In relation to algorithmic trading, such recovery action would be a 'digital clean up'. The authority would order the involved firms to engage in systematic changes of the algorithmic trading infrastructure. For example, programming a slowing down of algorithmic decision-making could mitigate the risk of systemic contagion.[63]

D. Finale: Google Autocomplete

The case we will conclude the book with is the famous google-autocomplete case. The reason is not only that this is by now one of the most often-mentioned examples of algorithmic failure that has found its way into the courts, and it did so in many jurisdictions.[64] It is also because the google-autocomplete case remarkably reveals the relevance of the distinctions we have introduced and the concepts that we have used.

Google-autocomplete cases have been brought against Google for violation of personality rights. The auto-complete function proposed compromising search terms for names of well-known personalities. The google autocomplete-function completes a search entry with similar terms. It is based on a complex combination of the search history of the individual user, previous searches by users in general, and personal indications such as the location from which the searching user is logging in. In the cases that became known as auto-complete cases,

[63] ibid 1097 ff.

[64] For Italy, Ordinario di Milano case number 10847/2011, 24 March 2011; for the US *Guy Hingston v Google Inc*, US District Court Central District of California, case number SACV12-02202-JST, case settled 7 March 2013; for Germany BGH GRUR 2013, 751 (Scientology). There are also reports about cases having taken place in Japan (2013, decided in favour of plaintiffs), France (2012, settled), Australia (2012, decided in favour of plaintiffs), Belgium (decided in favour of Google).

google searches combined, for instance the name of a company and its founder with the cult organisation scientology and, very prominently in Germany, the name of the wife of the at that time German President with an escort lady and prostitute. In the cases, Google argued that the algorithm's suggestions had been unforeseeable and uncontrollable for Google, thus Google was not responsible. In other cases, they argued that the unpredictability stems from the user input with Google just taking over the function of data collection and result publishing.[65] However, the courts have ruled so far that the search engine's results which violated personality rights are attributable to the company. The duty that the company has violated is an own duty to control. Consequently, it is liable in principle, but only once it obtains knowledge of personality rights violations by its autocomplete function.[66]

The requirement for Google to obtain knowledge in order to trigger the duty to control creates a massive evolving liability gap. For all those autocomplete functions that remain undetected by the company, Google cannot violate conceivably any duties. Our proposal would produce a different result. Google is per se liable for the violation of personality rights by its search algorithm, already in the very first case.

First of all, the case of the Google autocomplete algorithm demonstrates very well the development from automation to digital autonomy. The algorithm's operations are determined mathematical calculations, but the varying user input and the learning abilities of the algorithm in the light of such inputs as well as unforeseeable individual user's properties results in autonomous decision-making under uncertainty. 'Thus, Google provides for some decision premises by certain conditions via "input", But what becomes visible as "output" at the end, cannot be predicted with any certainty.'[67] The first autonomous algorithmic decision violating personality rights is the trigger for liability.

Second, it is not a wrongful decision by Google but the output of the autocomplete function, that counts as the violation of personality rights. It is not necessary to identify Google's knowledge of the infringement. Rather, it is the communicative act of auto-completion itself that the law treats as the violation. This distinction between Google's and the algorithm's behaviour is crucial for the complex determination of whether or not an illegal act has been committed. Particularly, for personality rights, this requires difficult weighing of legal principles, especially constitutional ones. As we argued in chapter three,[68] one does

[65] This was a central argument by Google in the Japanese case on autocomplete, see www.bbc.com/news/technology-17510651.

[66] BGH GRUR 2013, 751 recurs to the duties to control. Supportive D Wielsch, 'Die Haftung des Mediums: BGH 14.05.2013 (Google Autocomplete)', in B Lomfeld (ed), *Die Fälle der Gesellschaft: Eine neue Praxis soziologischer Jurisprudenz* (Tübingen, Mohr Siebeck, 2017).

[67] G Kastl, 'Eine Analyse der Autocomplete-Funktion der Google-Suchmaschine', (2015) 117 *Gewerblicher Rechtsschutz und Urheberrecht* 136, 140 (our translation).

[68] ch 3, V.D.

not need to find all the conditions for contractual or tortious liability (violation of a contractual obligation or a duty of care) in the human principal's behaviour, which becomes increasingly difficult with autonomous systems.[69] Rather it is exclusively the auto-complete output which needs to be qualified as illegal or not.

Third, the auto-complete cases demonstrate very well how inappropriate it is to apply the rules of strict liability for hazardous objects, as so many scholars suggest. These rules would not go far enough since they compensate only physical and bodily damage, excluding all other damages. On the other hand, they go much too far since they do not require to qualify the auto-completion as violating a legal obligation; sheer causation of the damage triggers liability. The floodgates would be open.

Finally, this case may very well illustrate overlaps between our three liability regimes. The Google autocomplete function occupies a somewhat strange intermediate place in-between an autonomous algorithmic decision and a hybrid human-machine interaction, in which user input, Google's management change of the search algorithm and the mathematical operations are all present. The reason for that ambivalence is that the action is not generated on the basis of training data, but is made by using real-time user input and personalised criteria of the users. In addition, the auto-complete function is only activated by user input in the search engine and its rules are constantly revised within the organisation. Google-autocomplete is, as an observer has it, not only a technical product evolving through the search engine itself; 'rather, it is a social process that at many points could be informed by social values'.[70] Is this then, according to our classification, a case of a hybrid or a case of digital assistance? Given our reasoning above, both qualifications are potentially conceivable. The Google-autocomplete results are based on the interaction between human user input and machine calculations. At the same time, the relation between human input and the algorithmic operations is not a clear-cut cooperative relation, but rather one of delegation. The act that amounts to a breach of a duty of care, ie the algorithm's autocompletion act, can be easily identified. This, together with the suggestion of treating hybrid liability as subsidiary to digital assistance, suggests that we are encountering a constellation of a digital agent violating personality rights for which the principal becomes vicariously liable.

This means that Google is liable as principal for the acts of the search algorithm as its agent. This solution, which is based on the general principles of contractual and tortious liability, would also solve the related legal problems that are discussed prominently on the applicability of liability rules for news providers. For our solution, Google's liability does not depend on whether the company is a news provider or an intermediary because this distinction does not affect its role as principal.

[69] See: M Ebers, 'Liability for Artificial Intelligence and EU Consumer Law', (2021) 12 *Journal of Intellectual Property, Information Technology and Electronic Commerce Law* 204, 211 f.

[70] F Pasquale, 'Reforming the Law of Reputation', (2015) 47 *Loyola University of Chicago Law Journal* 515, 522.

The Google auto-complete cases thus serve as a good illustration on how the law benefits from a deeper understanding of algorithmic autonomy, their output as the wrongful act and the dependence of liability regimes on socio-digital institutions. It shows how the law, if developed with an appropriate understanding for the socio-digital context, can evolve to close the liability gaps – for the real pressing problems at present and the foreseeable future.

BIBLIOGRAPHY

Abott, R, 'The Reasonable Computer: Disrupting the Paradigm of Tort Liability', (2018) 86 *George Washington Law Review* 1–45.

Adamowicz, E, *Dada Bodies: Between Battlefield and Fairground* (Manchester, Manchester University Press, 2019).

Agamben, G, *The Kingdom and the Glory: For a Theological Genealogy of Economy and Government* (Stanford, Stanford University Press, 2011).

Allain, JS, 'From Jeopardy! to Jaundice: The Medical Liability Implications of Dr. Watson and Other Artificial Intelligence Systems', (2013) 73 *Louisiana Law Review* 1049–1079.

Allen, T and Widdison, R, 'Can Computers Make Contracts?', (1996) 9 *Harvard Journal of Law & Technology* 25–52.

Ameri, F and McArthur, C, 'A Multi-Agent System for Autonomous Supply Chain Configuration', (2013) 66 *International Journal of Advanced Manufacturing Technology* 1097–1112.

Amstutz, M, 'The Constitution of Contractual Networks', in M Amstutz and G Teubner (eds), *Contractual Networks: Legal Issues of Multilateral Cooperation* 2009) 309–346.

Ananny, M and Crawford, K, 'Seeing without Knowing: Limitations of the Transparency Ideal and its Application to Algorithmic Accountability', (2016) 20 *New Media & Society* 973–989.

Andrade, F, Novais, P, Machado, J and Neves, J, 'Contracting Agents: Legal Personality and Representation', (2007) 15 *Artificial Intelligence Law* 357–373.

Anner, M, Bair, J and Blasi, J, 'Towards Joint Liability in Global Supply-Chains: Addressing the Root Causes of Labor Violations in International Subcontracting Networks', (2013) 35 *Comparative Labor Law and Policy Journal* 1–44.

Armbrüster, C, 'Verantwortungsverlagerungen und Versicherungsschutz: Das Beispiel des automatisierten Fahrens', in S Gless and K Seelmann (eds), *Intelligente Agenten und das Recht* (Baden-Baden, Nomos, 2016) 205–224.

Armour, J, 'Companies and Other Associations', in A Burrows (ed), *English Private Law* (Oxford, Oxford University Press, 2013) 115–169.

Armour, J and Eidenmüller, H, 'Self-Driving Corporations?', (2019) 475/2020 *ECGI-Law Working Paper* 1–44.

Arrow, K, 'A Difficulty in the Concept of Social Welfare', (1950) 58 *Journal of Political Economy* 328–346.

Asaro, PM, 'Determinism, Machine Agency, and Responsibility', (2014) 2 *Politica Società* 265–292.

Ashmarina, S, Mesquita, A and Vochozka, M (eds), *Digital Transformation of the Economy: Challenges, Trends and New Opportunities* (Cham, Springer, 2020).

Atiyah, PS, *The Rise and Fall of Freedom of Contract* (Oxford, Clarendon, 1979).

Auer, M, 'Rechtsfähige Softwareagenten: Ein erfrischender Anachronismus', (2019) *Verfassungsblog* 30 September 2019.

Austin, JL, *How to Do Things with Words* (Cambridge/Mass., Harvard University Press, 1962).

Aymerich-Franch, L and Fosch-Villaronga, E, 'What We Learned from Mediated Embodiment Experiments and Why It Should Matter to Policymakers', (2019) 27 *Presence* 63–67.

Baecker, D, 'Who Qualifies for Communication? A Systems Perspective on Human and Other Possibly Intelligent Beings Taking Part in the Next Society', (2011) 20 *TATuP - Zeitschrift für Technikfolgenabschätzung in Theorie und Praxis* 17–26.

—— 'Digitization as Calculus: A Prospect', (2020) *Research Proposal* 1–11.

Balkin, J, 'The Path of Robotics Law', (2015) 6 *California Law Review Circuit* 45–60.

Banteka, N, 'Artificially Intelligent Persons', (2021) 58 *Houston Law Review* 537–596.

Baquero, PM, *Networks of Collaborative Contracts for Innovation* (Oxford, Hart, 2020).
Barfield, W, 'Issues of Law for Software Agents within Virtual Environments', (2005) 14 *Presence* 747–754.
—— 'Liability for Autonomous and Artificially Intelligent Robots', (2018) 9 *Paladyn. Journal of Behavioral Robotics* 193–203.
Bashayreh, M, Sibai, FN and Tabbara, A, 'Artificial Intelligence and Legal Liability: Towards an International Approach of Proportional Liability Based on Risk Sharing', (2021) 30 *Information & Communications Technology Law* 169–192.
Bathaee, Y, 'The Artificial Intelligence Black Box and the Failure of Intent and Causation', (2018) 31 *Harvard Journal of Law & Technology* 889–938.
Beardsworth, T and Kumar, N, 'Going to Court Over Losses When Robot Is to Blame', [2019] *Insurance Journal*.
Becchetti, V, 'Max Ernst: Il surrealista psicoanalitico', (2020) *LoSpessore – Opinioni, Cultura e Analisi della Società* 10 November 2020.
Beck, S, 'Dealing with the Diffusion of Legal Responsibility: The Case of Robotics', in F Battaglia, N Mukerji and J Nida-Rümelin (eds), *Rethinking Responsibility in Science and Technology* (Pisa, Pisa University Press, 2014) 167–182.
—— 'The Problem of Ascribing Legal Responsibility in the Case of Robotics', (2016) 31 *AI & Society* 473–481.
Beckers, A, *Enforcing Corporate Social Responsibility Codes: On Global Self-Regulation and National Private Law* (Oxford, Hart, 2015).
Belia, A, 'Contracting with Electronic Agents', (2001) 50 *Emory Law Journal* 1047–1092.
Benhamou, Y and Ferland, J, 'Artificial Intelligence & Damages: Assessing Liability and Calculating the Damages', in P D'Agostino, C Piovesan and A Gaon (eds), *Leading Legal Disruption: Artificial Intelligence and a Toolkit for Lawyers and the Law* Thomson Reuters, 2021) forthcoming.
Bertolini, A, 'Robots as Products: The Case for a Realistic Analysis of Robot Applications and Liability Rules', (2013) 5 *Law, Innovation & Technology* 214–247.
Bertolini, A, *Artificial Intelligence and Civil Liability* (Brussels, European Parliament, Study Commissioned by the Juri Committee on Legal Affairs, 2020).
Bertolini, A and Palmerini, E, *Regulating Robotics: A Challenge for Europe* (Brussels, European Parliament, Study Commissioned by the Juri Committee on Legal Affairs, 2014).
Bertolini, A and Riccaboni, M, 'Grounding the Case for a European Approach to the Regulation of Automated Driving: The Technology-Selection Effect of Liability Rules', (2020) 51 *European Journal of Law and Economics* 243–284.
Blackstone, W, *Commentaries on the Laws of England: In Four Books* (Philadelphia, Robert Bell, 1771).
Blumer, H, 'Collective Behaviour', in A McClung Lee (ed), *New Outline of the Principles of Sociology* (New York, Barnes & Noble, 1946) 167–224.
Bora, A, 'Kommunikationsadressen als digitale Rechtssubjekte', (2019) *Verfassungsblog* 1 October 2019.
Borch, C, 'Crowds and Economic Life: Bringing an old figure back in', (2007) 36 *Economy and Society* 549–573.
Borges, G, 'New Liability Concepts: The Potential of Insurance and Compensation Funds', in S Lohsse, R Schulze and D Staudenmayer (eds), *Liability for Artificial Intelligence and the Internet of Things* (Baden-Baden, Nomos/Hart, 2019) 145–163.
Borghetti, J-S, 'How can Artificial Intelligence be Defective?', in S Lohsse, R Schulze and D Staudenmayer (eds), *Liability for Artificial Intelligence and the Internet of Things* (Baden-Baden/Oxford, Nomos/Hart, 2019) 63–76.
Borselli, A, 'Smart Contracts in Insurance: A Law and Futurology Perspective', in P Marano and K Noussia (eds), *InsurTech: A Legal and Regulatory View* (Cham, Springer, 2020) 101–125.
Bostrom, N, *Superintelligence: Paths, Dangers, Strategies* (Oxford, Oxford University Press, 2017).
Bradford, A, *The Brussels Effect: How the European Union Rules the World* (Oxford, Oxford University Press, 2020).
Braun, AC, *Latours Existenzweisen und Luhmanns Funktionssysteme: Ein soziologischer Theorienvergleich* (Heidelberg, Springer, 2017).

Braun, M, Hummel, P, Beck, S and Dabrock, P, 'Primer on an Ethics of AI-Based Decision Support Systems in the Clinic', (2020) 0 *Journal of medical ethics* 1–8.

Bräutigam, P and Klindt, T, 'Industrie 4.0, das Internet der Dinge und das Recht', [2015] *Neue Juristische Wochenschrift* 1137–1142.

Brownsword, R, 'Contracts with Network Effects: Is the Time Now Right?', in S Grundmann and F Cafaggi (eds), *The Organizational Contract: From Exchange to Long-Term Network Cooperation in European Contract Law* (London, Routledge, 2013) 137–163.

Brownsword, R, 'The E-Commerce Directive, Consumer Transactions, and the Digital Single Market – Questions of Regulatory Fitness, Regulatory Disconnection and Rule Redirection', in S Grundmann (ed), *European Contract Law in the Digital Single Age* (Antwerp/Cambridge, Intersentia, 2018) 165–204.

—— *Law 3.0* (London, Routledge, 2021).

Bryson, JJ, Diamantis, ME and Grant, TD, 'Of, for, and by the People: The Legal Lacuna of Synthetic Persons', (2017) 25 *Artificial Intelligence Law* 273–291.

Cafaggi, F and Iamiceli, P, 'Private Regulation and Industrial Organization: Contractual Governance and the Network Approach', in S Grundmann, F Möslein and K Riesenhuber (eds), *Contract Governance: Dimensions in Law and Interdisciplinary Research* (Oxford, Oxford University Press, 2015) 341–374.

Callon, M, 'What Does It Mean to Say That Economics Is Performative?', in D MacKenzie, F Muniesa and L Siu (eds), *Do Economists Make Markets? On Performativity in Economics* (Princeton, University Press, 2007) 311–357.

Canaris, C-W, *Die Vertrauenshaftung im Deutschen Privatrecht* (Munich, C.H. Beck, 1971).

Casey, A and Niblett, A, 'Self-Driving Contracts', (2017) 43 *Journal of Corporation Law* 1–33.

Cassels, J, 'The Uncertain Promise of Law: Lessons from Bhopal', (1991) 29 *Osgoode Hall Law Journal* 1–50.

Cauffman, C, 'Robo-Liability: The European Union in Search of the Best Way to Deal with Liability for Damage Caused by Artificial Intelligence', (2018) 25 *Maastricht Journal of European and Comparative Law* 527–532.

Čerka, P, Grigienė, J and Sirbikytė, G, 'Liability for Damages Caused by Artificial Intelligence', (2015) 31 *Computer Law & Security Review* 376–389.

—— 'Is it Possible to Grant Legal Personality to Artificial Intelligence Software Systems?', (2017) 33 *Computer Law & Security Review* 685–699.

Chagal-Feferkorn, KA, 'The Reasonable Algorithm', [2018] *University of Illinois Journal of Law, Technology & Policy* 111–147.

—— 'Am I an Algorithm or a Product? When Products Liability Should Apply to Algorithmic Decision-Makers', (2019) 30 *Stanford Law & Policy Review* 61–114.

—— 'How Can I Tell If My Algorithm Was Reasonable?', [2021] *Michigan Telecommunications and Technology Law Review* forthcoming.

Chandra, A, 'Liability Issues in Relation to Autonomous AI Systems', (2017) *SSRN Electronic Library* 1–8.

Chen, J and Burgess, P, 'The Boundaries of Legal Personhood: How Spontaneous Intelligence Can Problematize Differences Between Humans, Artificial Intelligence, Companies and Animals', (2019) 27 *Artificial Intelligence and Law* 73–92.

Chinen, MA, 'The Co-Evolution of Autonomous Machines and Legal Responsibility', (2016) 20 *Vanderbilt Journal of Law & Technology* 338–393.

—— *Law and Autonomous Machines* (Cheltenham, Elgar, 2019).

Chopra, SK and White, L, 'Artificial Agents and the Contracting Problem: A Solution via an Agency Analysis', (2009) *Journal of Law, Technology & Policy* 363–403.

—— *A Legal Theory for Autonomous Artificial Agents* (Ann Arbor, University of Michigan Press, 2011).

Ciborra, CU, *The Labyrinths of Information: Challenging the Wisdom of Systems* (Oxford, Oxford University Press, 2004).

Ciborra, CU, Braa, K, Cordella, A, Dahlbom, B, Failla, A, Henseth, O, Hepso, V, Ljungberg, J, Monteiro, E and Simon, KA, *From Control to Drift: The Dynamics of Corporate Information Infrastructures* (Oxford, Oxford University Press, 2001).

Ciborra, CU and Hanseth, O, 'From Tool to Gestell: Agendas for Managing the Information Infrastructure', (1998) 11 *Information Technology & People* 305–327.
Clarke, R, 'The Digital Persona and its Application to Data Surveillance', (1994) 10 *Information Society* 77–92.
Coeckelbergh, M, 'Moral Responsibility, Technology, and Experiences of the Tragic: From Kierkgeaard to Offshore Engineering', (2012) 18 *Science and Engineering Ethics* 35–48.
Cohen, JE, *Between Truth and Power: The Legal Constructions of Informational Capitalism* (Oxford, Oxford University Press, 2019).
Coleman, JS, *Foundations of Social Theory* (Cambridge/Mass., Harvard University Press, 1990).
Collingridge, D, *The Social Control of Technology* (New York, St. Martin's Press, 1980).
Collins, H, *Introduction to Networks as Connected Contracts* (Oxford, Hart, 2011).
Condon, R, *Network Responsibility: European Tort Law and the Society of Networks* (Cambridge, Cambridge University Press 2021 forthcoming).
Cook, RI, 'How Complex Systems Fail', (2002) *Unpublished Research Paper* 1–4.
Copp, D, 'The Collective Moral Autonomy Thesis', (2007) 38 *Journal of Social Philosophy* 369–388.
Corlett, JA, 'Collective Moral Responsibility', (2002) 32 *Journal of Social Philosophy* 573–584.
Crandall, JW, Oudah, M, Tennom, FI-O, Abdallah, S, Bonnefon, J-F, Cebrian, M, Shariff, A, Goodrich, MA and Rahwan, I, 'Cooperating With Machines', (2018) 9 *Nature Communications* Article 233, 1–12.
Crawford, K and Whittaker, M, *The AI Now Report: The Social and Economic Implications of Artificial Intelligence Technologies in the Near-Term* (New York, AI Now Institute, 2016).
Dafoe, A, 'AI Governance: A Research Agenda', (2018) *Centre for the Governance of AI Future of Humanity Institute University of Oxford* 1–54.
Dahiyat, E, 'Law and Software Agents: Are They "Agents" by the Way?', (2021) 29 *Artificial Intelligence and Law* 59–86.
Daniel, JL, 'Electronic Contracting under the 2003 Revisions to Article 2 of the Uniform Commercial Code: Clarification or Chaos?', (2004) 20 *Santa Clara Computer & High Technology Law Journal* 319–346.
Dannemann, G and Schulze, R (eds), *German Civil Code – Article by Article Commentary* (Munich / Baden-Baden, C.H. Beck / Nomos, 2020).
Davidson, A, *The Law of Electronic Commerce* (Cambridge, Cambridge University Press, 2012).
Dearborn, M, 'Enterprise Liability: Reviewing and Revitalizing Liability for Corporate Groups', (2009) 97 *California Law Review* 195–261.
Dennett, D, *The Intentional Stance* (Cambridge/Mass., MIT Press, 1987).
Diakopoulos, N, *Automating the News: How Algorithms are Rewriting the Media* (Cambridge/Mass., Harvard University Press, 2019).
Dijk, N van, 'In the Hall of Masks: Contrasting Modes of Personification', in M Hildebrandt and K O'Hara (eds), *Life and the Law in the Era of Data-Driven Agency* (Cheltenham, Edward Elgar, 2020) 230–251.
Döpke, C, 'The Importance of Big Data for Jurisprudence and Legal Practice', in T Hoeren and B Kolany-Raiser (eds), *Big Data in Context. Springer Briefs in Law* (Cham, Springer, 2018) 1–19.
Durkheim, E, *The Division of Labor in Society* (New York, Free Press, 1933 [1883]).
Dyrkolbotn, S, 'A Typology of Liability Rules for Robot Harms', in M Aldinhas Ferreira, J Silva Sequeira, M Tokhi, E Kadar and G Virk (eds), *A World with Robots: Intelligent Systems, Control and Automation* (Cham, Springer, 2017), 119–134.
Easterbrook, FH and Fischel, D, 'The Corporate Contract', (1989) 89 *Columbia Law Review* 1416–1448.
Ebers, M, 'Regulating AI and Robots: Ethical and Legal Challenges', in M Ebers and S Navas (eds), *Algorithms and Law* (Cambridge, Cambridge University Press, 2020) 37–99.
—— 'Liability for Artificial Intelligence and EU Consumer Law', (2021) 12 *Journal of Intellectual Property, Information Technology and Electronic Commerce Law* 204–220.
Eidenmüller, H, 'The Rise of Robots and the Law of Humans', (2017) 27/2017 *Oxford Legal Studies Research Paper* 1–15.

Eller, KH, 'Das Recht der Verantwortungsgesellschaft: Verantwortungskonzeptionen zwischen Recht, Moral- und Gesellschaftstheorie', (2019) 10 *Rechtswissenschaft* 13–40.

Erdélyi, OJ and Erdélyi, G, 'The AI Liability Puzzle and a Fund–Based Work-Around', (2020) *AIES '20: Proceedings of the AAAI/ACM Conference on AI, Ethics, and Society* 50–56.

Erdélyi, OJ and Goldsmith, J, 'Regulating Artificial Intelligence: Proposal for a Global Solution', (2018) *AIES '18: Proceedings of the AAAI/ACM Conference on AI, Ethics, and Society* 95–105.

Esposito, E, 'Artificial Communication? The Production of Contingency by Algorithms', (2017) 46 *Zeitschrift für Soziologie* 249–265.

Esposito, R, *Istituzione* (Bologna, Il Mulino, 2021).

Esser, J, *Grundlagen und Entwicklung der Gefährdungshaftung: Beiträge zur Reform des Haftungsrechts und zu seiner Wiedereinordnung in die Gedanken des allgemeinen Privatrechts* (Munich, Beck, 1941).

Evas, T, *Civil Liability Regime for Artificial Intelligence – European Added Value Assessment* (Brussels / Strasbourg, Study Commissioned by the European Parliamentary Research Service, 2020).

Ewald, W, 'Comparative Jurisprudence (I): What Was It Like to Try a Rat', (1995) 143 *American Journal of Comparative Law* 1889–2149.

Femia, P, 'Soggetti responsabili: Algoritmi e diritto civile', in P Femia (ed), *Soggetti giuridici digitali: Sullo status privatistico degli agenti software autonomi* (Napoli, Edizioni Scientifichi Italiane, 2019) 7–16.

Fischer-Lescano, A, 'Nature as a Legal Person: Proxy Constellations in Law', (2020) 32 *Law & Literature* 237–262.

Floridi, L and Sanders, JW, 'On the Morality of Artificial Agents', in M Anderson and SL Anderson (eds), *Machine Ethics* (Cambridge, Cambridge University Press, 2011) 184–212.

Foerster, Hv, 'Ethics and Second-Order Cybernetics', (1992) 1 *Cybernetics and Human Knowing* 9–19.

Förster, M, 'Automatisierung und Verantwortung im Zivilrecht', [2019] *Zeitschrift für die gesamte Privatrechtswissenschaft* 418–435.

Fosch-Villaronga, E and Golia, AJ, 'Robots, Standards and the Law: Rivalries between Private Standards and Public Policymaking for Robot Governance', (2019) 35 *Computer Law & Security Review* 129–144.

Galasso, A and Luo, H, 'Punishing Robots: Issues in the Economics of Tort Liability and Innovation in Artificial Intelligence', in A Agrawal, J Gans and A Goldfarb (eds), *The Economics of Artificial Intelligence: An Agenda* (Chicago, University of Chicago Press, 2019) 493–504.

Geistfeld, MA, 'The Coherence of Compensation-Deterrence Theory in Tort Law', (2012) 61 *DePaul Law Review* 383–418.

—— 'A Roadmap for Autonomous Vehicles: State Tort Liability, Automobile Insurance, and Federal Safety Regulation', (2017) 105 *California Law Review* 1611–1694.

Gellers, JC, *Rights for Robots: Artificial Intelligence, Animal and Environmental Law* (London, Routledge, 2021).

Gierke, O von, *Das Wesen der menschlichen Verbände* (Leipzig, Duncker & Humblot, 1902).

Gifford, DG, 'Technological Triggers to Tort Revolutions: Steam Locomotives, Autonomous Vehicles, and Accident Compensation', (2018) 11 *Journal of Tort Law* 71–143.

Giliker, P, *Vicarious Liability in Tort: A Comparative Perspective* (Cambridge, Cambridge University Press, 2010).

Gindis, D, 'Legal Personhood and the Firm: Avoiding Anthropomorphism and Equivocation', (2016) 12 *Journal of Institutional Economics* 499–513.

Gitter, R, *Softwareagenten im elektronischen Rechtsverkehr* (Baden-Baden, Nomos, 2007).

Gransche, B, Shala, E, Hubig, C, Alpsancar, S and Harrach, S, *Wandel von Autonomie und Kontrolle durch neue Mensch-Technik-Interaktionen: Grundsatzfragen autonomieorientierter Mensch-Technik-Verhältnisse* (Stuttgart, Fraunhofer, 2014).

Gruber, M-C, 'Zumutung und Zumutbarkeit von Verantwortung in Mensch-Maschine-Assoziationen', in J-P Günther and E Hilgendorf (eds), *Robotik und Gesetzgebung* (Baden-Baden, Nomos, 2013) 123–163.

—— *Bioinformationsrecht: Zur Persönlichkeitsentfaltung des Menschen in technisierter Verfassung* (Tübingen, Mohr Siebeck, 2015).

—— 'On Flash Boys and Their Flashbacks: The Attribution of Legal Responsibility in Algorithmic Trading', in M Jankowska, M Kulawiak and M Pawełczykai (eds), *AI: Law, Philosophy & Geoinformatics* (Warsaw, Prawa Gospodarczego, 2015) 88–102.
—— 'Was spricht gegen Maschinenrechte?', in M-C Gruber, J Bung and S Ziemann (eds), *Autonome Automaten: Künstliche Körper und artifizielle Agenten in der technisierten Gesellschaft* (Berlin, Berliner Wissenschaftsverlag, 2015) 191–206.
—— 'Legal Subjects and Partial Legal Subjects in Electronic Commerce', in T Pietrzykowski and B Stancioli (eds), *New Approaches to Personhood in Law* (Frankfurt, Lang, 2016) 67–91.
—— 'Why Non-Human Rights?', (2020) 32 *Law & Literature* 263–270.
Gunkel, DJ, 'Mind the Gap: Responsible Robotics and the Problem of Responsibility', (2020) 22 *Ethics and Information Technology* 307–320.
Günther, J-P, *Roboter und rechtliche Verantwortung: Eine Untersuchung der Benutzer- und Herstellerhaftung* (Munich, Utz, 2016).
Gurevich, Y, 'What Is an Algorithm?', [2012] *Theory and Practice of Computer Science* 31–42.
Hacker, P, 'Verhaltens- und Wissenszurechnung beim Einsatz von Künstlicher Intelligenz', (2018) 9 *Rechtswissenschaft* 243–288.
Hacker, P, Krestel, R, Grundmann, S and Naumann, F, 'Explainable AI under Contract and Tort Law: Legal Incentives and Technical Challenges', (2020) 28 *Artificial Intelligence and Law* 415–439.
Hage, J, 'Theoretical Foundations for the Responsibility of Autonomous Agents', (2017) 25 *Artificial Intelligence and Law* 255–271.
Hanisch, J, 'Zivilrechtliche Haftungskonzepte für Robotik', in E Hilgendorf (ed), *Robotik im Kontext von Recht und Moral* (Baden-Baden, Nomos, 2014) 27–61.
Hanson, FA, 'Beyond the Skin Bag: On the Moral Responsibility of Extended Agencies', (2009) 11 *Ethics and Information Technology* 91–99.
Harke, JD, 'Sklavenhalterhaftung in Rom', in S Gless and K Seelmann (eds), *Intelligente Agenten und das Recht* (Baden-Baden, Nomos, 2016) 97–118.
Haselager, P, 'Did I Do that? Brain-Computer Interfacing and the Sense of Agency', (2013) 23 *Minds & Machines* 405–418.
Hauriou, M, *Die Theorie der Institution* (Berlin, Duncker & Humblot, 1965).
Heath, S, Fuller, A and Johnston, B, 'Chasing Shadows: Defining Network Boundaries in Qualitative Social Network Analysis', (2009) 9 *Qualitative Research* 645–661.
Heine, K and Li, S, 'What Shall we Do with the Drunken Sailor? Product Safety in the Aftermath of 3D Printing', (2019) 10 *European Journal of Risk Regulation* 23–40.
Heinrichs, J-H, 'Artificial Intelligence in Extended Minds: Intrapersonal Diffusion of Responsibility and Legal Multiple Personality', in B Beck and M Kühler (eds), *Technology, Anthropology, and Dimensions of Responsibility* (Heidelberg/New York, Springer, 2020) 159–176.
Hennemann, M, *Interaktion und Partizipation: Dimensionen systemischer Bindung im Vertragsrecht* (Tübingen, Mohr Siebeck, 2020).
Hepp, A, 'Artificial Companions, Social Bots and Work Bots: Communicative Robots as Research Objects of Media and Communication Studies', (2020) 42 *Media, Culture and Society* 1410–1426.
—— *Deep Mediatization: Key Ideas in Media & Cultural Studies* (London, Routledge, 2020).
Herold, S, *Vertragsschlüsse unter Einbeziehung automatisiert und autonom agierender Systeme* (Hürth, Wolters Kluwer, 2020).
Heuer-James, J-U, Chibanguza, K and Stücker, B, 'Industrie 4.0: Vertrags- und haftungsrechtliche Fragestellungen', [2018] *Betriebsberater* 2818–2832.
Hildebrandt, M, *Smart Technologies and the End(s) of Law* (Cheltenham, Edward Elgar, 2015).
Hilgendorf, E, 'Können Roboter schuldhaft handeln? Zur Übertragbarkeit unseres normativen Grundvokabulars auf Maschinen', in S Beck (ed), *Jenseits von Mensch und Maschine* (Baden-Baden, Nomos, 2012) 119–132.
Horner, S and Kaulartz, M, 'Haftung 4.0: Rechtliche Herausforderungen im Kontext der Industrie 4.0', [2016] *InTeR Zeitschrift zum Innovations- und Technikrecht* 22–27.
Horwitz, MJ, 'Santa Clara Revisited: The Development of Corporate Theory', (1985) 88 *West Virginia Law Review* 173–224.

Hughes, B and Williamson, R, 'When AI Systems Cause Harm: The Application of Civil and Criminal Liability', (2019) *Digital Business Law - Blog.*

Hutchins, E, *Cognition in the Wild* (Boston, MIT Press, 1995).

Ingold, A, 'Grundrechtsschutz sozialer Emergenz: Eine Neukonfiguration juristischer Personalität in Art. 19 Abs. 3 GG angesichts webbasierter Kollektivitätsformen', (2014) 53 *Der Staat* 193–226.

Ishiyama, JT and Breuning, M, 'Neoinstitutionalism', (2014) *Encyclopedia Britannica.*

Janal, R, 'Extra-Contractual Liability for Wrongs Committed by Autonomous Systems', in M Ebers and S Navas (eds), *Algorithms and Law* (Cambridge, Cambridge University Press, 2020) 174–206.

Jansen, N, *Die Struktur des Haftungsrechts: Geschichte, Theorie und Dogmatik außervertraglicher Ansprüche auf Schadensersatz* (Tübingen, Mohr Siebeck, 2003).

Jasanoff, S, 'The Idiom of Co-Production', in S Jasanoff (ed), *States of Knowledge: The Co-production of Science and the Social Order* (London, Routledge, 2004) 1–12.

Jensen, M and Meckling, WH, 'Theory of the Firm: Managerial Behavior, Agency Costs and Ownership Structure', (1976) 3 *Journal of Financial Economics* 306–360.

Johnson, DG, 'Computer Systems: Moral Entities but not Moral Agents', (2006) 8 *Ethics and Information Technology* 195–204.

Kainer, F and Förster, L, 'Autonome Systeme im Kontext des Vertragsrechts', [2020] *Zeitschrift für die gesamte Privatrechtswissenschaft* 275–305.

Karanasiou, A and Pinotsis, D, 'Towards a Legal Definition of Machine Intelligence: The Argument for Artificial Personhood in the Age of Deep Learning', (2017) *ICAL'17: Proceedings of the 16th Edition of the International Conference on Artificial Intelligence and Law* 119–128.

Karner, E, 'Liability for Robotics: Current Rules, Challenges, and the Need for Innovative Concepts', in S Lohsse, R Schulze and D Staudenmayer (eds), *Liability for Artificial Intelligence and the Internet of Things* (Baden-Baden/Oxford, Nomos/Hart, 2019) 117–124.

Karnow, CEA, 'Liability for Distributed Artificial Intelligences', (1996) 11 *Berkeley Technology Law Journal* 147–204.

—— 'The Application of Traditional Tort Theory to Embodied Machine Intelligence', in R Calo, AM Froomkin and I Kerr (eds), *Robot Law* (Cheltenham, Edward Elgar, 2016) 51–77.

Kastl, G, 'Eine Analyse der Autocomplete-Funktion der Google-Suchmaschine', (2015) 117 *Gewerblicher Rechtsschutz und Urheberrecht* 136–141.

Kerr, IR, 'Ensuring the Success of Contract Formation in Agent-Mediated Electronic Commerce', (2001) 1 *Electronic Commerce Research* 183–202.

—— 'Providing for Autonomous Electronic Devices in the Uniform Electronic Commerce Act', [2006] *Uniform Law Conference* 1–55.

Kersten, J, 'Menschen und Maschinen: Rechtliche Konturen instrumenteller, symbiotischer und autonomer Konstellationen', [2015] *Juristenzeitung* 1–8.

—— 'Die Rechte der Natur und die Verfassungsfrage des Anthropozän', in J Soentgen, UM Gassner, Jv Hayek and A Manzel (eds), *Umwelt und Gesundheit* (Nomos, Baden-Baden, 2020) 87–120.

Kessler, O, 'Intelligente Roboter - neue Technologien im Einsatz: Voraussetzungen und Rechtsfolgen des Handelns informationstechnischer Systeme', [2017] *Multimedia und Recht* 589–594.

Kirchner, G, 'Big Data Management: Die Haftung des Big Data-Anwenders für Datenfehler', [2018] *InTeR Zeitschrift zum Innovations- und Technikrecht* 19–24.

Kirn, S and Müller-Hengstenberg, C-D, 'Intelligente (Software-)Agenten: Eine neue Herausforderung für die Gesellschaft und unser Rechtssystem?', (2014) *FZID Discussion Paper 86-2014* 1–21.

—— 'Intelligente (Software-)Agenten: Von der Automatisierung zur Autonomie? - Verselbstständigung technischer Systeme', [2014] *Multimedia und Recht* 225–232.

Kleiner, C, *Die elektronische Person: Entwurf eines Zurechnungs- und Haftungssubjekts für den Einsatz autonomer Systeme im Rechtsverkehr* (Baden-Baden, Nomos, 2021).

Klingbeil, S, 'Schuldnerhaftung für Roboterversagen: Zum Problem der Substitution von Erfüllungsgehilfen durch Maschinen', [2019] *Juristenzeitung* 718–725.

Koch, B, 'Product Liability 2.0 - Mere Update or New Version?', in S Lohsse, R Schulze and D Staudenmayer (eds), *Liability for Robotics and in the Internet of Things* (Baden-Baden/Oxford, Nomos/Hart, 2019) 99–116.

Konertz, R and Schönhof, R, *Das technische Phänomen „Künstliche Intelligenz" im allgemeinen Zivilrecht: Eine kritische Betrachtung im Lichte von Autonomie, Determinismus und Vorhersehbarkeit* (Baden-Baden, Nomos, 2020).

Koops, B-J, Hildebrandt, M and Jaquet-Chiffelle, D-O, 'Bridging the Accountability Gap: Rights for New Entities in the Information Society?', (2010) 11 *Minnesota Journal of Law, Science & Technology* 497–558.

Koops, B-J and Jaquet-Chiffelle, D-O, *New (Id)entities and the Law: Perspectives on Legal Personhood for Non-Humans* (Tilburg, FIDIS – Future of Identity in the Information Society, 2008).

Kovac, M, *Judgement-Proof Robots and Artificial Intelligence: A Comparative Law and Economics Approach* (London, Palgrave, 2020).

Ladeur, K-H (ed), *Innovationsoffene Regulierung des Internet: Neues Recht für Kommunikationsnetzwerke* (Baden-Baden, Nomos, 2003).

Lai, A, 'Artificial Intelligence, LLC: Corporate Personhood as Tort Reform', (2021) 2021 *Michigan State Law Review* forthcoming.

Latour, B, 'On Technical Mediation', (1994) 3 *Common Knowledge* 29–64.

—— *Politics of Nature: How to Bring the Sciences into Democracy* (Cambridge/Mass., Harvard University Press, 2004).

Laumann, EO, Marsden, PV and Prensky, D, 'The Boundary Specification Problem in Network Analysis', in RS Burt and M Minor (eds), *Applied Network Analysis* (Beverly Hills/Cal., SAGE Publications, 1983) 18–34.

Lemley, MA and Casey, B, 'Remedies for Robots', (2019) 86 *University of Chicago Law Review* 1311–1396.

Lerouge, J-F, 'The Use of Electronic Agents Questioned Under Contractual Law: Suggested Solutions on a European and American Level', (1999) 18 *John Marshall Journal of Computer Information Law* 403–433.

Lewinski, K von, Fritz, R de Barros and Biermeier, K, *Bestehende und künftige Regelungen des Einsatzes von Algorithmen im HR-Bereich* (Berlin, AlgorithmWatch/Hans-Böckler Stiftung, 2019).

Lewis, SC, Sanders, AK and Carmody, C, 'Libel by Algorithm? Automated Journalism and the Threat of Legal Liability', (2019) 98 *Journalism & Mass Communication Quarterly* 60–81.

Linardatos, D, 'Künstliche Intelligenz und Verantwortung', [2019] *Zeitschrift für Wirtschaftsrecht* 504–509.

—— *Autonome und vernetzte Aktanten im Zivilrecht: Grundlinien zivilrechtlicher Zurechnung und Strukturmerkmale einer elektronischen Person* (Tübingen, Mohr Siebeck, 2021).

Linarelli, J, 'Artificial General Intelligence and Contract', (2019) 24 *Uniform Law Review* 330–347.

Lindahl, H, 'We and Cyberlaw: The Spatial Unity of Constitutional Orders', (2013) 20 *Indiana Journal of Global Legal Studies* 697–730.

Linke, C, *Digitale Wissensorganisation: Wissenszurechnung beim Einsatz autonomer Systeme* (Baden-Baden, Nomos, 2021).

Lior, A, 'AI Entities as AI Agents: Artificial Intelligence Liability and the AI Respondeat Superior Analogy', (2020) 46 *Mitchell Hamline Law Review* 1043–1102.

—— 'The AI Accident Network: Artificial Intelligence Liability Meets Network Theory', (2021) 95 *Tulane Law Review* forthcoming.

Loh, W and Loh, J, 'Autonomy and Responsibility in Hybrid Systems', in P Lin, R Jenkins and K Abney (eds), *Robot Ethics 2.0: From Autonomous Cars to Artificial Intelligence* (Oxford, Oxford University Press, 2017) 35–50.

Lohmann, M, 'Ein europäisches Roboterrecht: überfällig oder überflüssig', (2017) *Zeitschrift für Rechtspolitik* 168–171.

Lohsse, S, Schulze, R and Staudenmayer, D, 'Liability for Artificial Intelligence', in S Lohsse, R Schulze and D Staudenmayer (eds), *Liability for Robotics and in the Internet of Things* (Baden-Baden/Oxford, Nomos/Hart, 2019) 11–26.

Loo, Rv, 'The Revival of Respondeat Superior and Evolution of Gatekeeper Liability', (2020) 109 *Georgetown Law Journal* 141–189.

Lorentzen, KF, 'Luhmann Goes Latour: Zur Soziologie hybrider Beziehungen', in W Rammert and I Schulz-Schaeffer (eds), *Können Maschinen handeln? Soziologische Beiträge zum Verhältnis von Mensch und Technik* (Frankfurt, Campus, 2002) 101–118.

Luhmann, N, *Grundrechte als Institution: Ein Beitrag zur politischen Soziologie* (Berlin, Duncker & Humblot, 1965).

—— 'Institutionalisierung – Funktion und Mechanismus im sozialen System der Gesellschaft', in H Schelsky (ed), *Zur Theorie der Institution.* (Düsseldorf, Bertelsmann, 1970) 27–41.

—— *A Sociological Theory of Law* (London, Routledge, 1985).

—— 'Systeme verstehen Systeme', in N Luhmann and E Schorr (eds), *Zwischen Intransparenz und Verstehen: Fragen an die Pädagogik* (Frankfurt, Suhrkamp, 1986) 72–117.

—— *Ecological Communication* (Cambridge, Polity Press, 1989).

—— 'Die Paradoxie des Entscheidens', (1993) 84 *Verwaltungsarchiv* 287–310.

—— *Risk: A Sociological Theory* (Berlin, de Gruyter, 1993).

—— *Social Systems* (Stanford, Stanford University Press, 1995).

—— *Die Politik der Gesellschaft* (Frankfurt, Suhrkamp, 2000).

—— *Organisation und Entscheidung* (Opladen, Westdeutscher Verlag, 2000).

—— *Law as a Social System* (Oxford, Oxford University Press, 2004).

—— *Theory of Society 1/2* (Stanford, Stanford University Press, 2012/2013).

Maas, MM, *Artificial Intelligence Governance under Change: Foundations, Facets, Frameworks* (Copenhagen, Dissertation University of Copenhagen, 2021).

Marchant, GE, 'The Growing Gap Between Emerging Technologies and the Law', in GE Marchant, BR Allenby and JR Herkert (eds), *The Growing Gap Between Emerging Technologies and Legal-Ethical Oversight: The Pacing Problem* (Dordrecht/Heidelberg/London/New York, Springer, 2011) 19–34.

Marchisio, E, 'In Support of "No-Fault" Civil Liability Rules for Artificial Intelligence', (2021) 1 *SN Social Sciences* 54, 1–25.

Markesinis, B, Unberath, H and Johnston, A, *The German Law of Contract: A Comparative Treatise* (Oxford, Hart Publishing, 2006).

Markou, C and Deakin, S, 'Is Law Computable? From the Rule of Law to Legal Singularity', in S Deakin and C Markou (eds), *Is Law Computable? Critical Perspectives on Law and Artificial Intelligence* (Oxford, Hart Publishing, 2020) 1–30.

Martone, I, 'Algoritmi e diritto: appunti in tema di responsabilità civile', (2020) 1 *Teconologie e diritto* 128–153.

Marttila, T, 'Post-Foundational Discourse Analysis: A Suggestion for a Research Program', (2015) 16 *Forum: Qualitative Social Research* 1.

Matthias, A, *Automaten als Träger von Rechten* 2nd edn (Berlin, Logos, 2010).

Mayinger, SM, *Die künstliche Person: Untersuchung rechtlicher Veränderungen durch die Installation von Softwareagenten im Rahmen von Industrie 4.0* (Frankfurt, Fachmedien Recht und Wirtschaft, 2017).

McLean, TR, 'Cybersurgery: An Argument for Enterprise Liability', (2002) 23 *Journal of Legal Medicine* 167–210.

Menke, K-H, *Stellvertretung. Schlüsselbegriff christlichen Lebens und theologische Grundkategorie,* (Freiburg, Johannes, 1991).

Messner, C, 'Listening to Distant Voices', (2020) 33 *International Journal for the Semiotics of Law – Revue internationale de Sémiotique juridique* 1143–1173.

Michalski, R, 'How to Sue a Robot', (2019) 2018 *Utah Law Review* 1021–1071.

Misselhorn, C, 'Collective Agency and Cooperation in Natural and Artificial Systems', in C Misselhorn (ed), *Collective Agency and Cooperation in Natural and Artificial Systems: Explanation, Implementation and Simulation* (Heidelberg, Springer, 2015) 3–24.

Mölders, M, 'Irritation Expertise: Recipient Design as Instrument for Strategic Reasoning', (2014) 2 *European Journal of Futures Research* 32–42.

Monteiro, E, 'Actor-Network Theory and Information Infrastructure', in CU Ciborra, K Braa, A Cordella, B Dahlbom, A Failla, O Hanseth, V Hepso, J Ljungberg, E Monteiro and KA Simon (eds), *From Control to Drift: The Dynamics of Corporate Information Infrastructures* (Oxford, Oxford University Press, 2001) 71–82.

Monterossi, MW, 'Liability for the Fact of Autonomous Artificial Intelligence Agents. Things, Agencies and Legal Actors', (2020) 6 *Global Jurist* 1–18.

Mosco, GD, 'AI and the Board Within Italian Corporate Law: Preliminary Notes', (2020) 17 *European Company Law Journal* 87–96.

Möslein, F, 'Robots in the Boardroom: Artificial Intelligence and Corporate Law', in W Barfield and U Pagallo (eds), *Research Handbook on the Law of Artificial Intelligence* (Cheltenham, Edward Elgar, 2017) 649–670.

Muhle, F, 'Sozialität von und mit Robotern? Drei soziologische Antworten und eine kommunikationstheoretische Alternative', (2018) 47 *Zeitschrift für Soziologie* 147–163.

Nake, F, 'Surface, Interface, Subface: Three Cases of Interaction and One Concept', in U Seifert, HK Jin and A Moore (eds), *Paradoxes of Interactivity* (Bielefeld, transcript, 2020) 92–109.

Nassehi, A, *Muster: Theorie der digitalen Gesellschaft* (Munich, C.H.Beck, 2019).

Navas, S, 'Robot Machines and Civil Liability', in M Ebers and S Navas (eds), *Algorithms and Law* (Cambridge, Cambridge University Press, 2020) 157–173.

Neuhäuser, C, 'Some Sceptical Remarks Regarding Robot Responsibility and a Way Forward', in C Misselhorn (ed), *Collective Agency and Cooperation in Natural and Artificial Systems* (Heidelberg, Springer, 2015) 131–147.

Nevejans, N, *European Civil Law Rules in Robotics* (Brussels, Study commissioned by the European Parliament's Juri Committee on Legal Affairs, 2016).

Neyland, D and Möllers, N, 'Algorithmic IF … THEN Rules and the Conditions and Consequences of Power', (2017) 20 *Information, Communication & Society* 45–62.

Nolan, D, 'Offer and Acceptance in the Electronic Age', in A Burrows and E Peel (eds), *Contract Formation and Parties* (Oxford, Oxford University Press, 2010) 61–87.

Nolan, D and Davies, J, 'Torts and Equitable Wrongs', in A Burrows (ed), *English Private Law* (Oxford, Oxford University Press, 2013) 927–1030.

Nonet, P and Selznick, P, *Law and Society in Transition: Toward Responsive Law* (New York, Harper & Row, 1978).

O'Callaghan, P, Brüggemeier, G and Ciacchi, A, *Personality Rights in European Tort Law* (Cambrige, Cambridge University Press, 2010).

On, D, *Strict Liability and the Aims of Tort Law* (Maastricht, Dissertation Maastricht University, 2020).

Oster, J, 'Haftung für Persönlichkeitsverletzungen durch Künstliche Intelligenz', [2018] *UFITA - Archiv für Medienrecht und Medienwissenschaft* 14–52.

Owen, DG, *Products Liability Law* 3rd edn (St. Paul, West Academic, 2015).

Pagallo, U, 'Three Roads to Complexity, AI and the Law of Robots: On Crimes, Contracts, and Torts', in M Palmirani, U Pagallo, P Casanovas and S Giovanni (eds), *AI Approaches to the Complexity of Legal Systems* (Berlin, Springer, 2012) 48–60.

—— 'From Automation to Autonomous Systems: A Legal Phenomenology with Problems of Accountability', (2017) *Proceedings of the Twenty-Sixth International Joint Conference on Artificial Intelligence* 17–23.

Panezi, A, 'Liability Rules for AI-Facilitated Wrongs: An Ecosystem Approach to Manage Risk and Uncertainty', in P García Mexía and F Pérez Bes (eds), *AI and the Law* (Alphen aan den Rijn, Wolters Kluwer, 2021) forthcoming.

Parsons, T and Shils, EA, *Toward a General Theory of Action: Theoretical Foundations for the Social Sciences* (New York, Harper & Row, 1951).

Pasquale, F, 'Reforming the Law of Reputation', (2015) 47 *Loyola University of Chicago Law Journal* 515–539.

Pearl, TH, 'Compensation at the Crossroads: Autonomous Vehicles & Alternative Victim Compensation Schemes', (2019) 60 *William & Mary Law Review* 1827–1891.

Pepito, JA, Vasquez, BA and Locsin, RC, 'Artificial Intelligence and Autonomous Machines: Influences, Consequences, and Dilemmas in Human Care', (2019) 11 *Health* 932–949.

Perlingieri, C, 'Responsabilità civile e robotica medica', (2020) 1 *Tecnologie e diritto* 161–180.

Pettit, P, 'Responsibility Incorporated', (2007) 117 *Ethics* 171–201.

Pieper, F-U, 'Die Vernetzung autonomer Systeme im Kontext von Vertrag und Haftung', [2016] *InTeR Zeitschrift zum Innovations- und Technikrecht* 188–194.

Powell, D, 'Autonomous Systems as Legal Agents: Directly by the Recognition of Personhood or Indirectly by the Alchemy of Algorithmic Entities', (2020) 18 *Duke Law & Technology Review* 306–331.

Powell, WW, 'Neither Market nor Hierarchy: Network Forms of Organization', (1990) 12 *Research in Organizational Behavior* 295–336.

Prescott, TJ, 'Robots are not Just Tools', (2017) 29 *Connection Science* 142–149.

Rabel, E, 'Die Stellvertretung in den hellenistischen Rechten und in Rom', in HJ Wolf (ed), *Gesammelte Aufsätze IV* (Tübingen, Mohr Siebeck, 1971 [1934]),

Rachum-Twaig, O, 'Whose Robot is it Anyway? Liability for Artificial-Intelligence-Based Robots', [2020] *University of Illinois Law Review* 1141–1175.

Rahwan, I, Cebrian, M, Obradovich, N, Bongard, J, Bonnefon, J-F, Breazeal, C, Crandall, JW, Christakis, NA, Couzin, ID, Jackson, MO, Jennings, NR, Kamar, E, Kloumann, IM, Larochelle, H, Lazer, D, McElreath, R, Mislove, A, Parkes, DC, Pentland, AS, Roberts, ME, Shariff, A, Tenenbaum, JB and Wellman, M, 'Machine Behaviour', (2019) 568 *Nature* 477–486.

Rammert, W, 'Distributed Agency and Advanced Technology: Or: How to Analyze Constellations of Collective Inter-agency', in J-H Passoth, B Peuker and M Schillmeier (eds), *Agency Without Actors: New Approaches to Collective Action* (London, Routledge, 2012) 89–111.

Rauer, V, 'Distribuierte Handlungsträgerschaft. Verantwortungsdiffusion als Problem der Digitalisierung sozialen Handelns', in C Daase, J Junk, S Kroll and V Rauer (eds), *Politik und Verantwortung: Analysen zum Wandel politischer Entscheidungs- und Rechtfertigungspraktiken* (Baden-Baden, Nomos, 2017) 436–453.

Reynolds, F, 'Agency', in A Burrows (ed), *English Private Law* (Oxford, Oxford University Press, 2013) 613–663.

Riehm, T and Meier, S, 'Künstliche Intelligenz im Zivilrecht', [2019] *DGRI Jahrbuch 2018* 1–63.

—— 'Product Liability in Germany: Ready for the Digital Age?', (2019) 8 *Journal of European Consumer and Market Law* 161–165.

Rott, P (ed), *Certification – Trust, Accountability, Liability* (Heidelberg/New York, Springer, 2019).

Säcker, FJ, Rixecker, R, Oetker, H and Limperg, B, *Münchener Kommentar zum Bürgerlichen Gesetzbuch. Band 1* 8th edn (Munich, C.H. Beck, 2018).

—— *Münchener Kommentar zum Bürgerlichen Gesetzbuch. Band 2* 8th edn (Munich, C.H.Beck, 2019).

Salminen, J, 'Contract-Boundary-Spanning Governance Mechanisms: Conceptualizing Fragmented and Globalized Production as Collectively Governed Entities', (2016) 23 *Indiana Journal of Global Legal Studies* 709–742.

—— 'From Product Liability to Production Liability: Modelling a Response to the Liability Deficit of Global Value Chains on Historical Transformations of Production', (2019) 23 *Competition & Change* 420–438.

Salomon, G, 'No Distribution Without Individuals' Cognition: A Dynamic Interactional View', in G Salomon (ed), *Distributed Cognitions: Psychological and Educational Considerations* (Cambridge, Cambridge University Press, 1993) 111–138.

Sanz Bayón, P, 'A Legal Framework for Robo-Advisors', in E Schweighofer, F Kummer, A Saarenpää and B Schafer (eds), *Datenschutz / LegalTech* (Bern, Weblaw, 2019) 311–318.

Sartor, G, 'Agents in Cyberlaw', in G Sartor (ed), *The Law of Electronic Agents: Selected Revised Papers. Proceedings of the Workshop on the Law of Electronic Agents (LEA 2002)* (Bologna, University of Bologna) 3–12.

—— 'Cognitive Automata and the Law: Electronic Contracting and the Intentionality of Software Agents', (2009) 17 *Artificial Intelligence and Law* 253–290.

Schaub, R, 'Interaktion von Mensch und Maschine: Haftungs- und immaterialgüterrechtliche Fragen bei eigenständigen Weiterentwicklungen autonomer Systeme', [2017] *Juristenzeitung* 342–349.

Scherer, MU, 'Regulating Artificial Intelligence Systems: Risks, Challenges, Competencies, and Strategies', (2016) 29 *Harvard Journal of Law & Technology* 353–400.

—— 'Of Wild Beasts and Digital Analogues: The Legal Status of Autonomous Systems', (2019) 19 *Nevada Law Journal* 259–292.

Schich, S and Kim, B-H, 'Guarantee Arrangements for Financial Promises: How Widely Should the Safety Net be Cast?', (2011) 2011 *OECD Journal: Financial Market Trends* 201–235.

Schirmer, J-E, 'Rechtsfähige Roboter', [2016] *Juristenzeitung* 660–666.

—— 'Artificial Intelligence and Legal Personality', in T Wischmeyer and T Rademacher (eds), *Regulating Artificial Intelligence* (Basel, Springer, 2019) 123–142.
Scholz, LH, 'Algorithmic Contracts', (2017) 20 *Stanford Technology Law Review* 128–169.
—— 'Algorithms and Contract Law', in W Barfield (ed), *The Cambridge Handbook on the Law of Algorithms* (Cambridge, Cambridge University Press, 2021) 141–52.
Schulz, T, *Verantwortlichkeit bei autonom agierenden Systemen: Fortentwicklung des Rechts und Gestaltung der Technik* (Baden-Baden, Nomos, 2015).
Schuppli, S, 'Deadly Algorithms: Can Legal Codes Hold Software Accountable for Code That Kills?', (2014) 187 *Radical Philosophy* 2–8.
Selbst, A, 'Negligence and AI's Human Users', (2020) 100 *Boston University Law Review* 1315–1376.
Selznick, P, *Law, Society, and Industrial Justice* (New York, Russell Sage, 1969).
Shavell, S, *Foundations of Economic Analysis of Law* (Harvard, Harvard University Press, 2004).
—— 'Liability for Accidents', in MA Polinsky and S Shavell (eds), *Handbook of Law and Economics, vol I* (North-Holland, Elsevier, 2007) 142–182.
Shidaro, H and Christanikis, NA, 'Locally Noisy Autonomous Agents Improve Global Human Coordination in Network Experiments', (2017) 545 *Nature* 370–374.
Smith, H and Fotheringham, K, 'Artificial Intelligence in Clinical Decision-Making: Rethinking Liability', (2020) 20 *Medical Law International* 131–154.
Solaiman, SM, 'Legal Personality of Robots, Corporations, Idols and Chimpanzees: A Quest for Legitimacy', (2017) 25 *Artificial Intelligence and Law* 155–179.
Solum, LB, 'Legal Personhood for Artificial Intelligences', (1992) 70 *North Carolina Law Review* 1231–1283.
Sommer, M, *Haftung für autonome Systeme: Verteilung der Risiken selbstlernender und vernetzter Algorithmen im Vertrags- und Deliktsrecht* (Baden-Baden, Nomos, 2020).
Specht, L and Herold, S, 'Roboter als Vertragspartner: Gedanken zu Vertragsabschlüssen unter Einbeziehung automatisiert und autonom agierender Systeme', [2018] *Multimedia und Recht* 40–44.
Spiecker, I, 'Zur Zukunft systemischer Digitalisierung: Erste Gedanken zur Haftungs- und Verantwortungszuschreibung bei informationstechnischen Systemen – Warum für die systemische Haftung ein neues Modell erforderlich ist', [2016] *Computer und Recht* 698–704.
Spindler, G, 'Zivilrechtliche Fragen beim Einsatz von Robotern', in E Hilgendorf (ed), *Robotik im Kontext von Recht und Moral* (Baden-Baden, Nomos, 2014), 63–80.
—— 'Digitale Wirtschaft – analoges Recht: Braucht das BGB ein Update?', (2016) 71 *Juristenzeitung* 805–856.
—— 'User Liability and Strict Liability in the Internet of Things and for Robots', in R Schulze, S Lohsse and D Staudenmayer (eds), *Liability for Robotics and in the Internet of Things* (Baden-Baden/Oxford, Nomos/Hart, 2019) 125–143.
Spindler, G and Schuster, F, *Recht der elektronischen Medien. Kommentar* 4th edn (Munich, C.H.Beck, 2019).
Sprenger, G, 'Communicated into Being: Systems Theory and the Shifting of Ontological Status', (2017) 17 *Anthropological Theory* 108–132.
—— 'Production is Exchange: Gift Giving between Humans and Non-Humans', in L Prager, M Prager and G Sprenger (eds), *Part and Wholes: Essays on Social Morphology, Cosmology, and Exchange* (Hamberg, Lit Verlag, 2018) 247–264.
Stäheli, U, 'Market Crowds', in J Schnapp and M Tiews (eds), *Crowds* (Stanford, Stanford University Press, 2006) 271–288.
Stone, CD, *Should Trees Have Standing? Toward Legal Rights for Natural Objects* (Los Altos, Kaufmann, 1974).
Storms, E, 'Exploring Actor-Network Theory in the Investigation of Algorithms', (2019) *Conference Paper, HCI workshop 'Standing on the Shoulders of Giants', May 4–9, 2019* 1–6.
Strzelczyk, BE, 'Rise of the Machines: The Legal Implications for Investor Protection with the Rise of Robo-Advisors', (2018) 16 *DePaul Business & Commercial Law Journal* 54–85.

Sullivan, HR and Schweikart, SJ, 'Are Current Tort Liability Doctrines Adequate for Addressing Injury Caused by AI?', (2019) 21 *AMA Journal of Ethics* 160–166.
Taddeo, M and Floridi, L, 'How AI can be a Force for Good: An Ethical Framework Will Help to Harness the Potential of AI while Keeping Humans in Control', (2018) 361 *Science* 751–752.
Taylor, SM and De Leeuw, M, 'Guidance Systems: From Autonomous Directives to Legal Sensor-Bilities', [2020] *AI & Society (Open Forum)* 1–14.
Teubner, G, 'Enterprise Corporatism: New Industrial Policy and the "Essence" of the Legal Person', (1988) 36 *The American Journal of Comparative Law* 130–155.
—— 'The Invisible Cupola: From Causal to Collective Attribution in Ecological Liability', in G Teubner, L Farmer and D Murphy (eds), *Environmental Law and Ecological Responsibility: The Concept and Practice of Ecological Self-Organization* (Chichester, Wiley, 1993) 19–47.
—— 'Legal Irritants: Good Faith in British Law or How Unifying Law Ends Up in New Divergences', (1998) 61 *Modern Law Review* 11–32.
—— 'Rights of Non-Humans? Electronic Agents and Animals as New Actors in Politics and Law', (2006) 33 *Journal of Law and Society* 497–521.
—— *Networks as Connected Contracts* (Oxford, Hart, 2011).
—— 'Law and Social Theory: Three Problems', [2014] *Ancilla Juris* 182–221.
—— 'Digital Personhood? The Status of Autonomous Software Agents in Private Law', [2018] *Ancilla Juris* 107–149.
Thacker, E, 'Networks, Swarms, Multitudes', [2004] *CTheory – Journal of Theory, Technology, and Culture.*
Thomadsen, T, *Hierarchical Network Design* (Kongens Lyngby, Technical University of Denmark, 2005).
Thürmel, S, 'The Participatory Turn: A Multidimensional Gradual Agency Concept for Human and Non-human Actors', in C Misselhorn (ed), *Collective Agency and Cooperation in Natural and Artificial Systems: Explanation, Implementation and Simulation* (Cham, Springer International, 2015) 45–62.
Tjong Tijn Lai, E, 'Liability for (Semi)autonomous Systems: Robots and Algorithms', in V Mak, E Tjong Tijn Lai and A Berlee (eds), *Research Handbook in Data Science and Law* (Cheltenham, Edward Elgar, 2018) 55–82.
Trüstedt, K, 'Representing Agency', (2020) 32 *Law & Literature* 195–206.
—— *Stellvertretung: Zur Szene der Person* (Konstanz, Konstanz University Press, 2021 forthcoming).
Turner, J, *Robot Rules: Regulating Artificial Intelligence* (London, Palgrave Macmillan, 2018).
Ubl, R, *Prehistoric Future: Max Ernst and the Return of Painting Between Wars* (Chicago, Chicago University Press, 2004).
Utku, D, 'Formation of Contracts via the Internet', in MH Bilgin, H Danis, E Demir and U Can (eds), *Eurasian Economic Perspectives* (New York, Springer, 2018) 289–308.
Viljanen, M, 'A Cyborg Turn in Law?', (2017) 18 *German Law Journal* 1277–1308.
Vladeck, DC, 'Machines without Principals: Liability Rules and Artificial Intelligence', (2014) 89 *Washington Law Review* 117–150.
Wagner, G, 'Transversale Vernunft und der soziologische Blick: Zur Erinnerung an Montesqieu', (1996) 25 *Zeitschrift für Soziologie* 315–329.
Wagner, G, 'Grundstrukturen des Europäischen Deliktsrechts', in R Zimmermann (ed), *Grundstrukturen des Europäischen Deliktsrechts* (Baden-Baden, Nomos, 2003) 189–340.
—— 'Produkthaftung für autonome Systeme', (2017) 216 *Archiv für die civilistische Praxis* 707–765.
—— 'Robot Liability', in R Schulze, S Lohsse and D Staudenmayer (eds), *Liability for Robotics and in the Internet of Things* (Baden-Baden/Oxford, Nomos/Hart, 2019) 27–62.
—— 'Robot, Inc.: Personhood for Autonomous Systems?', (2019) 88 *Fordham Law Review* 591–612.
—— 'Roboter als Haftungssubjekte? Konturen eines Haftungsrechts für autonome Systeme', in F Faust and H-B Schäfer (eds), *Zivilrechtliche und rechtsökonomische Probleme des Internet und der künstlichen Intelligenz* (Tübingen, Mohr Siebeck, 2019) 1–38.
—— 'Verantwortlichkeit im Zeichen digitaler Techniken', [2020] *Versicherungsrecht* 717–741.

Wagner, G and Luyken, L, 'Haftung für Robo Advice', in G Bachmann, S Grundmann, A Mengel and K Krolop (eds), *Festschrift für Christine Windbichler* (Berlin, de Gruyter, 2020) 155–176.

Wei, D, Deng, X, Zhang, X, Deng, Y and Mahadevan, S, 'Identifying Influential Nodes in Weighted Networks Based on Evidence Theory', (2013) 392 *PHYSICA A: Statistical Mechanics and its Applications* 2564–2575.

Weitzenboeck, EM, 'Electronic Agents and the Formation of Contracts', (2001) 9 *International Journal of Law and Information Technology* 204.

Welsch, W, *Vernunft: Die zeitgenössische Vernunftkritik und das Konzept der transversalen Vernunft* (Frankfurt, Suhrkamp, 1996).

Wendehorst, C, 'Strict Liability for AI and other Emerging Technologies', (2020) 11 *Journal of European Tort Law* 150–180.

Werle, R, 'Technik als Akteurfiktion', in W Rammert and I Schulz-Schaeffer (eds), *Können Maschinen handeln? Soziologische Beiträge zum Verhältnis von Mensch und Technik* (Frankfurt, Campus, 2002) 119–139.

Wettig, S, *Vertragsschluss mittels elektronischer Agenten* (Berlin, Wissenschaftlicher Verlag, 2010).

Wettig, S and Zehendner, E, 'The Electronic Agent: A Legal Personality under German Law?', [2003] *Proceedings of the Workshop on the Law of Electronic Agents (LEA)* 97–112.

Weyer, J and Fink, R, 'Die Interaktion von Mensch und autonomer Technik in soziologischer Perspektive', (2011) 20 *TATuP – Journal for Technology Assessment in Theory and Practice* 39–45.

White, TN and Baum, SD, 'Liability for Present and Future Robotics Technology', in P Lin, K Abney and R Jenkins (eds), *Robot Ethics 2.0: From Autonomous Cars to Artificial Intelligence* (Oxford, Oxford University Press, 2017) 5.2.

Wiedemann, C, 'Between Swarm, Network, and Multitude: Anonymous and the Infrastructures of the Common', (2014) 15 *Distinktion: Scandinavian Journal of Social Theory* 309–326.

Wielsch, D, 'Die Haftung des Mediums: BGH 14.05.2013 (Google Autocomplete)', in B Lomfeld (ed), *Die Fälle der Gesellschaft: Eine neue Praxis soziologischer Jurisprudenz* (Tübingen, Mohr Siebeck, 2017) 125–149.

—— 'Contract Interpretation Regimes', (2018) 81 *Modern Law Review* 958–988.

—— 'Die Ordnungen der Netzwerke. AGB – Code – Community Standards', in M Eifert and T Gostomzyk (eds), *Netzwerkrecht. Die Zukunft des NetzDG und seine Folgen für die Netzwerkkommunikation* (Baden-Baden, Nomos, 2018) 61–94.

—— 'Private Law Regulation of Digital Intermediaries', (2019) 27 *European Review of Private Law* 197–220.

—— 'Die Ermächtigung von Eigen-Sinn im Recht', in I Augsberg, S Augsberg and L Heidbrink (eds), *Recht auf Nicht-Recht: Rechtliche Reaktionen auf die Juridifizierung der Gesellschaft* (Weilerswist, Velbrück, 2020) 179–201.

Williamson, O, *The Economic Institutions of Capitalism: Firms, Markets, Relational Contracting* (New York, Free Press, 1985).

Winner, L, 'Do Artifacts Have Politics?', (1980) 109 *Daedalus* 121–136.

Wojtczak, S, 'Endowing Artificial Intelligence with Legal Subjectivity', [2021] *AI & Society (Open Forum)* 1–9.

Yadav, Y, 'The Failure of Liability in Modern Markets', (2016) 102 *Virginia Law Review* 1031–1100.

Yeung, K, *Responsibility and AI: A Study of the Implications of Advanced Digital Technologies (Including AI Systems) for the Concept of Responsibility within a Human Rights Framework* (Council of Europe study DGI(2019)05, 2019).

Zech, H, 'Zivilrechtliche Haftung für den Einsatz von Robotern: Zuweisung von Automatisierungs- und Autonomierisiken', in S Gless and K Seelmann (eds), *Intelligente Agenten und das Recht* (Baden-Baden, Nomos, 2016) 163–204.

—— 'Künstliche Intelligenz und Haftungsfragen', [2019] *Zeitschrift für die gesamte Privatrechtswissenschaft* 198–219.

—— 'Liability for Autonomous Systems: Tackling Specific Risks of Modern IT', in R Schulze, S Lohsse and D Staudenmayer (eds), *Liability for Robotics and in the Internet of Things* (Baden-Baden/Oxford, Nomos/Hart, 2019) 187–200.

—— 'Entscheidungen digitaler autonomer Systeme: Empfehlen sich Regelungen zu Verantwortung und Haftung?', (2020) I/A *73. Deutscher Juristentag* 11–111.

—— *Risiken digitaler Systeme: Robotik, Lernfähigkeit und Vernetzung als aktuelle Herausforderungen für das Recht* (Berlin, Weizenbaum Institute for the Networked Society, 2020).

—— 'Liability for AI: Public Policy Considerations', [2021] *ERA Forum* 147–158.

Zekos, GI, *Economics and Law of Artificial Intelligence: Finance, Economic Impacts, Risk Management and Governance* (Cham, Springer, 2021).

Zimmerman, EJ, 'Machine Minds: Frontiers in Legal Personhood', (2015) *SSRN Electronic Library* 1–43.

Policy Documents and Reports

Arbeitsgruppe 'Digitaler Neustart' der Konferenz der Justizministerinnen und Justizminister der Länder, Report of 1 October 2018 and 15 April 2019.

European Commission, Communication 'Artificial Intelligence for Europe' COM(2018) 237 final.

European Commission, 'Report on the Safety and Liability Implications of Artificial Intelligence, The Internet of Things and Robotics', COM(2020) 64 final.

European Commission, White Paper on Artificial Intelligence, COM(2020) 65 final.

European Commission, Communication 'Fostering a European Approach to Artificial Intelligence', COM (2021) 205 final.

European Commission, Proposal for a Regulation of the European Parliament and the Council Laying Down Harmonised Rules on Artificial Intelligence (Proposal Artificial Intelligence Act) and Amending Certain Union Legislative Acts, COM(2021) 206.

European Expert Group on Liability and New Technologies – New Technologies Formation, Report 'Liability for Artificial Intelligence and Other Emerging Technologies', 2019.

European Parliament, Resolution of 16 February 2017 with Recommendations to the Commission on Civil Law Rules on Robotics, 2015/2103(INL).

European Parliament, Civil Liability Regime for Artificial Intelligence, Resolution of 20 October 2020, 2020/2012(INL).

Open Letter to the European Commission, Artificial Intelligence and Robotics, available at www.robotics-openletter.eu.

U.S. Commodity Futures Trading Commission & U.S. Securities & Exchange Commission, Findings Regarding the Market Events of May 6, 2010, Report of the Staffs of the CFTC and SEC to the Joint Advisory Committee on Emerging Regulatory Issues.

INDEX

www.ingramcontent.com/pod-product-compliance
Ingram Content Group UK Ltd.
Pitfield, Milton Keynes, MK11 3LW, UK
UKHW020818290926
15470UKWH00003B/1230

9 781509 949335